PORTABLE
St. Maarten/ St. Martin, Anguilla & St. Barts

1st Edition

by Jordan Simon

Here's what critics say about Frommer's:

"Amazingly easy to use. Very portable, very complete."

—*Booklist*

"Detailed, accurate, and easy-to-read information for all price ranges."

—*Glamour Magazine*

Wiley Publishing, Inc.

Published by:

WILEY PUBLISHING, INC.

111 River St.
Hoboken, NJ 07030-5774

ISBN: 978-0-470-04900-6

Editor: Marc Nadeau
Production Editor: Suzanna R. Thompson
Cartographer: Tim Lohnes
Photo Editor: Richard Fox
Anniversary Logo Design: Richard Pacifico
Production by Wiley Indianapolis Composition Services

For information on our other products and services or to obtain technical
support, please contact our Customer Care Department within the U.S. at
800/762-2974, outside the U.S. at 317/572-3993 or fax 317/572-4002.

Wiley also publishes its books in a variety of electronic formats. Some con-
tent that appears in print may not be available in electronic formats.

Manufactured in the United States of America

5   4   3   2   1

Contents

List of Maps

ACKNOWLEDGMENTS

The author would like to thank some invaluable P.R. and tourism folk—Andria Mitsakos, William Bell, Rollina Bridgewater—and of course, his skilled, tireless, patient editor, Marc Nadeau.

—Jordan Simon

ABOUT THE AUTHOR

As a tot, **Jordan Simon**'s artist mother spirited him all over the Caribbean. He's authored and/or collaborated on several cookbooks and travel guides, including *Frommer's Irreverent U.S. Virgin Islands*, *Frommer's Irreverent Las Vegas*, and *Frommer's Madrid & Barcelona by Night*. He's gone tropical for *Condé Nast Traveler*, *Cooking Light*, *Town & Country*, *Diversion*, *Arthur Frommer's Budget Travel*, *USAir*, *Caribbean Travel & Life*, *Art & Antiques*, *Modern Bride*, *American Way*, *Food Arts*, *TravelAge*, *Palm Beach*, and ShermansTravel. com. He's currently Caribbean editor for I&MI and associate editor of Caribbean Escapes. Jordan codeveloped *Wine Country International* magazine as founding editor-in-chief of Wine Country Network, has served as food/wine or travel editor for national and regional publications, produced film festivals, and conducted corporate wine tastings/tours. He needs R&R and visits the Caribbean frequently—alas, to work.

AN INVITATION TO THE READER

In researching this book, we discovered many wonderful places—hotels, restaurants, shops, and more. We're sure you'll find others. Please tell us about them, so we can share the information with your fellow travelers in upcoming editions. If you were disappointed with a recommendation, we'd love to know that, too. Please write to:

Frommer's Portable St. Maarten/St. Martin, Anguilla & St Barts, 1st Edition
Wiley Publishing, Inc. • 111 River St. • Hoboken, NJ 07030-5774

AN ADDITIONAL NOTE

Please be advised that travel information is subject to change at any time—and this is especially true of prices. We therefore suggest that you write or call ahead for confirmation when making your travel plans. The authors, editors, and publisher cannot be held responsible for the experiences of readers while traveling. Your safety is important to us, however, so we encourage you to stay alert and be aware of your surroundings. Keep a close eye on cameras, purses, and wallets, all favorite targets of thieves and pickpockets.

FROMMER'S STAR RATINGS, ICONS & ABBREVIATIONS

Every hotel, restaurant, and attraction listing in this guide has been ranked for quality, value, service, amenities, and special features using a **star-rating system**. In country, state, and regional guides, we also rate towns and regions to help you narrow down your choices and budget your time accordingly. Hotels and restaurants are rated on a scale of zero (recommended) to three stars (exceptional). Attractions, shopping, nightlife, towns, and regions are rated according to the following scale: zero stars (recommended), one star (highly recommended), two stars (very highly recommended), and three stars (must-see).

In addition to the star-rating system, we also use **seven feature icons** that point you to the great deals, in-the-know advice, and unique experiences that separate travelers from tourists. Throughout the book, look for:

Finds	Special finds—those places only insiders know about
Fun Fact	Fun facts—details that make travelers more informed and their trips more fun
Kids	Best bets for kids and advice for the whole family
Moments	Special moments—those experiences that memories are made of
Overrated	Places or experiences not worth your time or money
Tips	Insider tips—great ways to save time and money
Value	Great values—where to get the best deals

The following **abbreviations** are used for credit cards:

AE	American Express	DISC	Discover	V	Visa
DC	Diners Club	MC	MasterCard		

FROMMERS.COM

Now that you have this guidebook to help you plan a great trip, visit our website at **www.frommers.com** for additional travel information on more than 3,500 destinations. We update features regularly to give you instant access to the most current trip-planning information available. At Frommers. com, you'll find scoops on the best airfares, lodging rates, and car rental bargains. You can even book your travel online through our reliable travel booking partners. Other popular features include:

- Online updates of our most popular guidebooks
- Vacation sweepstakes and contest giveaways
- Newsletters highlighting the hottest travel trends
- Online travel message boards with featured travel discussions

The Best of St. Maarten/ St. Martin with Anguilla & St. Barts

St. Maarten/St. Martin and its ritzy neighbors offer pristine beaches with gemlike coral reefs and baubles in duty-free jewelry and couture stores, natural wildlife sightings and nocturnal life on the wild side. You can stay in charming Creole cottages or Moorish-influenced marvels. And of course, you can eat . . . and eat . . . and eat again—at casual beach barbecues and grand temples of gastronomy. Whatever your tastes and budget, in this chapter I'll guide you to the best St. Maarten/St. Martin (as well as Anguilla and St. Barts) have to offer.

1 Frommer's Favorite Experiences

- **Going Off Island:** Some of my most memorable moments have been spent off the "mainland." Take a boat to one of the islands off Orient Bay at St. Martin's east end. There are few more relaxing diversions than sipping a *ti' punch* (a rum aperitif) while wading in a sandbank at Îlet Pinel, St. Martin's green curtain of mountains undulating in the distance, or taking a natural mud bath underneath the cliffs of Tintamarre. See p. 103.
- **Orient Beach:** Hanging out on this 3.2km (2-mile) stretch where everyone else lets it *all* hang out is a must. Activities aplenty exist other than ogling: Most beach bars double as watersports centers and/or chic boutiques. Some even offer massages on the sand. See p. 102.
- **Sidewalk Cafes:** For less obvious but equally enjoyable people-watching, find yourself a prime seat at the Marigot Waterfront or along the Front Street/Great Bay Boardwalk in Philipsburg, where leviathan cruise ships and mega-yachts make the fishing dinghies look like toy boats in a tub.
- **Grand Case:** Over the years this tiny fishing village earned the monikers "Caribbean Restaurant Row" and "Gourmet Capital

of the Caribbean," and you won't find such an amazing concentration of top-notch eateries anywhere in the world, let alone the Caribbean. See p. 101.

- **Loterie Farm:** Every time I fret over St. Maarten/St. Martin's increasing development, I head over to this nature reserve to handle the zip lines or hike through virgin rainforest, followed by a meal at its Hidden Forest Cafe. See p. 93.

- **12-Metre Challenge:** Seasoned sea salts and landlubbers alike will love the experience of racing a genuine America's Cup yacht. No swabbing required. See p. 105.

- **Kali's Full Moon Party:** Can you imagine a French frat party? Okay, I can't either, but this comes close. The pagan ritual is celebrated with terrific jazz and barbecue on delightful Friar's Bay. See p. 101.

- **Horseback Riding:** You actually swim astride your horse during champagne rides with **Bayside Riding Club** on the French side and **Lucky Stables** on the Dutch side (the latter also offers rugged 2-hr. jaunts down to Cay Bay). See p. 108.

- **Favorite Anguilla Experiences: Exploring beaches** is an evergreen delight on an island that resembles one big stretch of glittering sand. And touristy as it is, munching lobster on **Scilly Cay** is also idyllic. See p. 157.

- **Favorite St. Barts Experiences:** Again, anything on the **beaches,** of course. **Sunset cocktails** accompanied by live jazz at the "Goose," or Carl Gustav hotel, perched high on a hill overlooking Gustavia's fairy-tale harbor, somehow never gets old. See p. 188 and p. 172.

2 The Best Beaches

- **Orient Bay:** This hopping happening strand is clothing-optional. Shed your inhibitions and more, but don't gawk. Though I love the surreal sight of nude sunbathers snapping shots of passing cruise ships whose passengers are clicking away as well. See p. 102.

- **Baie Longue:** The loveliest, longest, and perhaps most private stretch of sand on St. Martin, and a fine place to spot celebrities staying at La Samanna. See p. 99.

- **Baie de l'Embouchure:** This ecru crescent is encircled (and protected) by a reef, making it a prime family beach. But the steady breezes lure windsurfers too. It's a great place to glide, and learn. See p. 102.

- **Happy Bay:** It's a short hike to this remarkably pretty, remarkably deserted scimitar of blinding sand where you can act out Robinson Crusoe fantasies. See p. 101.
- **Cupecoy Beach:** My favorite beach on the Dutch side, simply for the gorgeous multihued cliffs pocked with caves, and the occasional green flash sighting at sunset from the aptly named Cliffhanger Bar. See p. 96.
- **Dawn Beach:** Not that I'm up early enough to admire the sunrise here, but the views of St. Barts, great beach bars, excellent windsurfing, and superb snorkeling enchant at any time of day. See p. 98.
- **The Best Beaches on Anguilla:** It's almost impossible to go wrong on Anguilla, but **Shoal Bay** (not to be confused with Shoal Bay West) offers a near-perfect blend of activity and seclusion. I also love the dramatically situated, truly remote **Captain's Bay.** See p. 156.
- **The Best Beaches on St. Barts:** As with Anguilla, where to start? I adore **Anse du Gouverneur,** a perfect cove where I can never decide what's most beautiful: the water, the sunset, the snorkeling, or the bronzed buff bods in the buff . . . **Grande Saline,** practically "next door" on the south coast, is also clothing-optional but family-friendlier, with great swimming and windsurfing conditions. St-Jean and Grand Cul de Sac grab the headlines as the big hotel beaches, but I prefer the quieter **Flamands,** a long ribbon of sand the hue of Cristal champagne and just as apt to make me giddy. Lunch at La Langouste here is a must. See p. 188.

3 The Best Places to Get Away from It All

- **Mary's Boon Beach Plantation,** Simpson Bay, St. Maarten (© 599/545-7000), might seem like an odd getaway choice, given that its beautiful beach is buzzed a few times daily by jets. But this lovely enclave is peaceful, friendly, and outfitted with every modern necessity when civilization beckons. See p. 54.
- **Le Petit Hotel,** Grand Case, St. Martin (© 590/29-09-65), is small and intimate indeed, yet its chic suites are fully equipped. Even though it sits right in the middle of the Grand Case gourmet strip, serenity prevails once you're inside. It gets the nod over its slightly larger, equally sumptuous sister property, Hôtel L'Esplanade Caraïbes, simply for the beachfront setting. See p. 62.

- **Hostellerie des Trois Forces,** Vitet, St. Barts (© **590/27-61-25**), isn't about cash and cachet: It's a genuinely serene spiritual retreat that lures seers and CEOs, thanks to owner/astrologer Hubert Delamotte (a Gemini). The mountaintop setting, seemingly miles from civilization, makes life's frenzied, frantic, frenetic pace melt away. Rooms are decorated according to each astrological sign's characteristics, and where else could you book past life regression therapy with a gourmet dinner? The billeting and bill of fare live up to the billing for few bills. See p. 178.

- **Manoir de Marie,** Lorient, St. Barts (© **590/27-79-27**), isn't about cash and cachet either. In its own way, it's about getting back to basics and Nature at timbered cottages nestled in lavish gardens surrounding a genuine 17th-century Norman manor. See p. 180.

- **Salines Garden Cottages,** Grande Saline, St. Barts (© **590/51-04-44**), is a cozy, comfortable, and arty retreat for romantics and self-sufficient types, just steps from a gorgeous, relatively tranquil beach. See p. 180.

4 The Best Luxury Hotels

- **La Samanna,** Baie Longue, St. Martin (© **800/854-2252**), is stunningly beautiful and, rare among resorts in its class (in both senses of the word), offers posh pampering with nary a hint of pretension. The marvelous restaurant has a new chef but the *corps de cuisine* has remained the same for years, ensuring a graceful transition. The wine list comprising more than 410 entries and 10,000 bottles (the private house label is made by Burgundy's legendary Hospice de Beaune), will make oenophiles sing. See p. 61.

- **Cap Juluca,** Maundays Bay, Anguilla (© **888/858-8822**), is one of two Anguillian resorts that always takes my breath away. The Moroccan-themed posh pasha digs, the marvelous grounds, the superlative restaurants, and professional yet discreet service explain why it's a favorite of celebrities and titled Europeans. But regular folks receive the royal treatment, too. See p. 143.

- **Malliouhana,** Mead's Bay, Anguilla (© **800/835-0796**), is my other "if luxe could kill" option. The look and ambience are very different from Cap Juluca (perhaps reflecting the British management) but just as sybaritic. I adore the twin beaches, gorgeous landscaping, sublime food, lovely spa, stylish rooms, caring service, and owner Leon Roydon's collecting passions on display: Haitian art and arguably the Caribbean's finest wine cellar. See p. 146.

- **Eden Rock,** Baie de St-Jean, St. Barts (© **877/563-7105**), defines the old hotel mantra "location, location, location," its exquisite lodgings crowning or staggered on either side of the titular bluff that cleaves the bay, forming two perfect beaches. But delightful owners David and Jane Matthews never rest on their laurels, constantly improving one of the Caribbean's most elegant enclaves, where you'll be chic-by-jowl with perennial "Most Beautiful" and "Best Dressed" contenders. See p. 172.

5 The Best Restaurants

- **Temptation,** Cupecoy, St. Maarten (© **599/545-2254**), lives up to its admittedly silly if appropriate name with the island's most creative fare, not to mention an incredibly hip space. I have yet to experience a bad dish, let alone a poor meal. See p. 71.
- **Rare,** Cupecoy, St. Maarten (© **599/545-5714**), is the other brainchild of Temptation's wunderkind chef/owner, Dino Jagtiani. Aside from the witty decor and winning beef selection, his delightful side dishes are as "puckishly" inventive as anything devised by Wolfgang. See p. 71.
- **Le Gaïac,** Grand Case, St. Martin (© **590/51-97-66**), feels its "hautes" a bit too often, but I can take a little pretension to savor foie gras this exceptional. See p. 77.
- **L'Hibiscus,** Grand Case, St. Martin (© **590/29-17-91**), is tiny and on the "wrong side" of Grand Case Boulevard, so it gets overlooked. But not by savvy locals, including rival restaurateurs, who appreciate the marvelous blend of classic French and Creole fare. See p. 82.
- **Spiga,** Grand Case, St. Martin (© **590/52-47-83**), proves that Grand Case (and St. Martin) can *capisce* and cook Italian with equal panache. From tuna carpaccio to tiramisu, everything is perfection. See p. 85.
- **Lolos,** St. Martin/St. Maarten, is a term for the very basic shacks dishing out heaping helpings of heavenly Creole fare at more than fair prices. The biggest concentration lies along the beach in Grand Case. See p. 83.
- **Malliouhana,** Anguilla (© **264/497-6111**), exemplifies why this tiny, scrubby British island rivals the best of the French

West Indies in the dining department. The stellar French menu is personally supervised by two-star Michelin toque, Jo Rostang. The beachfront setting is simple yet stylish and the wine selection unparalleled. See p. 146.

- **Blanchards,** Anguilla (© 264/497-6100), ranks high on my list of near-perfect beachfront eateries. Owners Bob and Melinda Blanchard have become celebrities themselves, thanks to their witty books about the joys and perils of running a Caribbean restaurant. Fortunately you'll experience only the highs. See p. 151.

- **Hibernia,** Anguilla (© 264/497-4290), is an out-of-the-way gem whose owners brilliantly incorporate ingredients and techniques from their Asian travels into their exquisitely prepared and presented French fare. Their wanderings also inform the soothing, smart decor and adjacent gallery (a must-browse between courses). See p. 152.

- **Le Gaïac,** Anse de Toiny, St. Barts (© 590/27-88-88), in the ultra-plush Le Toiny hotel, may be the last bastion (or last gasp) of formal French dining on St. Barts. The ambience is swooningly romantic at dinner and the food sublime any time, but it's really a must for its extravagant (in both senses) Sunday brunches. See p. 188.

- **Le Sapotillier,** Gustavia, St. Barts (© 590/27-60-28), is my "default" reliably impressive dining experience. Charismatic owner Adam Rajner ensures that the food, service, and ambience are impeccable. And they always are. See p. 183.

- **Wall House,** Gustavia, St. Barts (© 590/27-71-83), lacks the sheer fanciness or even stellar people-watching of other St. Barts *boîtes,* but oh how it compensates with harbor-side setting, bonhomie, sensational grilled items, and prices (can't beat the special menus). See p. 183.

6 The Best Shopping

- **Front Street** in Philipsburg is simply an eye-popping, mind-boggling display of rampant consumerism. And it's all duty-free, from diamonds to Delft china. See p. 112.

- **Le West Indies Mall** and **Plaza Caraïbes** in Marigot feature the hautest of couture, well, at any rate prettily priced *prêt-à-porter* and accessories from such design legends as Cartier and Hermès. See p. 113.

- **Artists' ateliers** on the French side are particularly notable, showcasing Gallic expats working in a variety of media and traditions. Many open their studios to visitors, offering a wonderful insight into the creative process. See chapter 6.
- **Ma Doudou,** Cul de Sac, St. Martin (© 590/87-30-43), offers a series of delectable infused, charmingly bottled rums, which for my money (or yours) beats the more famous Guavaberry liqueurs for flavor. See p. 122.
- **La Ligne St. Barth,** Lorient, St. Barts (© 590/27-82-63), produces skin care, scents, and cosmetic products creatively crafted from Caribbean ingredients. The appetizing aroma in the traditional Creole cottage/factory surpasses that at many a restaurant. See p. 191.
- **Made in St-Barth,** St-Jean, St. Barts (© 590/27-56-57), is a fine source for local artworks and crafts, including superb intricate straw-work, as well as locally made essential oils and infused rums. See p. 192.

7 The Best Nightlife

- **Bamboo Bernie's,** St. Maarten (© 599/545-3622), is a sushi bar. No, it's a tiki bar. No, it's a grade-A meat market with preening pretties aplenty emerging from nooks and niches with that freshly ravaged look. Well, it's a pleasure palace, with fishbowl drinks, swimsuit competitions, even a climbing wall and movie screenings in its Kuta Beach "nightclub" section: something for almost everyone. See p. 127.
- **Bliss,** St. Maarten (© 599/545-3936), sounds like a spa, but it's actually Bernie's equally sizzling neighbor, another multipurpose, hedonistic beachfront nightclub-cum-restaurant-cum-live-music-venue. See p. 124
- **Casino Royale,** St. Maarten (© 599/524-0071), is the island's largest and glitziest casino, but really gets the nod over its competitors for its Vegas-style showroom and upstairs high-tech disco throwback, **Q-Club.**
- **Celine,** St. Maarten (© 599/545-3961), and her skipper/builder, Neil Roebert offer a unique experience. Among the many definitions in my dictionary, the crawl is a high-speed over-arm swim stroke and a leisurely journey between spots. Your head might be swimming after Celine's Lagoon Pub Crawl, sailing to three Simpson Bay hot spots for drinks and yummy apps. Sea legs optional. See p. 105.

- **Sunset Beach Bar,** St. Maarten (𝒞 **599/545-3998**), on the same beach as Bernie's and Bliss, is one of those places you either love or hate but it's a "must" experience. A dive in the best or worst sense of the word, you come here for live shows, dirty dancing, heavy drinking—and watching the planes take off and land right above your head. See p. 128.

- **Cheri's Café,** St. Maarten (𝒞 **599/545-3361**), is one of those institutions that manages to avoid becoming a cliché or a tourist trap: good relatively inexpensive food, congenial crowd, and fun entertainment. See p. 130.

- **StarBar,** St. Martin (𝒞 **590/29-65-22**), is the most sybaritic chichi club on the French side, which isn't as noted for its partying. But leaving StarBar out would be a nocturnal omission indeed, especially Mondays, Thursdays, and Saturdays (fab live acts, dizzying DJ spins, and wild costumes). See p. 126.

- **Johnno's Beach Stop,** Sandy Ground, Anguilla (𝒞 **264/497-2728**), is another enduringly popular haunt that draws everyone from locals to Hollywood elite for great barbecue and live music on the beach. See p. 161.

- **Dune Preserve,** Rendezvous Bay, Anguilla (𝒞 **264/497-2660**), opens irregularly, but it's jammed and jamming whenever its owner, Anguilla's best-known singer, "Bankie" Banx performs. See p. 162.

- **Nikki Beach,** Baie de St-Jean, St. Barts (𝒞 **590/27-64-64**), may be that chain's most absurdly decadent, debauched exclusive outpost. The A-list makes a beeline here to spray each other with champagne and canoodle in canopied four-poster beds on the sand, the paparazzi's popping bulbs (and everyone else's popping eyes) be damned. See p. 193.

- **Le Ti St. Barth,** Pointe Milou, St. Barts (𝒞 **590/27-97-71**), serves up uneven but often scrumptious food in a sensuous torchlit setting that lures the merely wealthy and beautiful for sizzling theme nights. Fortunately eye candy doesn't have calories. See p. 187.

2

Planning Your Trip to St. Maarten/St. Martin with Anguilla & St. Barts

Dickens may have had his *A Tale of Two Cities,* but St. Maarten/ St. Martin spins a tale of two nations, indeed two lifestyles, in just 96 sq. km (37 sq. miles)—the world's smallest land mass shared by two sovereign states, France and the Netherlands. So friendly are their relations that you don't even clear Customs when passing between them; only flags and welcome signs (BIENVENUE À PARTIE FRANÇAISE) stand guard over the obelisk marking the border at Mount Concordia. Everything about the island is similarly user-friendly. Though the euro and Netherlands Antilles florin are the official currencies, the dollar is accepted everywhere and English spoken throughout.

The island followed a similar historic path to its Caribbean sisters. Excavations suggest it was settled around 2,500 years ago by Amerindian Arawaks. Christopher Columbus sighted the island during his second voyage in November, 1493, naming it without setting foot on land. The Spaniards couldn't spare the expense of military maintenance after several devastating European wars, so they literally abandoned it in 1648, enabling opportunistic French and Dutch settlers from, respectively St. Kitts and St. Eustatius, to claim the island. After initial skirmishes, mostly political, the two nations officially settled their differences later that year. Even so, St. Maarten changed hands 16 times before it became permanently Dutch, while the French side endured the usual colonial tugs-of-war through the Napoleonic era. Alas, there appears to be no truth to the colorful legend of a wine-drinking Frenchman and gin-guzzling Dutchman walking the island to determine the border.

Returning visitors who haven't been to the island for a while are often shocked by today's St. Maarten. No longer a sleepy Caribbean backwater, it's now a boomtown (administered as part of the semi-autonomous Dutch Caribbean territory of the Netherlands

Antilles). Much has been lost to the bulldozer, and it isn't for those who hate crowds, especially when cruise ship hordes retake **Philipsburg,** the Dutch capital. Indeed, a fellow travel writer once described St. Maarten as Cleveland with palm trees; his wife quickly retorted that Cleveland had cleaned up its act.

In some respects, that uncharitable comment is true. Per square foot, the Dutch side is one of the Caribbean's most developed islands: Strip malls have stripped the landscape of character, and even residents joke that the local flower is the satellite dish. Indeed, the island, even the French side, is more notable for what it lacks: It has no major art museums or spectacular ruins, the native folk and craft traditions are disintegrating, everything has become increasingly homogenized. Ironically, that makes St. Maarten ideal entry-level Caribbean, cannily blending familiarity and exoticism. Despite problems like crime, occasional storms, traffic congestion, and corruption, St. Maarten continues to attract massive numbers of visitors who want a Caribbean island vacation with a splash of Las Vegas.

Despite increasing development, the French side (currently governed from Guadeloupe though it has petitioned for its separate status) remains quieter, more subtly European: a tropic St. Tropez. White stucco houses adorned with flowerpots and red-tile roofs cling to sapphire coves, the inimitable scent of galettes, Gauloises, and hibiscus hanging in the air. Police officers wear *kepis,* towns have names like Colombier and Orléans, and the French flag flies over the *gendarmerie* in **Marigot,** the capital. Advocates cite French St. Martin as more sophisticated, prosperous, stylish, and cosmopolitan than its fellow *départements d'outre-mer,* Guadeloupe and Martinique.

Dutch St. Maarten has its share of pastoral pockets, alluring beaches, and historic ruins, but the pace resembles a frenzied frat party by comparison, with nonstop neon-accented action well into the night (and next day) at its casinos and clubs. Both sides offer watersports aplenty, superb dining (you'll find not just some of the finest French fare outside La Belle France, but everything from rigatoni to *rijstaffel*), and duty-free shopping. It all depends on your definition of relaxation and hedonism, *n'est-ce pas?*

And underneath that splashy shell beats the heart of the islands' African roots. They emerge in the snatch of a racy reggae ditty along a street; in the brightly colored shirts and shifts that replace the crisp starched school uniforms at a weekend picnic; in the spices as hot as the tropic sun that enliven the local cuisine; in Carnival's jambalaya of sights, sounds, and smells that ranks with Rio, Trinidad, and The Big Easy for sheer flamboyance and excess.

It all adds up to a tale of two nations that offers the best of both worlds: activity and leisure. If you're seeking fun in the sun, even R&R *à deux,* they fit the bill (for fewer bills than many a Caribbean destination). If you want to get away from it all (and don't mind splurging), head for Anguilla and St. Barts, those twin hedonistic delights where I always advise people to go on their honeymoon or if they're on the verge of a nervous breakdown.

There's an old French adage: *Plus ça change, plus la même chose* ("The more things change, the more they remain the same"). Nearly 20 years after my first visit, I found myself walking down a Marigot street, frankly tired of the obsequious salesladies in the tonier shops. A woman was selling homemade "bush teas," touting their properties like any snake-oil salesman. I stopped to examine her mixtures, and we animatedly discussed local folklore, interrupted by several local ladies who purchased the blends of herbs, roots, and flowers designed to combat anything from impotence to impetigo. I turned to leave. *"Vous n'en voulez pas, char?"* she asked. ("You don't want anything?") *"Non, merci,"* I replied. She eyed me shrewdly, switching to English. "You worry too much, not enough sleep, *oui?*" And so saying, reached down for a bunch of soursop leaves. "Brew some tea, you will relax. Don't forget why you're here."

Indeed.

1 The Islands in Brief

ST. MAARTEN/ST. MARTIN   In the early 1990s, this comparatively minuscule speck exploded in popularity as a tourist destination thanks (or not) to fairly easy air access from the eastern U.S. and a boom in timeshare development. It's also one of the Caribbean's duty-free shopping meccas. Its unique political situation and remarkably varied populace (census figures allegedly list around 130 nationalities) lend it a cosmopolitan air even when it's overrun by cruise ship passengers, who tend to cluster on the more developed Dutch side. The population of roughly 75,000, huge number of tourists, and constant building combine to create traffic snarls, especially around the airport and just outside Marigot and Philipsburg.

ANGUILLA   Just 20 minutes by ferry from Marigot, flat, arid, scrubby Anguilla has become one of the Caribbean's chicest destinations. Despite its unprepossessing landscape and comparative lack of colonial grandeur, the reasons are obvious. The island resembles one big beach surrounded by water rippling from sapphire to turquoise. The locals are friendly and laid-back: You'll find very little hawking, pushiness, or overt poverty. The leading resorts and villa complexes redefine luxury. And despite its British heritage, the island teems with tempting eateries. Such delights do not come cheaply.

ST. BARTS   A quick flight or ferry ride 24km (15 miles) east of St. Maarten/St. Martin, this rugged, hilly, 21-sq.-km (8-sq.-mile) dot is practically synonymous with glitz, glamour, and glorious beaches. The cost for effortless chic is astronomical, but the jet set (once nick-named the Concorde Horde) has never minded. Despite its forbidding prices and luxury reputation, the 7,000 locals—most descended from the original hardy Norman and Breton settlers—remain matter-of-fact and supremely unimpressed, with such exceptionally pretty fishing villages as Colombier and Corossol retaining their cultural traditions. Despite the discovery of new stomping grounds, celebs still crowd the shops and cafes of the fairy-tale capital, Marigot, and the Caribbean equivalent of the Riviera in St-Jean.

2 Visitor Information

If you're going to either **Dutch St. Maarten** or **French St. Martin,** contact the St. Maarten/St. Martin Tourist Office, 675 Third Ave., Suite 1807, New York, NY 10017 (© **800/786-2278** or 212/953-2084 for the department servicing the Dutch side; © **877/956-1234** or 646/227-9440 for the department servicing the French side). In Canada, the office for information about the Dutch side of the island is located at 703 Evans Ave., Suite 106, Toronto, ON M9C 5E9 (© **416/622-4300**). For information about the French side of the island, contact 1981 Ave. McGill College, Suite 490, in Montreal (© **514/288-4264**). Once on the island, go to the **Tourist Information Bureau,** Vineyard Office Park, 33 W. G. Buncamper Rd., Philipsburg, St. Maarten, N.A. (© **599/542-2337**), open Monday to Friday from 9am to 5pm.

The tourist board on French St. Martin, called the **Office du Tourisme,** is at Rte. de Sandy Ground, Marigot, 97150 St. Martin, F.W.I. (© **590/87-57-21**), open Monday to Friday from 8:30am to 1pm and 2:30 to 5:30pm.

For information on the Web about the French side, go to **www.st-martin.org**. For information about the island's Dutch side, visit **www.st-maarten.com**. For details on Anguilla and St. Barts, see chapters 8 and 9, respectively.

3 Entry Requirements & Customs

ENTRY REQUIREMENTS
PASSPORTS

For information on how to get a passport, go to "Passports" in the "Fast Facts" section of this chapter—the websites listed provide downloadable passport applications as well as the current fees for processing passport applications. For an up-to-date, country-by-country listing of passport requirements around the world, go to the "Foreign Entry Requirement" Web page of the U.S. State Department at http://travel.state.gov. The DOS website includes information on obtaining passports for minors, who must hold the same documentation as adults.

VISAS

Visas are not required for U.S., Canada, E.U., Australia, or New Zealand citizens. Other nationalities should check the individual tourist board websites.

MEDICAL REQUIREMENTS

For information on medical requirements and recommendations, see "Health & Safety" on p. 21.

CUSTOMS
WHAT YOU CAN BRING INTO
ST. MAARTEN/ST. MARTIN

Visitors to St. Maarten/St. Martin (as well as St. Barts and Anguilla) may not carry any form of firearm, spear guns, pole spears, illegal drugs, live plants or cuttings, and raw fruits and vegetables. Visitors over 18 may bring in—duty-free—items intended for personal use (generally up to 4 liters of alcohol, a carton of cigarettes or 25 cigars), as well as laptops, cellphones, and cameras.

WHAT YOU CAN TAKE HOME FROM
ST. MAARTEN/ST. MARTIN
U.S. Citizens

The duty-free (or personal) exemption on merchandise acquired abroad for returning U.S. citizens or foreign nationals with proper documentation is $800. This includes 1 liter of alcohol and 200 cigarettes for persons over 21. You should collect all receipts for purchases made abroad. All items must be for personal or household use, or intended as gifts. For specifics on what you can bring back and the corresponding fees, download the invaluable free pamphlet

Know Before You Go online at **www.cbp.gov**. (Click on "Travel," and then click on "Know Before You Go! Online Brochure.") Or contact the **U.S. Customs & Border Protection (CBP),** 1300 Pennsylvania Ave., NW, Washington, DC 20229 (© **877/287-8667**) and request the pamphlet.

Canadian Citizens

For a clear summary of Canadian rules, write for the booklet *I Declare,* issued by the **Canada Border Services Agency** (© **800/ 461-9999** in Canada, or 204/983-3500; www.cbsa-asfc.gc.ca).

U.K. Citizens

For information, contact **HM Customs & Excise** at © **0845/010- 9000** (from outside the U.K., 020/8929-0152), or consult www. hmce.gov.uk.

Australian Citizens

A helpful brochure available from Australian consulates or Customs offices is *Know Before You Go.* For more information, call the **Australian Customs Service** at © **1300/363-263,** or log on to **www. customs.gov.au**.

New Zealand Citizens

Most questions are answered in a free pamphlet available at New Zealand consulates and Customs offices: *New Zealand Customs Guide for Travellers, Notice no. 4.* For more information, contact **New Zealand Customs,** The Customhouse, 17–21 Whitmore St., Box 2218, Wellington (© **04/473-6099** or 0800/428-786; www. customs.govt.nz).

4 Money

CURRENCY

Despite the dominance of the euro since January 2002 within the mother country, Holland, the legal tender on the Dutch side is still the **Netherlands Antilles florin (NAf);** the official exchange rate is NAf 1.79 for each US$1. U.S. dollars are widely accepted, and prices in hotels and most restaurants and shops are often designated in dollars as well. On the French side (as well as on St. Barts), the official monetary unit is the **euro,** with most establishments widely quoting and accepting either dollars or NAf guilders as well. At press time, the U.S. dollar was trading at $1.25 to the euro. **Anguilla**'s official currency is the **Eastern Caribbean Dollar,** though U.S. dollars are accepted everywhere; the exchange rate is set permanently at roughly 2.70EC to US$1. (Just before you leave home, you can check the current exchange rates at **www.xe.com/ucc.**) Prices throughout this book are given in U.S. currency for establishments on the Dutch side and Anguilla, and in either euros or U.S. dollars for establishments on the French side and St. Barts according to whether establishments quoted their prices in euros or dollars at the time of publication.

As the dollar is much weaker than the euro, some establishments on St. Barts and French St. Martin advertise a 1-to-1 exchange rate if you use cash. Always confirm before you get the bill.

ATMs

The easiest and best way to get cash away from home is from an ATM (automated teller machine). The **Cirrus** (© **800/424-7787;** www.mastercard.com) and **PLUS** (© **800/843-7587;** www.visa.com) networks span the globe; look at the back of your bank card to see which network you're on, then call or check online for ATM locations at your destination. Be sure you know your personal identification number (PIN) and daily withdrawal limit before you depart. *Note:* Remember that many banks impose a fee every time you use a card at another bank's ATM, and that fee can be higher for international transactions (up to $5 or more) than for domestic ones (where they're rarely more than $2). In addition, the bank from which you withdraw cash may charge its own fee. For international withdrawal fees, ask your bank. Most ATMs even dispense U.S. currency.

CREDIT CARDS

Credit cards are another safe way to carry money. They also provide a convenient record of all your expenses, and they generally offer relatively good exchange rates. You can withdraw cash advances from your credit cards at banks or ATMs, provided you know your PIN. Keep in mind that you'll pay interest from the moment of your withdrawal, even if you pay your monthly bills on time. Also, note that many banks now assess a 1% to 3% "transaction fee" on **all** charges you incur abroad (whether you're using the local currency or your native currency). Major establishments on all three islands accept major credit cards, though some don't take American Express or Discover.

TRAVELER'S CHECKS

You can buy traveler's checks at most banks. They are offered in denominations of $20, $50, $100, $500, and sometimes $1000. Generally, you'll pay a service charge ranging from 1% to 4%.

Foreign currency traveler's checks are unnecessary as the U.S. dollar is prevalent.

The most popular traveler's checks are offered by **American Express** (© **800/807-6233** or 800/221-7282 for card holders—this number accepts collect calls, offers service in several foreign languages, and exempts Amex gold and platinum cardholders from the 1% fee); **Visa** (© **800/732-1322**)—AAA members can obtain Visa checks for a $9.95 fee (for checks up to $1,500) at most AAA offices or by calling © **866/339-3378**; and **MasterCard** (© **800/223-9920**).

If you carry traveler's checks, keep a record of their serial numbers separate from your checks in the event that they are stolen or lost. You'll get a refund faster if you know the numbers.

5 When to Go

THE HIGH & LOW SEASONS

Hotels on all three islands charge their highest rates during the peak winter season, from mid-December to mid-April. Christmas week rates may double those tariffs. You should make reservations months in advance for Christmas and February, especially over Presidents' Day weekend.

The off-season on all three islands runs roughly mid-April to mid-December (though exact dates vary according to hotel). It's one big summer sale: Most hotels, inns, condos, and villas slash their prices 20% to 50%. The beaches are less crowded and many top lodgings and restaurants shutter for one, even two months as the owners take their own vacation or perform necessary renovations. Be sure to request a room away from noise if the hotel remains open during construction. We provide closing dates wherever possible, but visitors should double-check before booking.

WEATHER

High season on all three islands features a temperate climate, rarely exceeding 90°F (32°C), with lower humidity and the famed cooling trade winds blowing in from the northeast. It's ideal beach weather, with the occasional cloudy day. Usually rain showers are brief: Islanders call them "liquid sunshine."

Rainy season runs from late May to mid-November. This doesn't mean it rains for days at a time or even every day. But this also roughly corresponds to the official Atlantic hurricane season, June 1 to November 30. Fortunately, satellite surveillance provides enough advance warning to take precautions and, rarely, evacuate.

St. Maarten/St. Martin Average Daily Temperature & Rainfall

	Jan	Feb	Mar	Apr	May	June	July	Aug	Sept	Oct	Nov	Dec
Temp. (°F)	77	77	77	79	81	81	83	83	83	81	80	79
Temp. (°C)	25	25	25	26	27	27	28	28	28	28	27	26
Rainfall (in.)	2.5	1.3	1.6	2.3	2.3	3.8	3.8	3.5	3.7	4.4	3.8	3.7

ST. MAARTEN/ST. MARTIN CALENDAR OF EVENTS

For Anguilla and St. Barts, see chapters 8 and 9.

January & February

Carnival. Festivities on St. Martin last for nearly 2 months starting the second Sunday in January with parade rehearsals and band tryouts.

Carnival reaches its frenzied peak on the French side in February, with jump-ups, barbecues, and pageants. It all leads to J'ouvert, the weekend before Mardi Gras and lasts until Ash Wednesday. The wild dancing-in-the-streets parades represent the culmination of an entire year's preparation from creating the feathered, sequined costumes to writing the unique musical themes. The streets are crowded with young and old following trucks with enormous sound systems in Marigot until everyone congregates at "Carnival Village" come nightfall for concerts and events, including the crowning of the Carnival King and Queen.

March

Heineken Regatta. This annual series of major boat races debuted in 1980. More than 200 vessels, from converted family fishing dinghies to race prototypes, compete in several categories. It's a prime excuse for partying, particularly on the Dutch side. First weekend of March.

Anglers Big Fishing Tournament. This is the first of several year-round fishing competitions that lures an international roster. Last weekend of March.

April

Carnival. The Dutch side chimes in with its own, even more extravagant, version, beginning the Wednesday after Easter Sunday and continuing for 15 riotous days of beauty pageants, costume and calypso competitions, Mas bands, parades, shows, and assorted revels.

The Carnival Village features stands dishing out spicy local fare and an enormous stage where local and international musicians perform nightly. J'ouvert, the opening jump-up, showcases local and international bands and thousands of revelers line the streets and follow the bands until they arrive at Carnival Village.

More parades are held the next morning, and the grandest of all takes place on the Queen's Birthday. Crowds pack the streets of Philipsburg vying for a spot to see the musicians, the outrageous costumes, and the colorful floats. The Last Lap, the grand finale of the Carnival, includes a symbolic burning of King Momo, a straw figure who embodies the spirit of Carnival. Island legend claims that burning the King in effigy will purge the sins and consequent bad luck of the village. Check www.stmaarten carnival.com for more information.

May

St. Martin Challenge. Windsurfers and kite surfers descend on the east coast beaches of St. Martin for a series of races. Second weekend of May.

St. Maarten Open Golf Tournament. Residents and visitors alike are invited to participate in this 3-day 54-hole event at Mullet Bay Golf Course. Second weekend of May.

Ecotourism Day. Nature discovery organizations, activity operators, artisans, and local entertainers take over the Bellevue Estate on the French side. You can indulge in free sea kayaking, scuba diving, horseback tours, mountain bike riding, hiking, and treasure hunts. Cultural and culinary traditions are displayed: spice-growing, pottery-making, coffee-roasting. Typical island dishes and local bands are also on the menu. Usually second or third weekend of May.

Fête du Nautisme. This watersports festival organized by METIMER, the St. Martin Sea Trades Association, focuses on (re)discovering the rich marine environment. Free activities include yacht and motorboat excursions and regattas, jet-skiing, kayaking, and windsurfing, with lessons available. Usually second or third weekend of May.

June

Billfish Tournament. One of the Caribbean's most prestigious fishing competitions lasts nearly the entire week, attracting anglers from Europe and the Caribbean. About 30 fishing boats battle at the Marlin Boulevard area, rich fishing grounds about 48km (30 miles) east of St. Maarten. Usually second week of June.

July

Bastille Day. The French holiday is celebrated island-wide with fanfare and fireworks, races and revelry. July 14.

Schoelcher Day. Boat and bike races are held in honor of Victor Schœlcher, a Frenchman, who fought against slavery. July 21.

November

Fête de Cuisines. Several local and international cooking demonstrations and competitions are held throughout the island, especially in Grand Case. First week of November.

St. Maarten's Day. Christopher Columbus named the island St. Maarten/St. Martin because he discovered it in 1493 on November 11, the feast day of St. Martin of Tours. Island residents on both sides still celebrate it as an official holiday, organizing various sporting events, parades, and jump-ups over 2 to 3 days. November 11.

December

St. Maarten Charter Yacht Exhibition. One of the Caribbean's premier boat shows, a chance for brokers to display their leviathan ships to potential bookers. It's also an excuse for lots of partying on and off the water. First week of December.

6 Travel Insurance

The cost of travel insurance varies widely, depending on the cost and length of your trip, your age and health, and the type of trip you're taking, but expect to pay between 5% and 8% of the vacation itself. You can get estimates from various providers through **Insure-MyTrip.com.** Enter your trip cost and dates, your age, and other information, for prices from more than a dozen companies.

TRIP-CANCELLATION INSURANCE

Trip-cancellation insurance will help retrieve your money if you have to back out of a trip or depart early, or if your travel supplier goes bankrupt. Permissible reasons for trip cancellation can range from sickness to natural disasters to the State Department declaring a destination unsafe for travel.

For more information, contact one of the following recommended insurers: **Access America** (© 866/807-3982; www.access america.com); **Travel Guard International** (© 800/826-4919; www. travelguard.com); **Travel Insured International** (© 800/243-3174; www.travelinsured.com); and **Travelex Insurance Services** (© 888/ 457-4602; www.travelex-insurance.com).

MEDICAL INSURANCE

For travel overseas, most U.S. health plans (including Medicare and Medicaid) do not provide coverage, and the ones that do often

Travel in the Age of Bankruptcy

Airlines go bankrupt, so protect yourself by **buying your tickets with a credit card.** The Fair Credit Billing Act guarantees that you can get your money back from the credit card company if a travel supplier goes under (and if you request the refund within 60 days of the bankruptcy). **Travel insurance** can also help, but make sure it covers against "carrier default" for your specific travel provider. And be aware that if a U.S. airline goes bust mid-trip, a 2001 federal law requires other carriers to take you to your destination (albeit on a space-available basis) for a fee of no more than $25, provided you rebook within 60 days of the cancellation.

require you to pay for services upfront and reimburse you only after you return home. As a safety net, you may want to buy travel medical insurance, particularly if you're traveling to a remote or high-risk area where emergency evacuation might be necessary. If you require additional medical insurance, try **MEDEX Assistance** (© 410/453-6300; www.medexassist.com) or **Travel Assistance International** (© 800/821-2828; www.travelassistance.com; for general information on services, call the company's Worldwide Assistance Services, Inc., at © 800/777-8710).

LOST-LUGGAGE INSURANCE

On flights within the U.S., checked baggage is covered up to $2,500 per ticketed passenger. On international flights (including U.S. portions of international trips), baggage coverage is limited to approximately $9.07 per pound, up to approximately $635 per checked bag. If you plan to check items more valuable than what's covered by the standard liability, see if your homeowner's policy covers your valuables, get baggage insurance as part of your comprehensive travel-insurance package, or buy Travel Guard's "Bag-Trak" product.

If your luggage is lost, immediately file a lost-luggage claim at the airport, detailing the luggage contents. Most airlines require that you report delayed, damaged, or lost baggage within 4 hours of arrival. The airlines are required to deliver luggage, once found, directly to your house or destination free of charge.

7 Health & Safety

STAYING HEALTHY
GENERAL AVAILABILITY OF HEALTHCARE

There are no particular health concerns on St. Maarten/St. Martin, Anguilla, or St. Barts. The best medical facilities are on St. Maarten/ St. Martin, with good clinics on Anguilla and St. Barts. Emergency airlift to Puerto Rico is available from all three destinations.

It's fairly easy to obtain major over-the-counter medication, though the brands might be manufactured in Europe under unfamiliar names. Some leading prescription drugs for such common ailments as allergies, asthma, and acid reflux are also available over the counter, albeit by European pharmaceutical companies.

Contact the **International Association for Medical Assistance to Travelers (IAMAT;** ⓒ **716/754-4883** or, in Canada, 416/652-0137; www.iamat.org) for tips on travel and health concerns in the countries you're visiting, and for lists of local, English-speaking doctors. The United States **Centers for Disease Control and Prevention** (ⓒ **800/311-3435;** www.cdc.gov) provides up-to-date information on health hazards by region or country and offers tips on food safety. The website **www.tripprep.com**, sponsored by a consortium of travel medicine practitioners, may also offer helpful advice on traveling abroad. You can find listings of reliable clinics overseas at the **International Society of Travel Medicine** (www.istm.org).

Avoiding "Economy-Class Syndrome"

Deep vein thrombosis or, as it's know in the world of flying, "economy-class syndrome" is a blood clot that develops in a deep vein. It's a potentially deadly condition that can be caused by sitting in cramped conditions—such as an airplane cabin—for too long. During a flight (especially a long-haul flight), get up, walk around, and stretch your legs every 60 to 90 minutes to keep your blood flowing. Other preventative measures include frequent flexing of the legs while sitting, drinking lots of water, and avoiding alcohol and sleeping pills. If you have a history of deep vein thrombosis, heart disease, or another condition that puts you at high risk, some experts recommend wearing compression stockings or taking anticoagulants when you fly; always ask your physician about the best course for you. Symptoms of deep vein thrombosis include leg pain or swelling, or even shortness of breath.

Healthy Travels to You

The following government websites offer up-to-date health-related travel advice.

- **Australia:** www.dfat.gov.au/travel
- **Canada:** www.hc-sc.gc.ca/index_e.html
- **U.K.:** www.dh.gov.uk/PolicyAndGuidance/HealthAdvice ForTravellers/fs/en
- **U.S.:** www.cdc.gov/travel

COMMON AILMENTS

BUGS, BITES & OTHER WILDLIFE CONCERNS   The biggest menaces on all three islands are mosquitoes (none are disease vectors) and no-see-ums, which appear mainly in the early evening. Window screens aren't always sufficient, so carry insect repellent.

SUN EXPOSURE   The tropical sun can be brutal. Wear sunglasses and a hat, and apply sunscreen liberally. Increase your time on the beach gradually. If you do overexpose yourself, stay out of the sun until you recover. Sun and heatstroke are possibilities, especially if you engage in strenuous physical activity. See a doctor immediately if fever, chills, dizziness, nausea, or headaches follow overexposure.

WHAT TO DO IF YOU GET SICK AWAY FROM HOME

It's easy to find good English-speaking doctors on all three islands. You can find **hospitals** and **emergency numbers** under "Fast Facts" on p. 39. For Anguilla and St. Barts, refer to p. 141 and p. 169, respectively.

If you suffer from a chronic illness, consult your doctor before your departure. For conditions like epilepsy, diabetes, or heart problems wear a **MedicAlert identification tag** (© 888/633-4298; www.medicalert.org), which will immediately alert doctors to your condition and give them access to your records through MedicAlert's 24-hour hotline. Pack **prescription medications** in your carry-on luggage, and carry them in their original containers, with pharmacy labels—otherwise they won't make it through airport security. Carry the generic name of prescription medicines in case a local pharmacist is unfamiliar with the brand name. Take an extra pair of contact lenses and prescription eyeglasses.

You may have to pay all medical costs upfront and be reimbursed later. See "Medical Insurance," under "Travel Insurance," above.

STAYING SAFE

Violent crime is rare on Anguilla and St. Barts, though isolated incidents are reported on St. Maarten/St. Martin. Petty theft, pickpocketing, and purse snatching can occur anywhere. Visitors should exercise common sense and take basic precautions, including being aware of one's surroundings, avoiding walking alone after dark or in remote areas, and locking all valuables in a rental or hotel safe.

DEALING WITH DISCRIMINATION

See the discussion of unfortunate recent events under "Gay & Lesbian Travelers" within "Specialized Travel Resources," below.

8 Specialized Travel Resources

TRAVELERS WITH DISABILITIES

Most disabilities shouldn't stop anyone from traveling. There are more options and resources out there than ever before. Unfortunately, the islands aren't on the vanguard, though larger hotels usually offer handicap-accessible rooms. It's always advisable to call the hotel of your choice and personally discuss your needs before booking a vacation.

Many travel agencies offer customized tours and itineraries for travelers with disabilities. Among them are **Flying Wheels Travel** (*©* 507/451-5005; www.flyingwheelstravel.com); **Access-Able Travel Source** (*©* 303/232-2979; www.access-able.com); and **Accessible Journeys** (*©* 800/846-4537 or 610/521-0339; www.disabilitytravel.com).

Organizations that offer assistance to disabled travelers include **MossRehab** (www.mossresourcenet.org); the **American Foundation for the Blind** (AFB; *©* 800/232-5463; www.afb.org); and **SATH (Society for Accessible Travel & Hospitality;** *©* 212/447-7284; www.sath.org). **AirAmbulanceCard.com** is now partnered with SATH and allows you to preselect top-notch hospitals in case of an emergency.

The community website **iCan** (www.icanonline.net/channels/travel) has destination guides and several regular columns on accessible travel. Also check out the quarterly magazine *Emerging Horizons* (www.emerginghorizons.com), and *Open World* magazine, published by SATH.

GAY & LESBIAN TRAVELERS

The Caribbean in general isn't the LGBT-friendliest destination perhaps because of regrettably rampant "on the DL" hypocrisy in local communities. Anguilla, like many a British colony, is quite conservative in attitude, but individual deluxe resorts welcome gay and lesbian travelers. St. Barts is by far the most open of the islands covered in this book.

The French and Dutch are generally tolerant, but St. Maarten/ St. Martin is a mixed bag (though a gay-owned guesthouse thrives; see p. 56). Its self-proclaimed reputation as The Friendly Island took a beating after a horrific gay-bashing on April 6, 2006. Two men were attacked with tire irons, allegedly by four thugs shouting anti-gay epithets. Authorities on both sides, mindful of negative publicity and its impact on tourism, took action and apprehended the suspects within a month. But the *St. Maarten Daily Herald* actually published a decidedly un-P.C. editorial that stopped just short of condoning the hate assault. The trial was set to continue in late 2006.

The International Gay and Lesbian Travel Association (IGLTA; © 800/448-8550 or 954/776-2626; www.iglta.org) is the trade association for the gay and lesbian travel industry, and offers an online directory of gay- and lesbian-friendly travel businesses; go to their website and click on "Consumer Site."

Gay.com Travel (© 800/929-2268 or 415/644-8044; www.gay. com/travel or www.outandabout.com) is an excellent online complement to the popular *Out Traveler* print magazine. It provides regularly updated information about gay-owned, gay-oriented, and gay-friendly lodging, dining, sightseeing, nightlife, and shopping establishments in every important destination worldwide.

The following travel guides are available at many bookstores, or you can order them from any online bookseller: *Spartacus International Gay Guide* (Bruno Gmünder Verlag; www.spartacusworld. com/gayguide) and *Odysseus: The International Gay Travel Planner* (Odysseus Enterprises Ltd.); and the *Damron* guides (www. damron.com), with separate, annual books for gay men and lesbians.

SENIOR TRAVEL

Though the major U.S. airlines flying to St. Maarten no longer offer senior discounts or coupon books, some hotels extend deals, especially during slower periods. Members of **AARP** (formerly known as the American Association of Retired Persons), 601 E St. NW, Washington, DC 20049 (© **888/687-2277;** www.aarp.org), get discounts on hotels, airfares, and car rentals. AARP offers members a wide range of benefits, including *AARP: The Magazine* and a monthly newsletter. Anyone over 50 can join.

Many reliable agencies and organizations target the 50-plus market. **Elderhostel** (© 877/426-8056; www.elderhostel.org) arranges study programs for those aged 55 and over. **ElderTreks** (© 800/741-7956; www.eldertreks.com) offers small-group tours to off-the-beaten-path or adventure-travel locations, restricted to travelers 50 and older. **INTRAV** (© 800/456-8100; www.intrav.com) is a high-end tour operator that caters to the mature, discerning traveler (not specifically seniors), with trips around the world that include guided safaris, polar expeditions, private-jet adventures, and small-boat cruises down jungle rivers.

Recommended publications offering travel resources and discounts for seniors include: the quarterly magazine *Travel 50 & Beyond* (www.travel50andbeyond.com); *Travel Unlimited: Uncommon Adventures for the Mature Traveler* (Avalon); *101 Tips for Mature Travelers,* available from Grand Circle Travel (© 800/221-2610 or 617/350-7500; www.gct.com); and *Unbelievably Good Deals and Great Adventures That You Absolutely Can't Get Unless You're Over 50* (McGraw-Hill), by Joann Rattner Heilman.

FAMILY TRAVEL

Anguilla and St. Barts don't offer many kid-centric attractions, but they remain popular if pricey family destinations. St. Maarten/St. Martin has several activities children will find enjoyable and many restaurants feature kids' menus. Children traveling abroad should have plenty of documentation, especially if they're accompanied by adults other than parents (in which case a notarized form letter from a parent or guardian is strongly recommended).

To locate accommodations, restaurants, and attractions that are particularly kid-friendly, refer to the "Kids" icon throughout this guide.

Familyhostel (© 800/733-9753) takes the whole family, including kids ages 8 to 15, on moderately priced U.S. and international learning vacations. Lectures, field trips, and sightseeing are guided by a team of academics.

Recommended family travel websites include **Family Travel Forum** (www.familytravelforum.com); **Family Travel Network** (www.familytravelnetwork.com); **Traveling Internationally with Your Kids** (www.travelwithyourkids.com); **Family Travel Times** (www.familytraveltimes.com); and **Family Travel Files** (www.the familytravelfiles.com).

SINGLE TRAVELERS

On package vacations, single travelers are often hit with a "single supplement" to the base price. To avoid it, you can agree to room with other single travelers or find a compatible roommate before you go, from one of the many roommate-locator agencies.

For more information, check out Eleanor Berman's latest edition of *Traveling Solo: Advice and Ideas for More Than 250 Great Vacations* (Globe Pequot), a guide with advice on traveling alone, either solo or as part of a group tour. Other worthwhile books are Sharon Wingler's self-published *Travel Alone & Love It: A Flight Attendant's Guide to Solo Travel* (out of print but available via www.travelaloneandloveit.com, where you can sign up for a monthly newsletter, or Amazon) and upcoming revisit, *The Joy of Solo Travel.*

9 Planning Your Trip Online

SURFING FOR AIRFARE

The most popular online travel agencies are **Travelocity** (www.travelocity.com or www.travelocity.co.uk); **Expedia** (www.expedia.com, www.expedia.co.uk, or www.expedia.ca); and **Orbitz** (www.orbitz.com).

In addition, most airlines now offer online-only fares that even their phone agents know nothing about. For the websites of airlines that fly to and from your destination, go to "Getting There" on p. 28.

Other helpful websites for booking airline tickets online include:

- www.biddingfortravel.com
- www.cheapflights.com
- www.hotwire.com
- www.kayak.com
- www.lastminutetravel.com
- www.opodo.co.uk
- www.priceline.com
- www.sidestep.com
- www.site59.com
- www.smartertravel.com

SURFING FOR HOTELS

In addition to **Travelocity, Expedia, Orbitz, Priceline,** and **Hotwire** (see above), the following websites will help you with booking hotel rooms online:

Frommers.com: The Complete Travel Resource

For an excellent travel-planning resource, we highly recommend **Frommers.com** (www.frommers.com), voted Best Travel Site by *PC Magazine*. We're a little biased, of course, but we guarantee that you'll find the travel tips, reviews, monthly vacation giveaways, bookstore, and online-booking capabilities thoroughly indispensable. Among the special features are our popular **Destinations** section, where you'll get expert travel tips, hotel and dining recommendations, and advice on the sights to see for more than 3,500 destinations around the globe; the **Frommers.com Newsletter,** with the latest deals, travel trends, and money-saving secrets; our **Community** area featuring **Message Boards,** where Frommer's readers post queries and share advice (sometimes even our authors show up to answer questions); and our **Photo Center,** where you can post and share vacation tips. When your research is finished, the **Online Reservations System** (www.frommers.com/book_a_trip) takes you to Frommer's preferred online partners for booking your vacation at affordable prices.

- www.hotels.com
- www.quickbook.com
- www.travelaxe.net
- www.travelweb.com
- www.tripadvisor.com

It's a good idea to **get a confirmation number** and **make a printout** of any online booking transaction.

SURFING FOR RENTAL CARS

For booking rental cars online, the best deals are usually found at rental-car company websites, although all the major online travel agencies also offer rental-car reservations services. Priceline and Hotwire work well for rental cars, too; the only "mystery" is which major rental company you get, and for most travelers the difference between Hertz, Avis, and Budget is negligible.

10 Getting There

BY PLANE

There are two airports on the island. St. Maarten's **Princess Juliana International Airport** (© 599/545-4211; www.pjiae.com), SXM, is the Caribbean's second-busiest airport, topped only by San Juan, Puerto Rico. As of September 2006, a new, larger, more modern terminal was operational. You can also fly to the St. Martin's smaller **L'Espérance Airport,** in Grand Case (© 590/87-10-36). **American Airlines** (© 800/433-7300 in the U.S. and Canada; www.aa. com) offers more options and more frequent service into St. Maarten than any other airline—two daily nonstop flights from New York's JFK and one from Miami. Additional nonstop daily flights into St. Maarten are offered by American and its local affiliate, **American Eagle** (same number), from San Juan. Ask about American's package tours, which can save you a bundle. **Continental Airlines** (© 800/231-0856 in the U.S. and Canada; www.fly continental.com) has daily nonstop flights out of its hub in Newark, New Jersey, during the winter months. In low season flight times vary. **Delta** (© 800/241-4141 in the U.S. and Canada; www.delta. com) flies in from New York City, and **United** (© 800/538-2929) also offers flights from New York. Both leave from JFK. **US Airways** (© 800/428-4322 in the U.S. and Canada; www.usair.com) offers nonstop daily service from Charlotte and Philadelphia to St. Maarten.

Anguilla is served by more than 50 flights weekly, though nothing nonstop from the U.S. or U.K. The most reliable carrier is **American Eagle** (see above) out of San Juan, usually twice daily. You can also connect via inter-island carriers. **Winair** (Windward Islands Airways International; © 888/255-6889 in the U.S. and Canada; www.fly-winair.com) has eight daily flights to Anguilla from St. Maarten. **LIAT** (© 868/624-4727 in the U.S. and Canada, or 264/497-5002; www.liatairline.com) offers daily flights from Antigua. **Caribbean Star** (© 866/864-6272 in the U.S. and Canada, or 264/497-8690; www.flycaribbeanstar.com) wings in daily from Antigua.

St. Barts likewise has no nonstop or direct flights from North America or Europe. Again, **Winair** (see above) is your best bet out of St. Maarten, offering at least 10 daily flights. **St. Barth Commuter** (© 590/27-54-54; www.stbarthcommuter.com) flies several times daily from L'Espérance Airport in Grand Case, St. Martin and once daily from St. Maarten's Princess Juliana International Airport.

For more information on Anguilla and St. Barts, see "Getting There" in chapters 8 and 9.

GETTING INTO TOWN FROM THE AIRPORT

Most visitors use taxis to get around. Since they are unmetered on both sides of the island, always agree on the rate before getting into a cab. Rates are slightly different depending on which side of the island the taxi is based, though both Dutch and French cabs service the entire island.

St. Maarten taxis have minimum fares for two passengers; each additional passenger pays $4 extra. One piece of luggage per person is allowed free; each additional piece is $1 extra. Fares are 25% higher between 10pm and midnight, and 50% higher between midnight and 6am. Typical fares around the island are as follows: Queen Juliana Airport to Grand Case, $25; Marigot to Grand Case, $15; Queen Juliana Airport to anywhere in Marigot, $15 to $20; Queen Juliana Airport to the Maho Beach Hotel, $6; and from Queen Juliana Airport to Philipsburg, about $15. For late-night cab service on St. Maarten, call © **599/545-4317. Taxi Service & Information Center** operates at the port of Marigot (© **590/87-56-54**) on the French side.

FLYING FOR LESS: TIPS FOR GETTING THE BEST AIRFARE

- Passengers flying May through November will generally secure lower fares.
- Passengers who can book their ticket either **long in advance or at the last minute,** or who **fly midweek** or **at less-trafficked hours** may pay a fraction of the full fare. If your schedule is flexible, say so, and ask if you can secure a cheaper fare by changing your flight plans.
- Search **the Internet** for cheap fares (see "Planning Your Trip Online," earlier in this chapter).
- Keep an eye on local newspapers for **promotional specials** or **fare wars,** when airlines lower prices on their most popular routes. You rarely see fare wars offered for peak travel times, but if you can travel in the off-months, you may snag a bargain.
- **Consolidators,** also known as bucket shops, are great sources for international tickets, although they usually can't beat Internet fares within North America. Start by looking in Sunday newspaper travel sections; U.S. travelers should focus on the *New York Times, Los Angeles Times,* and *Miami Herald.* U.K. travelers should search in the *Independent, The Guardian,* or

---

Tips **Getting Through the Airport**

- Arrive at the airport 1 hour before a domestic flight and 2 hours before an international flight; if you show up late, tell an airline employee and he or she will probably whisk you to the front of the line.
- Beat the ticket-counter lines by using airport electronic kiosks or even online check-in from your home computer, from where you can print out boarding passes in advance. Curbside check-in is also a good way to avoid lines.
- Bring a current, government-issued photo ID such as a driver's license or passport. Children under 18 do not need government-issued photo IDs for flights within the U.S., but they do for international flights to most countries.
- Speed up security by removing your jacket and shoes before you're screened. In addition, remove metal objects such as big belt buckles. If you've got metallic body parts, a note from your doctor can prevent a long chat with the security screeners.
- Use a TSA-approved lock for your checked luggage. Look for Travel Sentry certified locks at luggage or travel shops and Brookstone stores (or online at www. brookstone.com).

The Observer. For less-developed destinations, small travel agents who cater to immigrant communities in large cities often have the best deals. *Beware:* Bucket shop tickets are usually nonrefundable or rigged with stiff cancellation penalties, often as high as 50% to 75% of the ticket price, and some put you on charter airlines, which may leave at inconvenient times and experience delays. Several reliable consolidators are worldwide and available online. **STA Travel** has been the world's leading consolidator for students since purchasing Council Travel, but their fares are competitive for travelers of all ages. **ELTExpress** (**Flights.com;** ② 800/TRAV-800; www.eltexpress. com) has excellent fares worldwide, particularly to Europe. They also have "local" websites in 12 countries. **FlyCheap** (② 800/FLY-CHEAP; www.1800flycheap.com), owned by package-holiday megalith MyTravel, has especially good fares to sunny destinations. **Air Tickets Direct** (© **800/778-3447;** www.airticketsdirect.com) is based in Montreal and leverages the currently weak Canadian dollar for low fares; they also book trips to places that U.S. travel agents won't touch, such as Cuba.

- Join **frequent-flier clubs.** Frequent-flier membership doesn't cost a cent, but it does entitle you to better seats, faster response to phone inquiries, and prompter service if your luggage is stolen or your flight is canceled or delayed, or if you want to change your seat. And you don't have to fly to earn points; **frequent-flier credit cards** can earn you thousands of miles for doing your everyday shopping. With more than 70 mileage awards programs on the market, consumers have never had more options. Investigate the program details of your favorite airlines before you sink points into any one. Consider which airlines have hubs in the airport nearest you, and, of those carriers, which have the most advantageous alliances, given your most common routes. To play the frequent-flier game to your best advantage, consult Randy Petersen's **Inside Flyer** (www.insideflyer.com). Petersen and friends review all the programs in detail and post regular updates on changes in policies and trends.

LONG-HAUL FLIGHTS: HOW TO STAY COMFORTABLE

- Your choice of airline and airplane will definitely affect your leg room. Find more details about U.S. airlines at **www.seat guru.com.** For international airlines, the research firm Skytrax has posted a list of average seat pitches at **www.airlinequality. com.**

- Emergency exit seats and bulkhead seats typically have the most legroom. Emergency exit seats are usually left unassigned

---

⟨Tips⟩ Don't Stow It—Ship It

Though pricey, it's sometimes worthwhile to travel luggage-free. Specialists in door-to-door luggage delivery include **Virtual Bellhop** (www.virtualbellhop.com), **SkyCap International** (www.skycapinternational.com), **Luggage Express** (www.usxp luggageexpress.com), and **Sports Express** (www.sportsexpress. com).

until the day of a flight (to ensure that someone able-bodied fills the seats); it's worth getting to the ticket counter early to snag one of these spots for a long flight. Many passengers find that bulkhead seating (the row facing the wall at the front of the cabin) offers more legroom, but keep in mind that bulkheads are where airlines often put baby bassinets, so you may be sitting next to an infant.

- To have two seats for yourself in a three-seat row, try for an aisle seat in a center section toward the back of coach. If you're traveling with a companion, book an aisle and a window seat. Middle seats are usually booked last, so chances are good you'll end up with three seats to yourselves.
- Ask about entertainment options. Many airlines offer seatback video systems where you get to choose your movies or play video games—but only on some of their planes. (Boeing 777s are your best bet.)
- To sleep, avoid the last row of any section or the row in front of an emergency exit, as these seats are the least likely to recline. Avoid seats near highly trafficked toilet areas. Avoid seats in the back of many jets—these can be narrower than those in the rest of coach. You also may want to reserve a window seat so you can rest your head and avoid being bumped in the aisle.
- Get up, walk around, and stretch every 60 to 90 minutes to keep your blood flowing. See "Avoiding 'Economy-Class Syndrome'" on p. 21.
- Drink water before, during, and after your flight to combat the lack of humidity in airplane cabins. Avoid alcohol, which will dehydrate you.
- If you're flying with kids, don't forget to carry on toys, books, pacifiers, and chewing gum to help them relieve ear pressure buildup during ascent and descent.

GETTING THERE BY FERRY

Ferries run between the ports of Marigot Bay, French St. Martin, and Blowing Point, Anguilla, every 30 to 45 minutes. The trip takes 20 to 25 minutes. The first ferry leaves St. Martin at 8am and the last at 7pm; from Blowing Point, the first ferry leaves at 7:30am and the last at 6:15pm. The one-way fare is $12 to $15 plus a $3 departure tax. No reservations are necessary; schedules and fares, of course, are always subject to change.

The **Voyager** vessels (© **590/87-10-68;** www.voyager-st-barths. com), which operate from a base in Gustavia harbor, make frequent (usually daily, sometimes twice a day) runs between St. Barts and either side of St. Maarten/St. Martin. The schedule varies according to the season, but the **Voyager II** usually departs Marigot Harbor for St. Barts every morning and evening. **Voyager I** travels from Oyster Pond to Gustavia. Advance reservations are a good idea. The technologically advanced, speedier, more luxurious, and stable catamaran **Rapid Explorer** (© **590/27-60-33;** www.st-barths.com/rapid-explorer) offers three daily 40-minute crossings between St. Maarten's Chesterfield Marina in Pointe Blanche and Marigot. Reservations are essential.

For additional details on Anguilla and St. Barts, see "Getting There" in chapters 8 and 9.

11 Packages for the Independent Traveler

Package tours are simply a way to buy the airfare, accommodations, and other elements of your trip (such as car rentals, airport transfers, and sometimes even activities) at the same time and often at discounted prices.

One good source of package deals is the airlines themselves. Most major airlines offer air/land packages, including **American Airlines Vacations** (© 800/321-2121; www.aavacations.com), **Delta Vacations** (© 800/221-6666; www.deltavacations.com), **Continental Airlines Vacations** (© 800/301-3800; www.covacations.com), and **United Vacations** (© 888/854-3899; www.unitedvacations.com). Several big **online travel agencies**—Expedia, Travelocity, Orbitz, Site59, and Lastminute.com—also do a brisk business in packages.

Reliable **Liberty Travel** (© **888/271-1584;** www.libertytravel.com) has more than 200 offices throughout New England, the mid-Atlantic, and Chicago. **Funjet Vacations** (© **888/558-6654;** www.funjet.com) is another tour operator that specializes in the Caribbean. **CheapCaribbean.com** (© **800/915-2322**) is a good clearing house, especially for last-minute discounts, and has its own user forum. **Apple Vacations** (© **800/888-7292;** www.applevacations.com) boasts 35 years of experience; it partners with USA3000 Airlines on charter and scheduled flights bringing down groups and individuals from several East Coast and Midwest gateways.

Travel packages are also listed in the travel section of your local Sunday newspaper. Or check ads in the national travel magazines such as *Arthur Frommer's Budget Travel Magazine, Travel + Leisure, National Geographic Traveler,* and *Condé Nast Traveler.*

> ### *Tips*   Ask before You Go
>
> Before you invest in a package deal or an escorted tour:
> - Always ask about the **cancellation policy.** Can you get your money back? Is there a deposit required?
> - Ask about the **accommodations choices and prices** for each. Then look up the hotels' reviews in a Frommer's guide and check their rates online for your specific dates of travel. Also find out what types of rooms are offered.
> - Request a complete **schedule** (escorted tours only).
> - Ask about the **size** and demographics of the group (escorted tours only).
> - Discuss what is included in the **price** (transportation, meals, tips, airport transfers, and such; escorted tours only).
> - Finally, look for **hidden expenses.** Ask whether airport departure fees and taxes, for example, are included in the total cost—they rarely are.

12 Getting Around St. Maarten/St. Martin

BY RENTAL CAR

Despite the islands' small size and ready availability of taxis, a car is the most efficient and often cost-effective way to experience and explore St. Maarten/St. Martin, Anguilla, and St. Barts. If you plan to stay at your resort, however, consider taking a day tour instead. Driving is on the right side of the road on St. Maarten/St. Martin and St. Barts, on the left on Anguilla. Parking is limited at most major tourist sites and in the capitals; costs vary. Expect traffic jams near the major towns and tourist areas on St. Maarten/St. Martin. International road signs are observed, and there are no Customs formalities at the border between the French and Dutch sides.

The St. Maarten taxi drivers' union strictly enforces a law that forbids anyone from picking up a car at the airport. As a result, every rental agency delivers cars directly to your hotel, where an employee will complete the paperwork. If you prefer to rent a car on arrival, head for one of the tiny rental kiosks across the road from the airport, but beware of long lines.

Avis maintains offices on both sides (© **800/331-1212** in the U.S. and Canada, 599/545-2847 on the Dutch side, or 590/87-50-60 on the French side; www.avis.com). **National** (© **800/328-4567** in the U.S. and Canada, or 599/545-5552 on the Dutch side; www.national car.com) is downtown on Airport Road, or at Queen Juliana Airport (© **599/545-4415**). **Budget** (© **800/472-3325** in the U.S. and Canada; www.budget.com) has offices at the airport (© **599/545-4030**), and at the cruise-ship terminal (© **599/543-0431**). All these companies charge roughly equivalent rates. All four major car-rental agencies require that renters be at least 25 years old. Your credit card issuer may provide insurance coverage, so check before your trip; otherwise, it may be wise to buy the fairly cheap collision-damage waiver (CDW) when you rent.

For information on Anguilla and St. Barts, see "Getting Around" in chapters 8 and 9.

BY BUS

All three islands feature wildly colored minivans that follow the main routes on a fairly regular basis from 8am to at least 8pm. It's a safe, cheap, if not always comfortable way to travel and learn more about the islands and their people. Cost varies, but is rarely more than $5 from one end of the island to the other. On St. Maarten/St. Martin, buses run daily from 6am to midnight and serve most of the major locations on both sides of the island. The most popular run is from Philipsburg on the Dutch side to Marigot on the French side. Privately owned and operated, minibuses tend to follow specific routes, with fares as follows: Grand Case to Marigot $1; Philipsburg to Marigot $1.50.

13 Tips on Accommodations

SAVING ON YOUR HOTEL ROOM

The **rack rate** is the maximum rate that a hotel charges for a room. I list these simply as a guideline. Hardly anybody pays this price, however, except in high season or on holidays. To lower the cost of your room:

- **Ask about special rates or other discounts.** You may qualify for corporate, student, military, senior, frequent flyer, trade union, or other discounts.
- **Dial direct.** When booking a room in a chain hotel, you'll often get a better deal by calling the individual hotel's reservation desk rather than the chain's main number.
- **Book online.** Many hotels offer Internet-only discounts, or supply rooms to Priceline, Hotwire, or Expedia at rates much lower than the ones you can get through the hotel itself.

- **Remember the law of supply and demand.** Resort hotels are most crowded and therefore most expensive on weekends, so discounts are usually available for midweek stays. Island hotels have high- and low-season prices, and booking even 1 day after high season ends can mean big discounts.
- **Look into group or long-stay discounts.** If you come as part of a large group, you should be able to negotiate a bargain rate. Likewise, if you're planning a long stay (at least 5 days), you might qualify for a discount. As a general rule, expect 1 night free after a 7-night stay.
- **Avoid excess charges and hidden costs.** When you book a room, ask whether the hotel charges for parking. Use your own cellphone, pay phones, or prepaid phone cards instead of dialing direct from hotel phones, which usually have exorbitant rates. And don't be tempted by the room's minibar offerings. Finally, ask about local taxes and service charges, which can increase the cost of a room by 15% or more.
- **Consider the pros and cons of all-inclusive resorts and hotels.** The term "all-inclusive" means different things at different hotels. Many all-inclusive hotels will include three meals daily, sports equipment, gym entry, and other amenities; others may include all or most drinks. In general, you'll save money going the "all-inclusive" way—as long as you use the facilities provided. The down side is that your choices are limited and you're stuck eating and playing in one place for the duration of your vacation.
- **Carefully consider your hotel's meal plan.** If you enjoy eating out and sampling the local cuisine, it makes sense to choose a **Continental Plan (CP),** which includes breakfast only, or a **European Plan (EP),** which doesn't include any meals and allows maximum flexibility. If you're more interested in saving money, opt for a **Modified American Plan (MAP),** which includes breakfast and one meal, or the **American Plan (AP),** which includes three meals. If you must choose a MAP, see if you can get a free lunch at your hotel if you decide to do dinner out.
- **Book an efficiency.** A room with a kitchenette allows you to shop for groceries and cook your own meals. This is a big money saver, especially for families on long stays.
- **Consider enrolling in hotel "frequent-stay" programs,** which are upping the ante lately to win the loyalty of repeat customers. Frequent guests can now accumulate points or

House-Swapping & Villa/Condo/Timeshare Rentals

House-swapping is becoming a more popular and viable means of travel; you stay in their place, they stay in yours, and you both get an authentic and personal view of the area, the opposite of the escapist retreat that many hotels offer. Try **HomeLink International** (Homelink.org), the largest and oldest home-swapping organization, founded in 1952, with over 11,000 listings worldwide ($75 for a yearly membership). **HomeExchange.org** ($50 for 6,000 listings) and **InterVac.com** ($69 for over 10,000 listings) are also reliable. Villas are particularly popular on St. Barts and, to a lesser degree, Anguilla and St. Maarten/St. Martin. **Wimco** (© 800/932-3222; www.wimco.com) is a reputable company handling properties on all three islands. For other suggestions for Anguilla and St. Barts, see chapters 8 and 9. In addition, St. Maarten is (in)famous for its timeshare complexes. For a few leading suggestions, see chapter 3. Members of **RCI** (© 317/805-9000; www.rci.com) or **Interval International** (© 888/784-3447; www.intervalworld.com) can look into the feasibility of exchanges.

credits to earn free hotel nights, airline miles, in-room amenities, merchandise, tickets to concerts and events, discounts on sporting facilities—and even credit toward stock in the participating hotel, in the case of the Jameson Inn hotel group. Perks are awarded not only by many chain hotels and motels (Hilton HHonors, Marriott Rewards, Wyndham ByRequest, to name a few), but individual inns and B&Bs. Many chain hotels partner with other hotel chains, car-rental firms, airlines, and credit card companies to give consumers additional incentive to do repeat business.

Refer to chapter 3 for information on St. Maarten/St. Martin lodging options and taxes/surcharges. For Anguilla and St. Barts, refer to chapters 8 and 9, respectively.

LANDING THE BEST ROOM

Somebody has to get the best room in the house. It might as well be you. You can start by joining the hotel's frequent-guest program, which may make you eligible for upgrades. A hotel-branded credit card usually gives its owner "silver" or "gold" status in frequent-guest programs for free. Always ask about a corner room. They're often larger and quieter, with more windows and light, and they often cost the same as standard rooms. When you make your reservation, ask if the hotel is renovating; if it is, request a room away from the construction. Ask about nonsmoking rooms, rooms with views, rooms with twin, queen- or king-size beds. If you're a light sleeper, request a quiet room away from vending machines, elevators, restaurants, bars, and discos. Ask for a room that has been most recently renovated or redecorated.

If you aren't happy with your room when you arrive, ask for another one. Most lodgings will be willing to accommodate you.

Ask the following questions before you book a room:

- What's the view like? Cost-conscious travelers may be willing to pay less for a back room facing the parking lot, especially if they don't plan to spend much time in their room.
- Does the room have air-conditioning or ceiling fans? Do the windows open? If they do, and the nighttime entertainment takes place alfresco, you may want to find out when show time is over.
- What's included in the price? Your room may be moderately priced, but if you're charged for beach chairs, towels, sports equipment, and other amenities, you could end up spending more than you bargained for.
- How far is the room from the beach and other amenities? If it's far, is there transportation to and from the beach, and is it free?

14 Tips on Dining

All three islands in this book are renowned for their fine dining. For St. Maarten/St. Martin specifics, see chapter 4. Consult chapters 8 and 9 for details on Anguilla and St. Barts.

To save money on St. Maarten/St. Martin and St. Barts, get take-out food for picnics. Several restaurants take the sting from the euro's strength by offering 1€ = US$1 exchange rates for customers paying cash (this rarely applies to credit card users). Several eateries, especially on the Dutch side, provide Internet coupons for free drinks or a second main course (note: *entrée* is actually the French term; *plat* means main course) at half price. Lunch is generally less expensive, and the menu selection often simpler. Look for multi-course prix-fixe (but not Chef's tasting or degustation) menus; these can represent bargains, often including a beverage. Tipping is usually hassle-free (the menu will state service included), but always confirm whether gratuities are added and give a little extra when you feel the staff warrants it. If there's no service charge, add 15% to 20% to your bill.

15 Recommended Books, Films & Music

The Caribbean has produced numerous fine authors, including Nobel Prize laureate Derek Walcott (St. Lucia), V. S. Naipaul (Trinidad), Anthony Winkler (Jamaica), Jean Rhys (Dominica), and Jamaica Kincaid (Antigua). Alas, none of the three islands in this book boast noted native writers. But there are a few literal "beach" reads worth mentioning. *The Captain's Fund* (Resource Power Publishing) by Raina Wissing Harris, a very purple "romance suspense" novel of murder, heiresses-in-distress, and black market diamonds is notable for its St. Maarten/St. Martin setting with such familiar landmarks as Friar's Beach Café, The Horny Toad Guesthouse, and Joe's Jewelry International. St. Martin inspired celebrity chef/author Anthony Bourdain's *Gone Bamboo* (Villard/Bloomsbury USA). This Leonard/Hiaasen-wannabe, transvestite-mafiosi-and-margaritas comic thriller is an improbable but likeable soufflé.

Melinda and Bob Blanchard's *A Trip to the Beach: Living on Island Time in the Caribbean* (Clarkson Potter/Three Rivers Press) and recent *Live What You Love: Notes from an Unusual Life* (Sterling) are the true-life restaurateurs' hilarious yet sympathetic, ungarnished version of Herman Wouk's riotous fictional account of an American hotelier in the Antilles, *Don't Stop the Carnival*. *Murder in St. Barts* (Beachfront Publishing), is a passable Gendarme Trenet novel by J. R. Ripley (note that teasing last name, mystery aficionados), better known for the Tony Kozol whodunits. Jimmy Buffet's *Tales from Margaritaville* (Fawcett Books) offers fictional short stories of West Indian life, many based on his years of St. Barts residency.

FAST FACTS: St. Maarten/St. Martin

American Express None of the three islands has an official AmEx representative.

Area Codes The country and area code for French St. Martin and St. Barts is 590/590, for Dutch St. Maarten 599, and for Anguilla 264.

ATM Networks See "Money" on p. 14.

Business Hours On the Dutch side, most banks are open Monday to Friday from 8:30am to 3:30pm, Saturday from 9am to noon. On the French side, they are usually open Monday to Friday 8:30am to 1:30pm. It's easy to find ATMs. On the Dutch side, several banks are clustered along Front Street in Philipsburg. On the French side, most banks are along rue de la République in Marigot. Store hours vary, but the French side shops generally open 10am to 5pm (closing for lunch), while Dutch side shops often stay open continuously and as late as 11pm.

Car Rentals See "Getting Around St. Maarten/St. Martin" on p. 34.

Currency See "Money" on p. 14.

Driving Rules See "Getting Around St. Maarten/St. Martin" on p. 34.

Drugstores Both sides have several pharmacies, though none are open 24 hours. On the **French** side, try **Pharmacie du Port** (rue de la Liberté, Marigot; ℭ 590/87-50-79; Mon–Sat 8am–7:30pm, Sun hours vary). On the **Dutch** side, try **Philipsburg Pharmacy** (4 E. Voges St., Philipsburg; ℭ 599/542-3001; Mon–Fri 7:30am–7pm, Sat 9am–1pm, Sun 10am–noon), **Simpson Bay Pharmacy** (Simpson Bay Yacht Club, 163 Welfare Rd.; ℭ 599/544-3653; Mon–Fri 8:15am–7pm, Sat 9am–1pm, Sun 5–7pm), and **The Druggist** (Airport Rd., Simpson Bay; ℭ 599/545-2777; Mon–Fri 8:30am–7:30pm, Sat noon–7pm, Sun 1–3pm). For pharmacies on Anguilla and St. Barts, see p. 142 and p. 170.

Electricity Dutch St. Maarten and Anguilla use the same voltage (110-volt AC, 60 cycles) with the same electrical configurations as the United States, so adapters and transformers are not necessary. However, on French St. Martin and St. Barts, 220-volt AC prevails, so you'll usually need transformers and adapters. To simplify things, many hotels on both sides of the island have installed sockets suitable for both European and North American appliances.

Embassies & Consulates There is no U.S. diplomatic representation on Anguilla. **U.S. citizens** are advised to register with the consulates at Bluff House, English Harbour on Antigua (ℭ 268/463-6531; ryderj@candw.ag), or Georgetown, Barbados (visit http://bridgetown.usembassy.gov or https://travelregistration.state.gov/ibrs/home.asp). Likewise **Canadian citizens** should register with the Canadian High Commission on Barbados.

Australian citizens can register with the Australian High Commission in Port-of-Spain, Trinidad and Tobago (© 868/628-4732). On St. Maarten/St. Martin, **citizens of the U.S.** are represented by its consulate at St. Anna Boulevard, Willemstad, Curaçao (© 599/961-3066). There is a Canadian conuslate at 16A Topaz Dr., St. Maarten (© 599/544-5023). **Citizens of the U.K.** can register with the consulate at 38 Jan Sofat in Willemstad, Curaçao (© 599/747-3322).

Emergencies On the **Dutch** side, call the **police** at © 542-2222 or an **ambulance** at © 542-2111; to report a **fire**, call © 911 or 120. On the **French** side, you can reach the **police** by dialing © 17 or 87-50-10. In case of **fire**, dial © 18. For an **ambulance** dial © 15 or 29-04-04. For Anguilla and St. Barts, see "Fast Facts" on p. 141 and p. 169, respectively.

Etiquette & Customs Despite the clothing-optional beaches on St. Martin, St. Maarten, and St. Barts, flaunting (or any flagrant display) is frowned upon, especially on proper British Anguilla. Except at casual beach bars, men should wear some kind of shirt, women a wrap. Smart resort wear is recommended for most restaurants, especially at dinner. "Sunday dress" is appropriate when visiting churches, though ties aren't mandatory for men. In general, profanity is frowned upon.

Holidays National holidays are New Year's Day, January 1; Epiphany, January 6 (French side); Carnival, early February; Good Friday and Easter Monday, usually April; Labor Day, May 1; Ascension Day, early May; Bastille Day, July 14 (French side); Schoelcher Day, July 21 (French side); Assumption Day, August 15; All Saints' Day, November 1; Concordia Day and St. Martin Day, November 11; Christmas Day, December 25; and Boxing Day, December 26. For more information, see "St. Maarten/ St. Martin Calendar of Events," earlier in this chapter.

Hospitals On the Dutch side, go to the **Medical Center,** Welegen Road, Cay Hill (© 599/543-1111). On the French side, the local hospital is **Hôpital Concordia Mont Accords,** near Marigot in Concordia (© 590/52-25-25). For Anguilla and St. Barts, refer to "Fast Facts" on p. 141 and p. 169, respectively.

Internet Access Cybercafes can be found in both Marigot and Philipsburg, but the hours are often limited.

Measurements See the chart on the inside front cover of this book for details on converting metric measurements to non-metric equivalents.

Newspapers & Magazines In addition to several local newspapers (*The Daily Herald* is the leading English-language publication), visitors can pick up one of several useful tourist magazines including *St. Maarten Nature, St. Maarten Events, Discover St. Martin/St. Maarten, St. Maarten Nights, Ti Gourmet,* and *Vacation St. Maarten.* For Anguilla and St. Barts, check "Fast Facts" in chapters 8 and 9.

Passports Allow plenty of time before your trip to apply for a passport; processing normally takes 3 weeks but can take longer during busy periods (especially spring). And keep in mind that if you need a passport in a hurry, you'll pay a higher processing fee.

For Residents of Australia: You can pick up an application from your local post office or any branch of Passports Australia, but you must schedule an interview at the passport office to present your application materials. Call the **Australian Passport Information Service** at ✆ **131-232,** or visit the government website at www.passports.gov.au.

For Residents of Canada: Passport applications are available at travel agencies throughout Canada or from the central **Passport Office,** Department of Foreign Affairs and International Trade, Ottawa, ON K1A 0G3 (✆ **800/567-6868;** www.ppt.gc.ca).

For Residents of Ireland: You can apply for a 10-year passport at the **Passport Office,** Setanta Centre, Molesworth Street, Dublin 2 (✆ **01/671-1633;** www.irlgov.ie/iveagh). Those under 18 and over 65 must apply for a €12 3-year passport. You can also apply at 1A South Mall, Cork (✆ **021/272-525**), or at most main post offices.

For Residents of New Zealand: You can pick up a passport application at any New Zealand Passports Office or download it from their website. Contact the **Passports Office** at ✆ **0800/225-050** in New Zealand or 04/474-8100, or log on to www.passports.govt.nz.

For Residents of the United Kingdom: To pick up an application for a standard 10-year passport (5-year passport for children under 16), visit your nearest passport office, major post office, or travel agency or contact the **United Kingdom Passport Service** at ✆ **0870/521-0410** or search its website at www.ukpa.gov.uk.

For Residents of the United States: Whether you're applying in person or by mail, you can download passport applications from the U.S. State Department website at

http://travel.state.gov. To find your regional passport office, either check the U.S. State Department website or call the **National Passport Information Center** toll-free number (© 877/ 487-2778) for automated information.

Police See "Emergencies," above.

Restrooms Public facilities are few and far betweem other than a couple of options in Marigot, Philipsburg, and Orient Beach. Hotel lobbies and restaurants are the best options, though you technically should be a guest or customer (you can always purchase a bottle of water or soft drink).

Safety See "Health & Safety," earlier in this chapter.

Smoking While many larger properties offer nonsmoking rooms, there are no regulations against smoking.

Taxes There is a 3€ ($3.60) departure tax for departures from L'Espérance Airport on the French side. However, for depar-tures from Princess Juliana Airport on the Dutch side, there's a tax of $30 ($10 if you're leaving the island for St. Eustatius or Saba; if you're leaving by ferry from Marigot Pier to Anguilla, the departure tax is $4); the tax is sometimes included in the airfare. On the Dutch side, a government tax of between 5% and 8%, depending on the category of hotel you stay in, is added to hotel bills. On the French side, hotels must levy a *taxe de séjour* (hotel tax); this differs from hotel to hotel, depending on its classification, but is often 5% a day. In addition to these taxes, most hotels add a (mandatory) serv-ice charge of around 10% to 15% to your hotel bill. For Anguilla and St. Barts, refer to "Fast Facts" (chapters 8 and 9).

Telephones To call **St. Maarten/St. Martin, Anguilla, and St. Barts:**

1. Dial the international access code: 011 from the U.S.; 00 from the U.K., Ireland, or New Zealand; or 0011 from Australia
2. Dial the country code 599 for St. Maarten and 590 for St. Barts and St. Martin
3. Dial the city code 590 (a second time) and then the six-digit number on St. Barts and St. Martin. The St. Maarten city code is 54, then dial the five-digit number. Dialing Anguilla from the U.S. doesn't require 011, just 1, then the 264 area code, followed by the seven-digit number.
4. To call the French side from the Dutch side and vice versa is an expensive international "long distance" call, going

through Byzantine routing to Europe and back. From the French to Dutch side, dial 00, then 599, 54 and the five-digit number. From the Dutch to the French side (and St. Barts), dial 00, then 590590 (590690 for cell phones) and the six-digit number.

To make international calls: From St. Maarten/St. Martin and St. Barts, first dial 00 and then the country code (U.S. or Canada 1, U.K. 44, Ireland 353, Australia 61, New Zealand 64). Next dial the area code and number. For example, if you wanted to call the British Embassy in Washington, D.C., you would dial 00-1-202-588-7800. From Anguilla to the U.S., dial 1, then the number.

On the Dutch side there are facilities for overseas calls, but from the French side you cannot make collect calls to the States and there are no coin-operated phones. At the Marigot post office you can purchase a *Telecarte,* giving you 40 units. A typical 5-minute call to the States takes up to 120 units. There are two public phones at the Marigot tourist office from which it's possible to make credit card calls. There are six public phones at the post office.

For directory assistance: Dial 150 if you're looking for a number inside St. Maarten/St. Martin, and dial 0 for numbers to all other countries.

For operator assistance: If you need operator assistance in making a call, dial 0 if you're trying to make an international call and a number within St. Maarten/St. Martin.

Toll-free numbers: There are no toll-free numbers on St. Maarten/St. Martin, Anguilla, or St. Barts, and calling a 1-800 number in the States from them is not toll-free. In fact, it costs the same as an overseas call.

Time Zone St. Maarten/St. Martin, Anguilla, and St. Barts operate on Atlantic Standard Time year-round. Thus in winter, if it's 6pm in Philipsburg, it's 5pm in New York. During daylight saving time in the United States, the islands and the U.S. East Coast are on the same time.

Tipping See "Tips on Dining," earlier in this chapter, for restaurant guidelines. Otherwise, porters and bellmen expect $1 per bag. Taxi drivers should receive 10% of the fare, more if they offer touring or other suggestions.

Useful Phone Numbers **U.S. Dept. of State Travel Advisory:** ℂ 202/647-5225 (manned 24 hr.); **U.S. Passport Agency:** ℂ 202/647-0518; **U.S. Centers for Disease Control International Traveler's Hot Line:** ℂ 404/332-4559.

Water The water on St. Maarten/St. Martin, Anguilla, and St. Barts is safe to drink. In fact, most hotels serve desalinated water.

3

Where to Stay on St. Maarten/St. Martin

Despite its small size, St. Maarten/St. Martin offers a surprising range of accommodations: large sterile high-rise all-inclusive resorts, medium-size chain hotels catering to tour groups, a luxury enclave, small "bourgeois" hotels, locally owned guesthouses ranging from boutique-y to budget, not to mention villas, apartments, and—the scourge of the island—timeshare complexes. As you leave the airport, it seems you can't go more than a few feet without someone hawking a new or expanded development. Hurricanes, particularly Luis in 1995, delayed or destroyed many a property, but the mania is experiencing a resurgence, even on the quieter French side.

Frankly, it's getting increasingly difficult to distinguish hotels from timeshares, which are no longer restricted to annexes—especially on the Dutch side. As a result, maintenance isn't always as diligent as it should be: Be prepared to find more wear and tear from ripped fabric to rusted faucets. In general, the French resorts are more intimate and romantic, though the flip side is periodic problems with electricity and water pressure at smaller hostelries. What the Dutch properties lack in ambience, they compensate for in functional, comfortable rooms with all the "extras."

1 Dutch St. Maarten

Remember, a government tax of between 5% and 8%, plus a service charge of 10% to 15% will be added to your hotel bill. Ask whether it's included in the original rates you're quoted to save yourself a shock when you check out.

VERY EXPENSIVE

Divi Little Bay Beach Resort *☞*   About a 10-minute drive east of the airport, this hotel sits on a sandy sheltered beach caught between two craggy headlands. It originated as a simple guesthouse in 1955, and soon became famous as the vacation home of the Netherlands' Queen Juliana, Prince Bernhard, and Queen Beatrix.

(Tips) Other Options

Although I've recommended some hotel-timeshare combos below, several others can represent excellent value, especially during low season, and offer all the facilities of any beach resort. Units in the rental pool usually meet certain standards in terms of amenities. Possibilities include **Pelican Resort** (© 800/550-7088 in the U.S. or 599/544-2503; www.pelican resort.com), **Caravanserai** (© 877/786-1002 in the U.S. or 599/545-4000; www.caravanseraibeachresort.com), and **Princess Port de Plaisance Resort, Marina & Casino** (© 800/622-7836 in the U.S. or 599/544-5222; www.princessresortandcasino.com). Another route is villa rentals. Expect to pay anywhere from $2,000 to $68,000 per week in high season. **Wimco** (© 800/932-3222 or 800/449-1553; www.wimco.com) is the acknowledged king of Caribbean villa living and represents dozens of properties from one- to nine-bedrooms. For high-end properties, look no further than **Pierres Caraïbes,** affiliated with Christie's Great Estates (on the French side: rue Kennedy, Marigot, © 590/29-21-46; on the Dutch side: Plaza del Lago, Simpson Bay Yacht Club, © 599/544-2622; www.pierres-caraibes.com). **Jennifer's Vacation Villas** (Plaza del Lago, Simpson Bay Yacht Club; © 599/544-3107; www.jennifers vacationvillas.com) arguably boasts the largest selection, and caters to all budgets. All three companies will source chefs, drivers, even personal trainers.

Severely damaged during the hurricanes of the early 1990s, it was rebuilt in 1997 as the flagship of the Divi chain. Its design evokes a European seaside village, with pastel stucco walls and terra-cotta roofs, accented by Dutch colonial touches. The property's upper reaches encompass the ruins of Fort Amsterdam, once Dutch St. Maarten's most prized military stronghold. Gardens are carefully landscaped, and Divi improved the beach (whose southwest point offers sublime snorkeling) after it suffered massive erosion; alas, it's often overrun by cruise ship passengers.

This hotel development is larger than its 265 units imply, since part of it is devoted to the maintenance and marketing of timeshare units, which crawl up the promontory. It evokes a large residential apartment complex enhanced by hotel-style amenities and services. Accommodations are airy, accented with ceramic tiles and pastel

On the Horizon

Two new major American-based chain hotels (actually renovations and expansions of previous incarnations) debut in
2007. The **Westin St. Maarten Dawn Beach Resort & Spa** and
Westin St. Maarten Dawn Beach Residences (www.starwood
hotels.com) are slated to open January 2007. The 317 mostly
oceanview guest rooms will feature all the expected amenities. Facilities will include a full-service, European-style Hibiscus Spa, fitness center (with the brand's patented private
workout rooms), retail shops with duty-free shopping, a large
casino, freshwater infinity pool complete with swim-up bar
and whirlpool, two oceanfront restaurants, watersports
galore including dive shop, car rental, expansive meeting
facilities, and Westin Kid's Club®—Camp Scallywag.

Carlson Hotels Worldwide will inaugurate the **Radisson
St. Martin Resort and Spa** (www.radisson.com/stmartin)—
formerly Le Meridien/L'Habitation de Lonvilliers—in summer
2007 after a $60-million investment that transforms the exist-
ing buildings and grounds (including extensive tropical gardens and artificial lagoons) along 480m (1,600 ft.) of Anse
Marcel, one of St. Martin's prettiest coves, surrounded on
three sides by mountains. The 250 units feature flatscreen
TVs, complimentary Wi-Fi, and premium amenities. Facilities
will include two pools (one free-form, one recreational "lazy
river"), Radisson's second Larimar spa, a watersports center
and dive shop, meeting space, two restaurants, and a contemporary upscale lounge.

colors; deluxe units have kitchenettes. Bathrooms tend to be small
and compact, but have adequate shelf space and a tub/shower combination. There's wide disparity between units as management
embarked on a diligent refurbishment program (ensure when booking that your room was recently redone).

Little Bay (P.O. Box 961), Philipsburg, St. Maarten, N.A. © **800/367-3484** in the
U.S., or 599/542-2333. Fax 599/542-4336. www.divilittlebay.com. 265 units. Winter
$277–$300 double, $310–$352 1-bedroom apt, $495 2-bedroom apt; off season
$208–$255 double, $249–$305 1-bedroom apt, $375 2-bedroom apt. Modified
American Plan (breakfast and dinner) $48 per day adult, $28 per day child (3–12).
All-Inclusive (1-week minimum) $90 per day adult, $55 per child. Children under 15
stay free in parent's room. AE, DC, MC, V. **Amenities:** 3 restaurants; bar; cybercafe;
3 outdoor pools; 2 lit tennis courts; gym; spa; watersports center; dive shop; jet skis;
kayaks; sailing; snorkeling; water-skiing; windsurfing; activities coordinator; car

rental; salon; laundry service; coin-operated laundry; nonsmoking rooms; meeting rooms; minimart. *In room:* A/C, TV, kitchenette (in some), beverage maker, hair dryer, iron, safe, Jacuzzi (in some).

Princess Heights ☞ *(Finds)*   This luxury boutique condo-hotel and intimate hideaway climbs the hills above Dawn Beach, just across the road, showcasing smashing views of the water. Opening onto St. Barts in the distance, the tastefully appointed suites contain one or two bedrooms, with separate living rooms opening onto balconies offering vistas (only slightly compromised by the new Westin eyesore). Granite-topped counters, Italian-clay-tiled terraces, lots of marble (including fabulous bathrooms with whirlpool tubs), and well-crafted kitchens make for fine living, and the hillside location spells privacy. Thoughtful touches include two entrances and elevators (ensuring you won't hike more than two flights) and forms to stock your kitchen prior to arrival. A new building will double the number of suites by 2008.

156 Oyster Pond Rd., Oyster Pond, St. Maarten, N.A. ✆ **800/441-7227** or 599/543-6906. Fax 599/54-36007. www.princessheights.com. 15 units (31 by 2008). Winter $350–$450 double; off season $225–$375 double. Extra person $45, off season $35. Children under 12 stay free in parent's room. AE, DISC, MC, V. **Amenities:** Outdoor pool; fitness room; car rental; limited room service; massage; babysitting; laundry service; dry cleaning; computer with Internet access. *In room:* A/C, TV, VCR or DVD, minibar, kitchen, safe, washer/dryer (in some).

Sonesta Maho Beach Hotel & Casino ☞   Separated into three distinct sections, this megaresort, practically a self-contained village with its sprawling convention facilities, is the island's largest hotel. Even with its failings, it's the closest thing on either the Dutch or French side to a Las Vegas–style blockbuster resort. It has a rather anonymous feeling (it's always full of conventioneers and giant tour groups), but it is completely modern and up-to-date, thanks to continual upgrades and renovations. Set on a 4-hectare (10-acre) tract that straddles the busy, and often congested, coastal road adjacent to the crescent-shaped Maho Beach, the hotel's scattered structures are painted a trademark cream and white.

The commodious rooms are conservatively but comfortably furnished. Each has wicker and rattan furniture, Italian tiles, a 27-inch TV, plush upholstered pieces, a walk-in closet, pillow-top mattresses, and good soundproofing (which is important, since you hear the thunder of planes landing at the nearby airport several times a day when you're on the hotel's beach).

The hotel contains three separate, directly managed restaurants (The Point is excellent but avoid The Palms, where karaoke blasts

St. Maarten/St. Martin

Pointe Arago

Pointe du Bluff

Pointe du Plum
Baie aux Prunes **2**

Baie Rouge

Baie Nettlé

Baie de Marigot

Nettlé Beach **8**

Marigot

3 4 **5-6 7**

Marigot Fort

Baie Longue **1**

Cupecoy Bay Beach

88 **83-87**

82

Simpson Bay Lagoon

Border Monument

Mullet Bay Beach **81**

75-76

Queen Juliana International Airport

68-69

64-65

77-80

74

70

67

66

Simpson Bay Beach

61-63

48

57-60

Maho Bay Beach

71-73

Kimsha Beach

Koolbaai

50-52

53-56

49

Caribbean Sea

Cole Bay

Airport ✈
Beach 🏖
Mountain ⛰

0 ___ 1 Mile
0 ___ 1 Kilometer

N

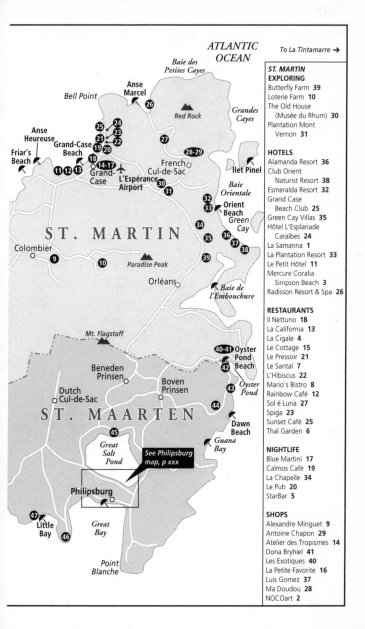

Philipsburg

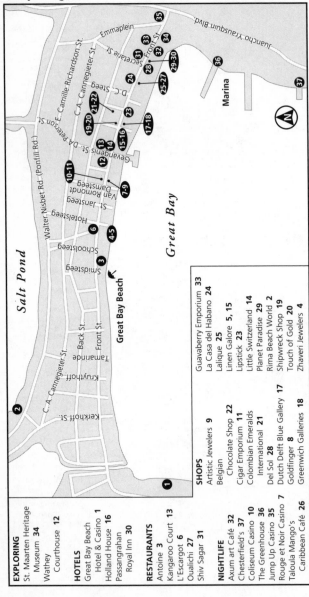

EXPLORING
St. Maarten Heritage
  Museum **34**
Wathey
  Courthouse **12**

HOTELS
Great Bay Beach
  Hotel & Casino **1**
Holland House **16**
Passangrahan
  Royal Inn **30**

RESTAURANTS
Antoine **3**
Kangaroo Court **13**
L'Escargot **6**
Oualichi **27**
Shiv Sagar **31**

NIGHTLIFE
Axum art Café **32**
Chesterfield's **37**
Coliseum Casino **10**
The Greenhouse **36**
Jump Up Casino **35**
Rouge et Noir Casino **7**
Taloula Mango's
  Caribbean Café **26**

SHOPS
Artistic Jewelers **9**
Belgian
  Chocolate Shop **22**
Cigar Emporium **11**
Colombian Emeralds
  International **21**
Del Sol **28**
Dutch Delft Blue Gallery **17**
Goldfinger **8**
Greenwich Galleries **18**

Guavaberry Emporium **33**
La Casa del Habano **24**
Lalique **25**
Linen Galore **5, 15**
Lipstick **23**
Little Switzerland **14**
Planet Paradise **29**
Rima Beach World **2**
Shipwreck Shop **19**
Touch of Gold **20**
Zhaveri Jewelers **4**

louder than the jets), with another half-dozen on-site that are independently operated but accept all-inclusive guests. The glitzy Casino Royale, across the street from the accommodations, includes a cabaret theater for glittery shows and Q-Club, the island's splashiest late-night dance spot. Maho Plaza, which occupies the resort's street front, contains several dozen shops open late, restaurants, Internet center, scuba-diving center, dance club, piano bar, even a classy gentleman's club.

Maho Bay, 1 Rhine Rd., St. Maarten, N.A. *C* 800/223-0757 in the U.S., or 599/545-2115. Fax 599/545-3180. www.sonesta.com/stmaarten. 537 units. Winter $250–$350 double, $400–$600 suite, from $860 2-bedroom unit; off season $200–$270 double, $340–$420 suite, from $675 2-bedroom unit. AE, DC, DISC, MC, V. **Amenities:** 9 restaurants; 5 bars; cybercafe; 2 outdoor pools; golf (nearby); 4 tennis courts; fitness center; spa; business services; shopping arcade; babysitting; laundry service; rooms for those w/limited mobility; casino; showroom; dance club. *In room:* A/C, TV, dataport, Wi-Fi, fridge (in some), beverage maker (in some), hair dryer, safe.

EXPENSIVE

Great Bay Beach Hotel & Casino ✦   This hurricane-ravaged property, ideally located on a less deserted section of the eponymous strand a few minutes' walk from downtown Philipsburg, reopened in 2005 after a $10-million renovation. Virtually every area was completely refurbished; several facilities, including the fine La Cucina Italian restaurant and a splendid infinity pool with swim-up bar were added or expanded. Handsome Art Deco touches enliven the public spaces and halls, though the sizable rooms (more than half with an ocean view) feature standard decorative tropical trappings. Studios and one- and two-bedroom suites include kitchens and Murphy or sofa beds. Friendly management, extensive facilities (including a full-service spa), and an enviable location make it a fine bet for honeymooners and families alike.

19 Little Bay Rd. (P.O. Box 910), Philipsburg, St. Maarten, N.A. *C* 800/223-0757 in the U.S. or 599/542-2446. Fax 599/544-3008. www.greatbaybeachresort.com. 262 units. $240–$350 double ($410–$550 all-inclusive), $490–$625 suite ($720–$880 all-inclusive); off season $180–$290 double ($350–$470 all-inclusive), $390–$550 suite ($600–$790 all-inclusive). AE, DISC, MC, V. **Amenities:** 4 restaurants; 4 bars; 3 outdoor pools; lit tennis court; fitness center; spa; outdoor hot tub; boating; jet-skiing; snorkeling; windsurfing; car rental; business services; babysitting; casino. *In room:* A/C, ceiling fan, TV, dataport, kitchenette (in some), fridge (in some), beverage maker, hair dryer, safe.

The Horny Toad Guesthouse ✦ *Value*   This homey, welcoming place is run by an expatriate from Maine, Betty Vaughan. Unfortunately, the hotel is near the airport, but the roar of jumbo jets is heard only briefly a few times a day. Children 7 and under are not allowed, but families with older children often come here to avoid the megaresorts, and second-timers quickly become "part of the family."

Seven immaculate, individually decorated units sit in an amply proportioned 1950s beachside house built by the island's former governor. The eighth room is in half of an octagonal "round house," with large windows and sea views. Guest rooms range from medium-size to spacious, and each has a fully equipped kitchen, and a small but well-kept shower-only bathroom. Prime lodgings open right onto the beach but second-floor units boast especially sensational views of Saba, Statia, St. Kitts, and Nevis. There's no pool, no restaurant, and no organized activities of any kind. However, the beach is a few steps away and there are often impromptu get-togethers around the pair of gas-fired barbecues.

2 Vlaun Dr., Simpson Bay, St. Maarten, N.A. ℂ **800/417-9361** in the U.S., or 599/545-4323. Fax 599/545-3316. www.thtgh.com. 8 units. Winter $198 double; off season $107 double. Extra person $40 in winter, $25 off season. MC, V. No children under 7 allowed. **Amenities:** Laundry service; nonsmoking rooms; grills; computer with Internet access. *In room:* A/C (in most), ceiling fan, kitchen, fridge, safe, no phone.

Mary's Boon Beach Plantation ℛℛ *(Finds)*   This is the most charming and well-managed small inn on Dutch St. Maarten. It's very near the airport (so you do hear jets taking off and landing a few times a day), but it's also only minutes from casinos, shops, and restaurants. Mary's Boon draws a loyal repeat clientele, including CEOs and literati who appreciate its understated barefoot elegance and intimacy. Everything's relaxed and informal, though the service is alert and attentive. Owners Mark and Karla Cleveland continually tinker with paradise, improving the grounds, the rooms, the amenities, the experience. Hospitable little behind-the-scenes touches include walkways named for longtime staffers and an in-house carpenter who fashions the intricate moldings and carved doors.

Accommodations have verandas or terraces, but each varies architecturally. Those directly facing the sea are breezy, high-ceilinged, and comfortably unpretentious, with decor that wouldn't be out of place in a 1970s-era Florida motel. I adore the exceptionally stylish, newer units set within the lush garden. Done in jewel tones, they usually contain four-poster cherry-wood beds, gold gilt frames, quilts, tapestries, Balinese teak carvings, even African masks or other fanciful artful touches. Regardless of their age, most units have king-size beds, kitchenettes, Wi-Fi access, and Italian-tile shower-only bathrooms. The inn enjoys direct access to one of St. Maarten's finest beaches. The family-style restaurant offers good-value fixed-price dinners (with seconds included).

117 Simpson Bay Rd. (P.O. Box 2078), St. Maarten, N.A. (or P.O. Box 523882, Miami, FL 33152). © **599/545-7000.** Fax 599/545-3403. www.marysboon.com. 34 units. Winter $175–$275 double, $225–$300 1-bedroom suite, $300–$425 2-bedroom suite; off season $75–$200 double, $125–$200 1-bedroom, $195–$275 2-bedroom. Extra person $30. AE, MC, V. **Amenities:** Restaurant; bar; outdoor pool; limited room service; babysitting; massage. In room: A/C, ceiling fan, TV, dataport, Wi-Fi, kitchenette, kitchen (in some), fridge, beverage maker, hair dryer, iron, safe.

Oyster Bay Beach Resort ☞ Crowning a promontory at the end of a twisting, scenic road, a 1-minute walk from Dawn Beach near the French border, this elegant retreat was originally designed for vacationers who don't like overly commercialized megaresorts, like the Sonesta Maho. Once an intimate isolated inn, it continues growing by leaps and bounds. It no longer qualifies as cozy, but it's still not overwhelming. The crenellated fortresslike structure stands guard over a 14-hectare (35-acre) protected marina. There's a central stone courtyard and an alfresco lobby, with brown wicker, woven straw, and fine paintings. Several units are being aggressively marketed as timeshares, prompting ongoing renovations, reconfiguring, and refurbishment. Travelers with disabilities may have trouble with the hilly layout and abundance of stairs.

More than half the units have kitchens (with dishwasher), and most have West Indian decor with lots of rattan and wicker, soft color schemes, bold local paintings, and striking close-up photos of magnified blossoms. The bedrooms offer balconies overlooking the pond, marina, or sea; the deluxe and superior rooms are preferable to the tower suites. Rooms are airy and fairly spacious, and suites have a bathroom with a tub and a shower.

The resort's handsome restaurant, Jade, overlooks the beautiful free-form infinity pool and beach beyond, serving international Asian-tinged food for breakfast, lunch, and dinner. Beau Beau's, on the beach, serves seafood and international fare at lunch and dinner, along with karaoke and Calypso revues starring King Beau Beau and the Beaubettes.

10 Emerald Merit Rd., Oyster Pond (P.O. Box 239), St. Maarten, N.A. © **866/978-0212** in the U.S., or 599/543-6040. Fax 599/543-6695. www.obbr.com. 178 units (of those, 153 are timeshares). Winter $200–$290 double, $310–$600 suite; off season $120–$190 double, $200–$400 suite. Extra person $50. Children under 12 stay free in parent's room. AE, DISC, MC, V. **Amenities:** 2 restaurants; 3 bars; outdoor pool; 4 tennis courts; fitness center; outdoor Jacuzzi; boating; snorkeling; bike rentals; activities desk; car rental; babysitting; coin-operated laundry; 1 room for those w/limited mobility; computer stations (dial-up); minimart. In room: A/C, TV, DVD (in

some), VCR (in some), dataport, kitchen (in most), fridge, beverage maker, hair dryer, iron, safe, washer/dryer (in some).

MODERATE/INEXPENSIVE

Delfina Hotel 𝒢 This delightful little retreat is run by a very convivial gay German couple ("but don't worry: we don't discriminate"). Boris and Michael (the family chef and social director who'd put the *Love Boat*'s Julie McCoy to shame) have lived on island for 20 years ("make it 15, darling") and offer plenty of tips and even mothering when necessary. The garden setting is idyllic, with green vervet monkeys plundering the banana trees in early morning and late afternoon (when guests relax in the pool or clothing-optional Jacuzzi). Massages, facials, and yoga classes are arranged on-site ("so important now that we're . . . 29," notes Boris). The sun-drenched breakfast room has views of the water (Cupecoy and Mullet Bay beaches are 10 minutes' walk), and doubles for happy hour cocktails and Friday evening art openings in season. The rooms have large, vaulted ceilings, white tile floors, and touches like handmade quilts or local crafts. Each is dedicated to a showbiz gay icon, with photos of the legend at his or her peak: Marilyn Monroe, Princess Di, Tina Turner, Bette Davis, Bette Midler, James Dean, Liz Taylor, and Ricky Martin.

14–16 Tigris Rd., Cupecoy, St. Maarten, N.A. ℂ/fax **599/545-3300**. www.delfina hotel.com. 12 rooms. Winter $149 double; off season $89–$105 double. Buffet continental breakfast included. AE, MC, V. **Amenities:** Pool; gym; hot tub; massage; computer with Internet access. *In room:* A/C, ceiling fan, TV, fridge, beverage maker.

Holland House The lobby of this well-run "city" hotel runs uninterrupted from bustling Front Street to Great Bay Beach. The public areas are quite stylish, with rotating local and Dutch artworks for sale on the walls. The lively global clientele enjoys the little touches (free international newspapers, beach chairs, and freshwater beach shower). Most rooms have gorgeous polished hardwood floors, large arched balconies, and small full bathrooms. The muted color scheme favors cream and canary yellow. The one-bedroom penthouse includes kitchenette, large screen TV, DVD, and fax machine. The $36 surcharge is well worth it for the popular oceanview rooms; but weekly stays in any unit lasso huge savings.

The beachfront restaurant and bar (crowned by a billowing tent) rock weekends with live jazz; the regular menu is surprisingly good, but opt for the chef's creative affordable tapas (including Dutch finger food, Vietnamese spring rolls, and Spanish meatballs).

43 Front St. (P.O. Box 393), Philipsburg, St. Maarten, N.A. ℂ **800/223-9815** in the U.S. or 599/542-2572. Fax 599/542-4673. www.hhbh.com. 54 units. Winter

$149–$275 double, $295 1-bedroom suite, $325 penthouse; off season $109–$175 double, $195 1-bedroom suite, $215 penthouse. AE, MC, V. **Amenities:** Restaurant; bar; salon; snorkeling; massage; Wi-Fi throughout; computer with Internet access; conference room. *In room:* A/C, ceiling fan, TV, Wi-Fi, kitchenette, hair dryer, iron, safe, Jacuzzi (in some).

La Vista 🍴   This small West Indian–style complex lies at the foot of Pelican Key. For a fee, guests can use the more elaborate facilities of the nearby Pelican Resort, with its casino, shops, and spa. The resort consists of two parts—La Vista Resort, a series of blue-and-white semi-detached bungalows amid gardens staggered up a hill, and the newer La Vista Beach Resort across the road, whose sunnily decorated studios and two-bedroom apartments open directly on the poky beach. Rooms with a view come in seven different categories, including a junior suite, deluxe suite, penthouse, or cottage. Accommodations feature fully equipped kitchenettes, cramped bedrooms, and medium-size shower-only bathrooms. The most desirable are the one-bedroom Antillean cottages with front porch (suitable for occupancy by four) whose panoramic views live up to the name. Maintenance can be spotty, but management is extremely solicitous, and the resort offers several intriguing activities like weekly art workshops.

Popular with locals, The Hideaway serves well-prepared French cuisine adjacent to the infinity pool, with live entertainment and dancing several nights a week.

53 Billy Folly Rd., Pelican Key (P.O. Box 2086), Simpson Bay, St. Maarten, N.A. ☎ 599/544-3005. Fax 599/544-3010. www.lavistaresort.com. 50 units. Winter $180 double, $270–$425 suites for 4; off season $95 double, $200–$300 suites for 4. Children under 12 stay free when sharing with 2 adults. Extra person $20. AE, DISC, MC, V. **Amenities:** Restaurant; bar; 2 outdoor pools; massage; coin-operated laundry. *In room:* A/C, ceiling fan, TV, kitchenette, fridge, coffeemaker, hair dryer, iron, safe.

Pasanggrahan Royal Inn 🍴 *Value*   *Pasanggrahan* is the Indonesian word for guesthouse, and this 1707 West Indian–style former governor's residence lies steps from a quiet part of Great Bay Beach. A small, informal place, it's right on Philipsburg's busy, narrow main street but set back under tall trees, with a gingerbread-trim white wooden veranda. The interior has peacock bamboo chairs, Indian spool tables, Balinese shadow puppets, and a gilt-framed oil portrait of Queen Wilhelmina. The adjacent bar, named the Sydney Greenstreet though he never stayed here, does seem atmospherically suited to sweaty shady expats and disgraced diplomats. The small- to medium-size, mostly oceanview bedrooms have queen-size, double, or king-size beds with good mattresses; some occupy the main building, others an adjoining annex. The finest sing with colonial flair: antique secretaries and four-posters swaddled in mosquito netting, madras valances, hand-stitched quilts, beamed ceilings, and still life paintings. Bathrooms are small but tidy, and all have tub/shower combinations.

Set among a tangle of palms and shrubbery dotted with rusting copper pots, the beachfront Pasanggrahan Restaurant specializes in freshly caught fish. The two-course dinners (with soup or salad and carb du jour) represent terrific value.

19 Front St. (P.O. Box 151), Philipsburg, St. Maarten, N.A. ℰ **599/542-3588.** Fax 599/542-2885. www.pasanhotel.com. 30 units. Winter $158–$250 double; off season $98–$165 double. Extra person winter $75, off-season $55. DISC, MC, V. Closed Sept. **Amenities:** Restaurant; 2 bars; laundry service. *In room:* A/C, ceiling fan, TV, dataport, kitchenette (in some), fridge, beverage maker (in some), safe (in some).

Turquoise Shell Inn *Value* The surrounding area isn't as nice and clean (or safe) as this trim yellow-and-white apartment complex steps from Simpson Bay Beach, but the price and location are right. Each one-bedroom suite has a fully equipped kitchen, though the restaurants and bars along the Simpson Bay "strip" are easy walking distance (not recommended if you're alone after a night's carousing). The plumbing is noisy, the A/C patchy, the shower-only bathrooms cramped, and the decor unassuming, but the friendly, obliging management keeps everything tidy.

34 Simpson Bay Rd., Simpson Bay, St. Maarten, N.A. ℰ **599/545-2875** or 599/545-5642. Fax 599/545-2846. www.tshellinn.com. 10 units. Winter $145 double; off season $95–$115 double. MC, V. **Amenities:** Pool. *In room:* A/C, ceiling fan, TV, Wi-Fi access.

2 French St. Martin

Hotels on French St. Martin add a 10% service charge and a *taxe de séjour.* This visitors' tax on rooms differs from hotel to hotel, depending on its classification, but is often $4 a day. Expect higher rates during Christmas week. Rates are quoted in either euros or dollars depending upon how establishments quoted them at the time of publication.

VERY EXPENSIVE

Alamanda Resort ℛ Orient Bay's newest "luxury" resort is a small gathering of Creole-style *cazes* with traditional pastel-hued galleries, gables, and gingerbread surrounding a lushly landscaped pool, steps from the beach. The spacious units regrettably lack real views as they're set back and obstructed by resplendent trees and

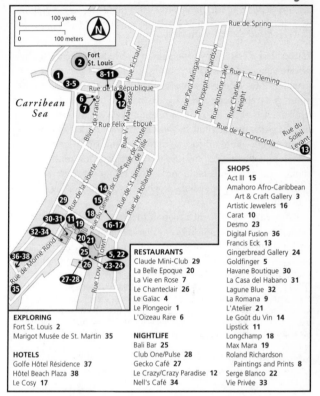

SHOPS
Act III **15**
Amahoro Afro-Caribbean
  Art & Craft Gallery **3**
Artistic Jewelers **16**
Carat **10**
Desmo **23**
Digital Fusion **36**
Francis Eck **13**
Gingerbread Gallery **24**
Goldfinger **5**
Havane Boutique **30**
La Casa del Habano **31**
Lagune Blue **32**
La Romana **9**
L'Atelier **21**
Le Goût du Vin **14**
Lipstick **11**
Longchamp **18**
Max Mara **19**
Roland Richardson
  Paintings and Prints **8**
Serge Blanco **22**
Vie Privée **33**

RESTAURANTS
Claude Mini-Club **29**
La Belle Epoque **20**
La Vie en Rose **7**
Le Chanteclair **26**
Le Gaïac **4**
Le Plongeoir **1**
L'Oizeau Rare **6**

NIGHTLIFE
Bali Bar **25**
Club One/Pulse **28**
Gecko Café **27**
Le Crazy/Crazy Paradise **12**
Nell's Café **34**

EXPLORING
Fort St. Louis **2**
Marigot Musée de St. Martin **35**

HOTELS
Golfe Hôtel Résidence **37**
Hôtel Beach Plaza **38**
Le Cosy **17**

flowering bushes. That said, they're the chicest option on Orient Bay. Sunny yellow walls and vivid fabrics from tomato to turquoise contrast with pristine white accents, mahogany crown moldings, pineapple-pattern throw pillows, framed lantana weavings, and four-poster or elegantly carved curvaceous hardwood-and-wicker beds. The two fine restaurants include Kakao Beach on the water, but each unit has a fully equipped kitchenette. Guests also enjoy privileges at the so-called "Five Stars of Orient Bay" beach bars and neighboring sister property, Esmeralda. Ocean view two-bedroom duplexes (as opposed to the pricier oceanfront version) offer excellent value with second bathroom and TV.

Baie Orientale (B.P. 5166), St. Martin, F.W.I. © **800/622-7836** in the U.S. or 590/52-87-40. Fax 590/52-87-41. www.alamanda-resort.com. 42 units. Winter $330–$495 double, $495–$605 suite; off season $240–$330 double, $330–$420 suite. AE, MC, V. Closed Sept. **Amenities:** 2 restaurants; 2 bars; outdoor pool; gym; car rental; laundry service; Wi-Fi access; meeting rooms. *In room:* A/C, ceiling fan, TV, dataport, kitchenette, hair dryer, iron, safe.

Esmeralda Resort ★ Originally conceived as a site for a single private villa, and then for a semiprivate club, this hillside property opening onto Orient Beach resembles a well-maintained Sunbelt housing development given Creole flair in colors from mint to mauve. Each of the 18 Spanish mission–style, tile-roofed villas can be configured into separate lock-off units or combined in any number up to five-bedroom palatial digs. Each individual unit contains a beamed cathedral ceiling (the nicest architectural touch), kitchenette, shower or tub bathroom, a terrace, and private entrance. Each villa has a communal pool, which creates the feeling of a private club.

L'Astrolabe serves French food at breakfast and dinner daily. At lunch, the hotel issues an ID card that can be used for discounts at any of a half-dozen restaurants along the nearby beach.

Parc de la Baie Orientale (B.P. 5141), 97071 St. Martin, F.W.I. ✆ **590/87-36-36.** Fax 590/87-35-18. www.esmeralda-resort.com. 65 units. Winter $330–$485 double, $605–$880 suite; off season $240–$320 double, from $370 suite. AE, MC, V. Closed Sept. **Amenities:** 2 restaurants; bar; 18 outdoor pools; 2 tennis courts; parasailing; scuba diving; snorkeling; water-skiing; car rental; limited room service; massage; babysitting; laundry service; horseback riding (nearby). *In room:* A/C, ceiling fan, TV, dataport, kitchenette, fridge, beverage maker, hair dryer, safe.

Green Cay Villas ★ This gated hillside community overlooking the sweep of Orient Bay features 16 fully equipped, three-bedroom, 418-sq.-m (4,500-sq.-ft.) villas with private pools at—comparatively—bargain rates, especially off season. Each can be configured into individual units; even the studio contains a modern kitchen. The design emphasizes cool blue, pristine off-whites, and rich tropical accents mirroring sea, sand, and sunset. White and natural wicker and hardwood furnishings are juxtaposed with boldly hued art naïf, throw pillows, fabrics, ceramics, and whimsical touches like painted parrots dangling from the high coffered ceilings. Daily maid service and breakfast are included.

Parc de la Baie Orientale (B.P. 3006), St. Martin, F.W.I. ✆ **866/592-4213** in the U.S., or 590/87-38-63. Fax 590/87-39-27. www.greencayvillas.com. 16 units. Winter $300 studio, $672–$756 1-bedroom suite, $792–$858 2-bedroom suite, $900–$960 3-bedroom villa; off season $228 studio, $402–$510 1-bedroom, $474–$540 2-bedroom, $522–$600 3-bedroom. Rates include continental breakfast. Minimum stay 5 nights. AE, MC, V. **Amenities:** 16 pools; gym; Jacuzzis; airport shuttle. *In room:* A/C, TV, VCR, Internet, kitchen, beverage maker, hair dryer, safe.

Hôtel L'Esplanade Caraïbe 🏵🏵   This elegant collection of suites lies on a steeply sloping hillside above the road leading into the village of Grand Case from Marigot. Covered with cascades of bougainvillea, and accented with a vaguely Hispanic overlay of white walls, exquisite hand-painted tiles, and light-blue-colored roofs, the resort's various elements are connected by a network of stairways that add to the layout's drama, accentuating the dazzling prospects at every turn. There's a multitiered pool with swim-up bar (Alain, the main bartender, is a font of local lore and information . . . typical of the splendid, warm service), a series of gorgeous terraced gardens, and access to a beach via a 6-minute walk on a winding, stair-dotted pathway. There's no restaurant, but Grand Case is celebrated for its stellar eateries.

All views from the guest rooms and their terraces angle out toward the sea and the sun setting behind Anguilla. Each individually decorated unit contains a kitchen with up-to-date cookware, Italian porcelain tile floors, beamed ceilings, plasma-screen TVs, DVDs, mahogany and wicker furniture, and very comfortable queen- or king-size beds (many four-poster). Slate and tumbled marble bathrooms are beautifully equipped right down to refined toiletries baskets and enormous showers. The loft suites on the upper floors are worth the extra charge, as they include a sofa bed, an upstairs master bedroom with a king-size bed, and a partial bathroom downstairs. The cordial owners, Marc and Kristin Petrelluzzi will have completely redone each suite (during the hotel's slow season from summer through early fall) by 2008; additional, even posher villas are in the works.

Grand Case (B.P. 5007), 97150 St. Martin, F.W.I. 🕻 **866/596-8365** in the U.S., or 590/87-06-55. Fax 590/87-29-15. www.lesplanade.com. 24 units. Winter $320–$370 double studio, $370–$470 suite; off season $220 double studio, $270–$320 suite. Extra person winter $70, off season $50. AE, MC, V. **Amenities:** Bar (winter season); outdoor pool; car rental; babysitting; laundry service; rooms for those w/limited mobility. *In room:* A/C, ceiling fan, TV, DVD, dataport, kitchen, beverage maker, hair dryer, iron, safe.

La Samanna 🏵🏵🏵   Sybaritic, sleek, sexy, and as meticulously groomed as its celebrity clientele, this world-class resort (a member of the Orient Express collection) commands the wide grin of alabaster sand called Baie Longue. Rows of mature royal palms, part of the glorious landscaping fragrant with orchids and oleander, embellish the 22-hectare (54-acre) property's front entrance. The overall aesthetic harmoniously blends Mediterranean flourishes from the Costa del Sol to Santorini: arches, stucco walls, azure doors, navy blue awnings, red barrel-tile roofs, and terra-cotta floors. Ornate Moroccan and Thai objets d'art adorn the *Architectural Digest*–worthy interior. Yet despite the stratospheric price tag and equally haute design, La Samanna isn't stuffy: service is warm and professional, the staffers (many here since its 1973 inception) knowing their business but not yours.

Regardless of their size, most units are awash in mahogany and marble; private terraces and picture windows transform Baie Longue into a living canvas. Suites and villas have spacious bedrooms with luxurious beds, fully equipped kitchens, living and dining rooms, and large patios. The bathrooms are simple but well-designed, with bidets, hand-painted Mexican tiles, and (mostly) tub/shower combinations. Five of its deluxe suites were upgraded in 2005 with rooftop terraces and plunge pools. The resort has cannily added gadgetry sans gaucherie including flatscreen TVs and in-room Wi-Fi access planned for 2007. But charming island touches like conch shells instead of Do Not Disturb signs happily remain.

Posh pampering includes the exclusive Elysées Spa and superb French cuisine alfresco, on a candlelit terrace overlooking Baie Longue. After dinner, the bar becomes a dance club. At the poolside grill, waiters serve food, St-Tropez style, on the beach.

Baie Longue (B.P. 4077), 97064 St. Martin CEDEX, F.W.I. ℂ **800/854-2252** in the U.S., or 590/87-64-00. Fax 590/87-87-86. www.lasamanna.com. 81 units. Winter $875 double, from $1,650 suite or villa; off season $425–$640 double, from $795 suite or villa. Rates include breakfast. AE, MC, V. Closed late Aug to late Oct. **Amenities:** Restaurant; 2 bars; outdoor pool; 3 tennis courts; fitness center; spa; sailing; snorkeling; water-skiing; windsurfing; boutiques; room service; babysitting; laundry service; dry cleaning; nonsmoking rooms; computer center with Internet access; library. *In room:* A/C, ceiling fan, TV, minibar, beverage maker, hair dryer, iron, safe, plunge pool (in some).

Le Petit Hotel 🏝🏝 *(Finds)* This well-managed, thoughtfully designed hotel that opens directly onto the sands of Grand Case Beach practically defines quiet chic, starting with the magnificent hand-painted tiles throughout the public spaces and hallways. It shares the same meticulous, near-obsessive attention to detail that distinguishes its splendid sister property, L'Esplanade. Furnishings and accents are sourced around the globe, including Balinese teak and Brazilian mahogany that offset natural wicker beds topped with white down duvets and pillows. The usual luxury accessory culprits range from Frette linens to Damana toiletries. The smallish bathrooms are mostly shower-only and the kitchenettes stylish if basic with a microwave, fridge, and a two-burner stovetop, but no oven. Each has a huge, beautifully appointed terrace or balcony overlooking the sand. The overall effect is of serene sanctuary, the only "noise" the percussive surf. Though there's no restaurant, the warm, gracious staff offers advice on the town's many superb dining options.

248 bd. de Grand Case, Grand Case, 97150 St. Martin, F.W.I. ℂ **590/29-09-65.** Fax 590/87-09-19. www.lepetithotel.com. 10 units. Winter $340–$380 studio for 2, $450 1-bedroom apt for up to 4; off season $240–$280 studio for 2, $350 1-bedroom apt for up to 4. Extra person $70, off season $50. Children under 7 stay free in parent's room. AE, MC, V. **Amenities:** Activities desk; babysitting; laundry service; 1 room for those w/limited mobility. *In room:* A/C, ceiling fan, TV, DVD (in some), kitchenette, fridge, beverage maker, hair dryer, iron, safe.

EXPENSIVE

Club Orient Naturist Resort ⪰ Occupying an isolated spot, this is the only true nudist resort in the French West Indies, but it's definitely *not* a wild, swinging, party place. It's very clean, decent, middle-class, even family-friendly. Very few singles check in, so "Club O" won't stimulate those seeking titillation. Despite their lack of clothing, many of the guests are older and very conservative—looking for a quiet, reclusive getaway with like-minded nudists. There's no pool on the premises, but the chalets are right on an excellent beach, with plentiful activities to facilitate hanging out (in every sense). Accommodations, set in red-pine chalets imported from Finland, are utterly plain and simple, sporting an IKEA-meets-campground-cabin look though decor is being spruced up. All have outside showers and most have both front and back porches. At Papagayo you can dine alfresco; the popular 5 to 7pm happy hour allows guests to compare . . . notes. However, each unit has a kitchenette and there's a minimarket on-site for those wishing to cook their own meals.

1 Baie Orientale, 97150 St. Martin, F.W.I. ℂ **800/690-0199** in the U.S., or 590/87-33-85. Fax 590/87-33-76. www.cluborient.com. 136 units. Winter 215€–270€ ($269–$338) studio and suite, 330€–395€ ($413–$494) chalet, 1,000€ ($1,250) villa; off season 120€–200€ ($150–$250) studio and suite, 175€–220€ ($219–$275) chalet, 600€ ($750) villa. AE, DC, DISC, MC, V. **Amenities:** Restaurant; 2 bars; gym; spa; kayaks; sailboats; snorkeling; windsurfing; car rental; babysitting; laundry service; coin-operated laundry; library; minimart; 1 room for those w/limited mobility. *In room:* A/C, ceiling fan, Ethernet access, kitchen, beverage maker, safe.

Grand Case Beach Club ⪰ This cheerful bundling of bougainvillea-draped buildings sits trapped between two beaches just a short stroll from the action in "downtown" Grand Case. There are several different room categories, including duplex units, but all have well-stocked kitchens with granite counters, sizable bathrooms, and private balconies (the best offering smashing views of Anguilla). Some units could use cosmetic touch-ups (and new plumbing) but the property is otherwise immaculately maintained. Families will particularly appreciate the gated entrance (making the lovely "Petite Plage" practically private) and 24-hour security guard and video surveillance. Little extras include a sampling of island CDs and a bottle of wine at check-in. General manager Steve Wright is conscientious, cordial, and helpful, qualities he inculcates in the staff.

Sunset Café (see chapter 4), set spectacularly on the rocks overlooking the water, serves a yummy breakfast, lunch, and dinner.

Grand Case 97150, St. Martin, F.W.I. © **800/344-3016** in the U.S. or 590/87-51-87. Fax 590/87-59-93. www.grandcasebeachclub.com. 73 units. Winter $275–$350 studio, $330–$385 1-bedroom suite, $485–$515 2-bedroom suite; off season $130–$225 studio, $145–$245 1-bedroom suite, $255–$365 2-bedroom suite. Continental breakfast included. Children under 12 stay free in parent's room. Extra person $35. AE, MC, V. **Amenities:** Restaurant; bar; outdoor pool; tennis court; fitness room; dive shop; sailing; snorkeling; kayaking; water-skiing; car rental; laundry facilities; computer with Internet access. *In room:* A/C, ceiling fan, TV, kitchen, hair dryer, safe.

Hotel Beach Plaza ✸   This stunner is set on a decent beach within a reasonable walking distance of Marigot's commercial heart. Its three-story buildings center on a soaring, skylit, colonnaded atrium festooned with live banana trees and climbing vines and filigreed with faux waterfalls. Elegant artful touches abound in the marbled public spaces, including violently hued Francis Eck seascapes, Klimt posters, and a dazzling blue-tile floor that creates the illusion of walking on water. Its location midway between the open sea and the lagoon ensures all units have water views. Each room contains a balcony, white tile floors, madras fabrics, native art, and varnished hardwood furniture, including a writing desk and comfortable beds. Bathrooms have tub/shower combinations and generous shelf space.

The hotel's poolside restaurant, Le Corsaire, serves surprisingly creative French food except for the all-you-can-eat buffets on Tuesday and Friday nights, which feature Creole and seafood, respectively. Its bar lures Marigot movers-and-shakers after work.

Baie de Marigot, 97150 St. Martin, F.W.I. © **590/87-87-00.** Fax 590/87-18-87. www.hotelbeachplazaxm.com. 144 units. Winter $238–$381 double, from $547 suite; off season $193–$270 double, from $438 suite. Rates include buffet breakfast. AE, MC, V. **Amenities:** Restaurant; 2 bars; outdoor pool; jet skis; kayaks; scuba diving; snorkeling; bike rental; car rental; limited room service; babysitting; laundry service; nonsmoking rooms; computer with Wi-Fi; complimentary casino shuttle; rooms for those w/limited mobility. *In room:* A/C, TV, minibar, fridge, hair dryer, safe.

Mercure Simson Beach   This is one of the French side's most stylish hotels in its price bracket. The complex occupies a flat, sandy stretch of land between a saltwater lagoon and the beach. Decorated throughout in ocean-inspired fabrics, its five three-story buildings evoke many-balconied Antillean houses. A large central pool serves as the focal point for a bar built out over the lagoon, an indoor/outdoor restaurant known for theme buffets, and a flagstone terrace that hosts steel bands, casino and karaoke nights, and cocktail parties. Flight crews and a generally youthful European clientele keep things hopping. Each unit offers an outdoor kitchenette, simple wicker and rattan furniture, plus a tiled, shower-only bathroom. The most desirable accommodations, on the third floor, contain sloping ceilings sheltering sleeping lofts and two bathrooms.

Baie Nettlé (B.P. 172), Marigot, 97052 St. Martin, F.W.I. ✆ **800/221-4542** in the U.S., or 590/87-54-54. Fax 590/87-92-11. www.mercure.com. 178 units. Winter from $306 studio, from $372 duplex; off season from $205 studio, from $249 duplex. Rates include buffet breakfast. AE, DC, MC, V. **Amenities:** Restaurant; 2 bars; outdoor pool; children's pool; tennis court; fitness room; dive center; kayaking; snorkeling; water-skiing; windsurfing; bikes; car rental; airport shuttle; babysitting; laundry service; dry cleaning; rooms for those w/limited mobility. *In room:* A/C, TV, dataport, kitchenette, beverage maker (in some), hair dryer (in some), safe.

MODERATE/INEXPENSIVE

Golfe Hôtel   This intimate, peaceful family-run hotel nestles amid exotic gardens in a Marigot "suburb" just 5 minutes' walk from bustling Marina Port la Royale. Public spaces are relatively stylish but rooms are clean if nothing special—the usual white-tile floors, local artworks, and predominantly yellow, chartreuse, or (much smarter) blue color schemes. Half feature a sliver of balcony overlooking Simpson Bay Lagoon. There's a car rental on-site and the owners offer deep-sea fishing, snorkeling, and other excursions on their boat, the "Magic Fish."

Résidence St. Jean, Bellevue (B.P. 974), Marigot, St. Martin, F.W.I. ✆ **590/87-92-08.** Fax 590/87-83-92. www.golfehotelstmartin.com. 24 units. Winter $115–$125 double; off season $90–$105 double. MC, V. **Amenities:** Bar; outdoor pool; deep-sea fishing; diving; car rental; airport transfer (free with car rental). *In room:* A/C, TV.

La Plantation Resort ✟   Although the gorgeous white-sand beach is a few minutes' walk down a steep slope, this is one of the most appealing hotels at Orient Bay. Seventeen colonial-style villas are scattered around the lavishly landscaped grounds and pool; each villa contains a suite and two studios, which can be rented separately or combined. The spacious units, all with oceanview terrace, are stylishly furnished in a Polynesian/Creole theme with hand-painted stenciling and murals, mosquito netting, beamed ceilings, and bamboo furnishings. If there's a surface it's painted, usually in such psychedelic hues as turquoise, sunshine yellow, forest green, scarlet, or mango. Studios have kitchenettes and queen-size or twin beds; the suites have separate bedrooms with king-size beds, spacious living rooms, full kitchens, and beautifully tiled full bathrooms.

Café Plantation serves French/Creole dinners; it's quite popular for its Monday lobster special. At lunch, clients use an ID card to buy meals and drinks at any of five beachfront restaurants loosely associated with the resort.

C 5 Parc de la Baie Orientale, Orient Bay, 97150 St. Martin, F.W.I. © **590/29-58-00.** Fax 590/29-58-08. www.la-plantation.com. 52 units. Winter $245 studio, $360 suite; off season $160–$185 studio, $220–$250 suite. Rates include breakfast. DISC, MC, V. Closed Sept 1 to mid-Oct. **Amenities:** 2 restaurants; outdoor pool; 2 tennis courts; health club; diving; jet ski; parasailing; windsurfing; bike rental; car rental; boutiques; massage. *In room:* A/C, ceiling fan, TV, kitchen, fridge, beverage maker, hair dryer, safe.

Le Cosy   In the commercial center of Marigot (and favored by business travelers), Le Cosy's concrete facade is enlivened with gingerbread fretwork and magenta awnings. A bar with a soaring tent serves drinks to guests relaxing on wicker and bentwood furniture. The small bedrooms are arranged around a landscaped central courtyard with a fish-shaped fountain and funky island murals. A lime or cherry throw pillow suffices for decor in the worn, minimalist rooms, most of them duplexes with mahogany-trimmed stairs climbing to a sleeping loft. Tiny bathrooms are shower-only.

The simple restaurant serves dinner only. The staff grandly defines meals as French *cuisine gastronomique;* they're more prosaic than that, but the open-air rooftop location is *charmant.*

Rue du Général-de-Gaulle (B.P. 679), Marigot, 97150 St. Martin, F.W.I. © **590/87-63-93.** Fax 590/87-43-95. lecosy@wanadoo.fr. 12 units. Year-round 80€–100€ ($100–$125) double. MC, V. **Amenities:** Restaurant. *In room:* A/C, TV, minibar.

4

Where to Dine on
St. Maarten/St. Martin

True confession time: I don't go to St. Maarten/St. Martin for its
lovely beaches, sizzling nightlife, duty-free shopping, or abundant
aquatic activities. No, I'm a foodie on a mission, a pilgrimage. Both
the French and Dutch sides offer epicurean experiences galore, with
nearly 500 eateries. Though you'll still encounter classic, even nos-
talgic (tableside flambé, anyone?) fare, most restaurants entered the
millennium with gastronomic abandon, importing whatever they
can't grow, raise, or catch locally. Otherwise by-the-book bouilla-
baisse might be accented by Thai lemon grass, or stolid smoked
salmon juiced with juniper. And, especially in duty-free St. Martin,
you'll find incredible wine buys—often cheaper than in France itself.

I give the French side the nod for overall excellence, as diners ben-
efit from the gastronomic gallivanting of young Gallic chefs eager to
see the world before returning home to pursue Michelin recogni-
tion. Though many sow their wild hautes, as it were, the leading
eateries are often shackled by tradition. The Dutch side is more
uneven and Americanized (KFC, Burger King, and their ilk litter
the islandscape here), but the top toques are arguably even more creative. Even when the operatives—often C.I.A. (Culinary Institute of
America) grads—only last a season, the owners, many of whom lend
a hand in the kitchen, remain the real stars.

Fortunately, although fab finds exist on back roads, restaurants
are concentrated in the heavily trafficked tourist areas. Shopping?
Enjoy lunch at Marigot's Waterfront and Marina Port la Royale, or
along Philipsburg's Front Street. Beaching it? Orient Bay makes a
splash with several beach bar/restaurants, including those like
Kakao, Bikini Beach, and Kontiki comprising the so-called "Five
Stars of Orient Bay" (see "Beaches" in chapter 5). Taking advantage
of the nightlife? Numerous fine options have sprouted around the
Sonesta Maho, while Simpson Bay has a walkable strip of strip malls

La Belle Créole

Befitting its turbulent colonial history, St. Maarten/St. Martin is a rich culinary melting pot. The local cuisine, symbol of the island's voyage on many levels, is primarily a savvy, savory blend of Arawak (the indigenous people), French, African, even East Indian influences. The Arawaks contributed native tubers like yuca (aka cassava) and dasheen (whose leaves, similar to spinach, are also used), as well as cilantro, lemon grass, and achiote for flavoring. The slave ships introduced plantains, sweet potato, green pigeon peas, and assorted peppers. The various European influences bore fruit in fresh garden staples like onions (and breadfruit imported from Tahiti because it proved cheaper for feeding slaves). The East Indians brought curry with them, an essential ingredient of Colombo, a meat or chicken dish of Tamil origin, as well as exotic spices.

True Creole cuisine is fast vanishing: It requires patience and work, long hours marinating and pounding. But you can still find authentic dishes whose seasonings ignite the palate. Look for specialties such as *crabe farci* (stuffed crab), *féroce* (avocado with shredded, spicy codfish called *chiquetaille*), *accras* (cod fritters), *blaff* (seafood simmered in seasoned soup), *boudin* (spicy blood sausage), *bébélé* and *matéte* (tripe dishes stewed with anything from breadfruit to bananas). Conch *(lambi)* and whelks are found in fritters and stews with fiery *sauce chien*. Wash them down with local juices: mango, guava, papaya, and less familiar flavors like the tart tangy tamarind; milky mouth-puckering soursop; pulpy passion fruit; bitter yet refreshing mauby (made from tree bark); and the milkshakelike, reputedly aphrodisiacal sea moss (as locals say, "Puts lead in your pencil, man"). And try a *ti' punch* aperitif: deceptively sweet, fruit-infused 100-proof rum (quite the knockout punch).

with dozens of watering holes overlooking the lagoon where fresh seafood reflects the community's longtime fishing heritage. But mecca is the sleepy fishing village of Grand Case perched near the northern tip of St. Martin: No other Caribbean town offers so many marvelous restaurants per capita, sitting chic-by-jowl along the mile-long main drag fronting the beach. *Bon appétit!*

1 Dutch St. Maarten

PHILIPSBURG
EXPENSIVE

Antoine ⓘ FRENCH   In a lovely seaside setting, Antoine serves fine, comfortingly retro-bistro food with sophistication and style. The handsome room decked with jungle-themed Haitian masterworks, Delft tile, hurricane lanterns, old phonographs, and towering floral arrangements further sets the scene for romance. I always start with the chef's savory kettle of fish soup, escargots de Bourgogne, or homemade pâté. Specials might include exquisitely gossamer, almost translucent scallops Nantaise. As with most restaurants, beef, veal, and duck are shipped frozen, and I occasionally find them stringy or overcooked, and the kitchen could use a lighter touch with flour and garlic. But you can't go wrong with the baked red snapper filet delicately flavored with lemon-shallot beurre blanc, lobster thermidor, or shrimp scampi flambéed with Pernod. And desserts are satisfyingly sinful. Antoine occasionally opens for basic lunches (though some dinner items are available).

119 Front St., Philipsburg. ⓒ **599/542-2964.** www.antoinerestaurant.com. Reservations recommended. Main courses lunch $10–$17, dinner $16–$37. AE, DISC, MC, V. Daily 11am–10pm.

L'Escargot FRENCH   You can't miss the wildly painted shutters and tropical Toulouse-Lautrec murals of revelers (and snails in toques) on the otherwise yellow exterior of this 160-year-old Creole cottage. The high spirits continue within, thanks to the mellow staff which does double duty performing the "must" Friday night cabaret drag show called, *bien sûr,* "La Cage aux Folles." The chef moonlights as Maurice Chevalier, the owners channel Kenny Rogers and Dolly Parton on "Islands in the Stream," and divas—Cher, Diana Ross, Patti LaBelle, Tina Turner—sashay in gold lamé and wigs whose colors don't exist in nature. The chef smartly sticks to stick-to-your-ribs bistro classics like Dover sole meunière, duck terrine, quiche Lorraine, herbed rack of lamb, frogs' legs Provençal, and roast duck with signature pineapple/banana sauce. And oh yes,

---

ⓘ **Tips Mapping It**

For locations of dining establishments listed in this chapter, please refer to the St. Maarten/St. Martin, Marigot, or Philipsburg maps on p. 50, p. 59, and p. 52, respectively.

snails, with at least six preparations on the menu (try the sampler plate): *millefeuille* (phyllo pastry) with saffron sauce to *profiteroles aux escargots forestière* (wild mushrooms, shallots, white wine).

96 Front St., Philipsburg. ✆ 599/542-2483. www.lescargotrestaurant.com. Reservations recommended. Main courses $20–$35. AE, DISC, MC, V. Daily noon–2pm and 6–10:30pm.

MODERATE

Oualichi FRENCH/INTERNATIONAL   Ideally situated on the boardwalk (there's even beach service), this French-owned brasserie is a local favorite frequented by island dignitaries and a big yachter hangout during boat shows and regattas. The jungle interior (glass bar embedded with shells, sand, and driftwood) is fun, but I prefer sitting on the patio, listening to occasional live music wafting across the courtyard and counting berths on the cruise ships. The menu offers fabulous mahimahi tartare, tuna sashimi, chicken breast in coconut curry, or escargots in garlic butter, as well as perfectly fine burgers, pizzas, and the like. A bucket of beers is $10 and lick-your-lips libations include the eponymous house specialty (vodka, Myer's rum, passion fruit, strawberry): the island's original Arawak name, meaning "land of women" after its curvaceous hills.

St. Rose Arcade, Front St., Philipsburg. ✆ 599/542-4313. Main courses $13–$30. AE, MC, V. Daily 11:30am–11pm.

Shiv Sagar INDIAN   The island's first Indian eatery remains its best, emphasizing Kashmiri and Mughlai specialties. The best tables in the large second floor split-level space oversee Front Street. Black lacquer chairs, hand-carved chess tables, and traditional Indian silk-screens depicting scenes from such great epics as the *Mahabharata* set the stage for tempting tandooris, Madras fish curry, and splendid vegetarian dishes like *saag panir* (spinach in garlicky curried yogurt), hearty enough to convert even the most dedicated carnivore.

20 Front St., Philipsburg. ✆ 599/542-2299. Main courses $12–$20. AE, DISC, MC, V. Mon–Sat noon–10pm; Sun noon–3pm.

INEXPENSIVE

Kangaroo Court SANDWICHES/SALADS   This down-to-earth coffeehouse is set on a side street between Front and Back streets, adjacent to Wathey Courthouse (named for the owners' fore-bears). The thick red-brick and black-stone walls, crafted 200 years ago from the ballast bricks of ships that sailed to the island for salt, have withstood many an act of God and war. Within an interior that's splashed in vibrant Creole colors, you'll find display racks loaded with fresh-baked pastries and constantly chugging espresso machines. Sandwiches and salads (including sesame chicken, or shrimp, avocado, and papaya) are sold at a roaring pace, mostly to passengers from the nearby cruise-ship docks, throughout the day. Continue through the back to a more tranquil interior garden courtyard with blue canvas chairs and nets strategically slung to catch falling leaves from shady almond and banyan trees. The pizzas are especially yummy (try the roast chicken or salmon-caper sour cream), as are the sweet potato fries with garlic pepper.

10 Hendrickstraat, Philipsburg. ℭ **599/542-7557.** Sandwiches and salads $8–$13. AE, DISC, MC, V. Mon–Fri 8am–5pm; Sat 8am–4pm.

MAHO & CUPECOY BEACH AREAS
VERY EXPENSIVE

Rare *&& STEAKHOUSE* Dino Jagtiani, the whiz behind the adjacent Temptation (see below) opened this take on the classic chophouse in 2005. The futuristic-yet-*Jetsons*-retro space is wittily design-infected. The only steakhouse in St. Maarten (and supposedly the entire Caribbean) to carry USDA Prime dry-aged CAB (certified Angus beef), Rare offers choices from a 12-ounce filet mignon to a 28-ounce porterhouse that can be deconstructed several ways. Those seeking lighter fare can savor mahimahi with lemon-coconut sauce, sashimi-grade tuna in red wine–mint glaze, or ostrich steak with wild mushroom fricassee. Anyone could make a meal of the home-baked bread and dips (hummus, pesto, tapenade). Dino's creativity truly shines in the sides (truffled mac 'n' cheese, wasabi mashed potatoes, polenta fries, Gouda-bacon croquettes) and sauces (nine including chipotle-ketchup and spicy peanut). Over-the-top desserts include the 1.2m (4-ft.) chocolate "Liquid of Love" fountain for dunking strawberries. Finish your meal (and yourself) off with a dessert wine or brandy from the fine if pricey list.

Atlantis Casino, Cupecoy. ℭ **599/545-5714.** www.dare-to-be-rare.com. Reservations recommended. Main courses $24–$54. AE, DISC, MC, V. Daily 6–10:30pm.

Temptation *&&& CONTEMPORARY* The name may sound like a strip club, but this impressive, innovative gem may well be the finest restaurant on island. Owner/chef Dino Jagtiani, who hails from a multigenerational East Indian family, is the only native St. Maarten grad of the prestigious C.I.A. His mother Asha graciously greets diners "as if it were our house, only for 100 guests." Dino's "nouvelle Caribbean" cuisine is exciting, even unusual, often utilizing unorthodox pairings. Witness such witty, stellar, slyly sophisticated dishes as seared foie gras "PB&J" (roasted peanut sauce and Port-fig jelly), his take on surf and turf (sea scallops in vanilla sauce with Italian sausage and curried lentil), or the McDino (Granny Smith apple tempura with honey-thyme ice cream and caramel sauce). He brilliantly juxtaposes flavors and textures in perfect balance, as they detonate on the palate. Tempura mussel shooters with coconut curry and *wakame* (seaweed), duck with mashed sweet potatoes and red cabbage (sweet and sour), or arugula-mushroom ravioli in basil jelly are crispy yet slippery, chunky yet satiny, multilayered yet subtle, respectively. You'll find the perfect vinous complement on one of the island's top wine lists, with extremely pricey if intriguing boutique selections such as producers Didier Dagueneau and Napa's Philip Togni. Alas, it regrettably apes *Wine Spectator* by listing its scores as if gospel, as well as dividing selections by "Best Buy," "Spectator Selector," and "Collectable." But what the hell: You're here to give in to Temptation.

Atlantis Casino, Cupecoy. ⓒ 599/545-2254. www.nouveaucaribbean.com. Main courses $28–$37. AE, MC, V. Tues–Sun 6:30–10:30pm.

EXPENSIVE

Le Montmartre ⓡ FRENCH   Convivial owner/hostess Karen Narm (who also operates the excellent Grand Case eateries, L'Auberge Gourmande and Sunset Café with husband, Pascal) and maitre d' Olivier Tillionbois preside over this very Parisian bistro. Art Nouveau–inspired lamps, pilasters, crown moldings, and Second Empire–style furnishings set the tone for equally classic fare. Start with cold duck foie gras terrine with Monbazillac, truffle oil and fresh figs, house-smoked salmon plate, or impeccable fish soup. Main courses run the gamut from innovative (tandoori prawns with saffron ratatouille, monkfish piccata with artichoke *millefeuille* in lime–green pepper sauce) to superbly executed standards (roasted veal chop with porcini-morel sauce, tournedos Rossini, beef filet with a foie gras medallion and truffles in brioche, duck à l'orange, whole Dover sole, rack of lamb, and prime rib). Many items are filleted or carved tableside with a flourish by an enthusiastic waitstaff. Decadent desserts include some of the best crème brûlées (try the raspberry or Tahitian vanilla) and soufflés on island. The wine list is comprehensive and fairly priced; Karen or Olivier will bring you complimentary infused rum after dinner.

Atlantis Casino, Cupecoy. ⓒ 599/545-3939. www.lemontmartre.com. Reservations recommended. Main courses $15–$36. AE, MC, V. Daily 6–10:30pm.

Terra ⓡ *finds* CONTEMPORARY   This stylish, wildly inventive eatery is often overlooked by the hordes descending on the Maho area. The food reflects American chef/owner and C.I.A. grad Scott Clagett's peripatetic postings from Greece to Indochina. The merry mélange of influences and ingredients results in such beautifully prepared and presented stunners as pumpkin mascarpone ravioli with duck confit, apples, mâche, and sage-Parmesan chicken broth; tuna tartare with mango salsa, daikon sprouts, crispy plantain, and coconut lime sauce; and pan-seared foie gras in spiced cider glaze with tempura Turkish fig and watercress-apple-and-almond salad. Those are just appetizers. You might segue into pan-roasted duck breast with duck cracklings, shepherd's pie of wild mushroom and duck confit, baby spinach and fresh fig rosemary glaze, or grilled lemon grass–skewered Scottish salmon with Asian-style ratatouille, crispy coconut polenta, crab-and-avocado relish, and warm citrus soy vinaigrette. The three-course dinner menu is an especially good buy. The space is sleek yet warm in earth tones with black accents, gilt mirrors, and bronze valances. Come by for live jazz and dessert, if nothing else.

14 Maho Plaza. ℂ 599/545-3829. www.terrasxm.com. Reservations recommended. Main courses $21–$36. AE, MC, V. Mon–Sat 6–10:30pm.

MODERATE

La Gondola ⍟ ITALIAN This traditional trattoria offers Mamma Mia Italian, all garlic and attitude, unfortunately at non-*paisano* prices. But I'll overlook the pretension, prices, and overdone decor in questionable taste (neoclassical Davids, cherubs, gilt frames). The renderings of standards (and casino setting) would have pleased the Chairman of the Board: lasagna; linguini in clam sauce; veal Milanese and parmigiana; and desserts from tiramisu to *tartufo*. I do have a soft spot (bordering on a paunch) for the risotti, especially the seafood and homemade *salsiccia* (sausage) and broccoli di rabe versions. The warm, attentive service is another plus.

Atlantis Casino, Cupecoy. ℂ 599/545-3938. Reservations recommended. Pastas and main courses $18–$36. AE, MC, V. Daily 6–10:30pm.

SIMPSON BAY AREA
EXPENSIVE

Saratoga ⍟ INTERNATIONAL/SEAFOOD This cutting-edge restaurant run by C.I.A. (Culinary Institute of America) grad John Jackson occupies a beautiful setting, resembling a Spanish colonial structure from the outside, and lined with rich mahogany inside. Seating is either indoors or on a marina-side veranda. The menu changes frequently, but there's always an artfully contrived low-fat selection like onion-crusted salmon served on a compote of lentils and sweet corn. Not that fat is banned: Witness torchon of foie gras with arugula chiffonade and apricot marmalade, fusilli with spinach-Gorgonzola cream sauce, or sautéed veal scallops with golden chanterelle raspberry-butter sauce. The presentation is invariably attractive and the execution rivals the setting.

Simpson Bay Yacht Club, Airport Rd. ✆ **599/544-2421**. Reservations recommended. Main courses $24–$37. AE, MC, V. Mon–Sat 6:30–10pm. Closed Aug to mid-Oct.

MODERATE

The Boathouse AMERICAN/INTERNATIONAL Funky, irreverent, and friendly, this is one of the Dutch side's most enduringly popular bars/restaurants. The whimsical seafaring theme of the interior includes a soaring network of heavy timbers accented with soft yellows, blues, greens, and lots of nautical accessories like dangling boats, buoys, and fish nets. Come here for the bar, a wraparound affair that attracts good-natured expatriates and locals alike, and for the generous portions. Lunches consist of sandwiches, wraps, pastas, and salads. (Especially good are the shrimp salad and the grilled chicken Caesar salad.) Main courses at dinner are more substantial, including filet mignon, pepper steak, surf and turf, scallops Madagascar (light cream curry), and beer-battered coconut shrimp. Terrific live jazz or blues animate weekend evenings (avoid eating at The Wharf next door, but stop there later for still more entertainment every night).

74 Airport Rd., Simpson Bay. ✆ **599/544-5409**. Reservations not required. Main courses lunch $8–$18, dinner $14–$20. DISC, MC, V. Mon–Sat 11:30am–3pm; daily 5:30–10:30pm.

Jimbo's Rock & Blues Café *Kids* TEX-MEX "Party and eat hearty" could be the motto of this rocking, rollicking family-friendly frat-house masquerading as a restaurant. The huge neon guitar at the entrance hints at the ambience, reinforced by the amazing sound system, cocktails with *cojones* (try the 32-ounce "megarita"), and fun watery decor: split-level platforms surrounding fountains and a pool with swim-up bar (if you forgot your bathing suit, try the boutique, which also sells marvelous Mexican glassware). Yes, you'll find lots of kids splashing about here—during the day. Come happy hour (with numerous specials), anything goes, as the place devolves into a meat market. Food is surprisingly good, emphasizing mesquite-grilled items like fajitas, as well as baby back ribs, more creative fare such as grouper stuffed with chipotle crab cake or goat cheese–roasted pepper enchiladas, lots of salads for the calorie- and cholesterol-conscious, as well as homemade low-carb tortillas for the Atkins and Zone crowd. You earn one Jimbo Dollar per drink (five gets a freebie, and some folks stockpile them for a last-night bender).

Plaza del Lago, Airport Rd., Simpson Bay. ✆ 599/544-3600. www.jimboscafe.com. Main courses $9–$27. AE, MC, V. Mon–Sat 11am–midnight; Sun 5pm–midnight.

Los Gauchos ✿ ARGENTINE/STEAKHOUSE   Steak lovers will be bullish about this prime eatery whose owner, Liesa Euton, also operates Mariano Imports, an Argentine beef supplier. You might forgo the excellent starters (empanadas or *hongos rellenos,* mushrooms stuffed with shallots, Gouda, and prosciutto) in favor of pampas-raised *vacio* (12- and 24-ounce cuts of beef loin), served with salad, garlic potatoes, and your choice of honey mustard, rosemary, peppercorn, or mushroom sauce. Liesa ensures the atmosphere is authentic from clubby decor (beamed ceilings, cowhide chairs, wagon-wheel chandeliers, diagrams of cow's anatomical parts) to tango exhibitions every evening in high season.

87 Nisbeth Rd., Pelican Resort Club, Simpson Bay. ✆ 599/542-4084. www.los-gauchos.com. Main courses $17–$29. AE, MC, V. Daily 6–11pm.

Peg Leg Pub ✿ AMERICAN/STEAKHOUSE   This lagoon-side tavern does a brisk business in beer (more than 35 available at allegedly the Caribbean's longest bar). The antics of maitre d' Shawn and yo-ho-hokum-meets-clubby-steakhouse decor (wood beams, brass ceiling fans, model boats, Jolly Rogers, peg legs dangling from rafters) belie the serious food. Invariably fine entrees range from tuna teriyaki to filet mignon. Even pub grub (coconut shrimp, beer-battered onion rings, fried calamari) is elevated to an art form; sample half-priced appetizers and two-for-one drinks at happy hour.

Three Palm Plaza, Simpson Bay. ✆ 599/544-5859. www.peglegpub.com. Main courses $18–$37. AE, DISC, MC, V. Daily noon–11pm. Closed Sun lunch.

SkipJack's Bar, Grill and Fish Market ✿ SEAFOOD   Of the many shipshape seafood spots on Simpson Bay, this recent newcomer gets the nod over the nearby, more established Lee's Roadside Grill, though the latter will cook any fish you catch on their three boats (see "Deep-Sea Fishing" in chapter 5). You can pick your fish on ice and both Maine and Caribbean lobster from a tank and pool, then enjoy the breezes (and live music Wed and Fri) on the expansive marina-front terrace. Excellent starters include tuna carpaccio, crab-corn chowder, mahimahi ceviche, fried calamari, and crab cakes with caper mayo. Entrees also taste like they jumped from the sea to your plate, from salmon béarnaise to shrimp scampi. Skip-Jack's does justice to its namesake, the old-time single-mast fishing boats that plied the Chesapeake.

Airport Rd., Simpson Bay. ℂ **599/544-2313**. www.skipjacks-sxm.com. Main courses $15–$28. MC, V. Daily noon–10:30pm. Closed Sun lunch.

Turtle Pier Bar & Restaurant SEAFOOD Though turtles swim in a large protected pool in the nearby lagoon, they're not destined for the stew pot, but are released upon becoming adults. This restaurant does, however, offer some of the island's freshest seafood, much of it caught in waters off neighboring islands. The location across from the Juliana airport is not its greatest asset, but once inside, you forget all about jets, their roar drowned out by chattering macaws and the occasional monkey. By day admire the yachts and sun-silvered tarpon pirouetting off the pier. Fine Creole specialties scented with garlic, cumin, and thyme include *blaff,* tamarind pork, coconut shrimp with ginger-pear chutney, and goat Colombo. Fish such as mahimahi, snapper, tuna, or grouper can be grilled, poached, served meunière, or blackened. On Wednesday, lobster prepared many different ways takes center stage ($30 also buys an appetizer, dessert, and dancing to live bands). Chops, poultry, and steaks round out the menu.

116 Airport Rd., Simpson Bay. ℂ **599/545-2562**. www.turtlepier.com. Main courses lunch $11–$19, dinner $16–$22. AE, DISC, MC, V. Daily 7:30am–11pm.

Wajang Doll INDONESIAN Indonesia was once a Dutch colony and literally spiced up that country's dining scene. The restaurant's name is derived from the puppet used in traditional shadow plays, and several exquisite examples adorn the walls. Typically, the food is fiery, though they temper heat according to request. Musts include *nasi* (various fried rices), *sate* (chicken or beef in peanut sauce), soy-glazed snapper, *gulai ikan* (mixed seafood pot), and fresh mango pudding. Adventuresome palates should dive into the original tapas: *rijsttafel* (literally, rice table), a parade of 14 to 20 small dishes from pickled to piquant.

56 Welfare Rd., Simpson Bay. ℂ **599/544-2255**. Reservations recommended. Main courses $16–$26. AE, MC, V. Mon–Sat 6–10pm.

INEXPENSIVE

Bavaria GERMAN Sauerbraten, schnitzel, spaetzle, and strudel might seem heavy for the climate, but they go down well with a frosty draft German beer. Annette Krabbe's little slice of home lures locals in droves for its fine fare at fair prices and cheap cocktails. While the kitchen turns out a proper beef roulade with red cabbage, it also offers "international" selections, from Italian to Indian (surprisingly good chicken curry). There's plenty of oomph in the oompah band (replete with accordion) Wednesday nights.

103 Airport Rd., Simpson Bay. © **599/544-2665.** www.bavariarestaurant.com. Main courses $13–$15. MC, V. Daily 5–10pm.

Ric's Place AMERICAN/TEX-MEX The American expat owners wanted "a small neighborhood bar on an island" and this breezy multipurpose hangout is that and more. Everybody comes to Ric's, to paraphrase *Casablanca.* Team pennants (Canadiens, Georgia Bulldogs), games (air hockey, darts, video), and large-screen TVs lure sports buffs. More than a dozen beers, retro cocktails (sidecars, Rusty Nails, coladas like the house BBC—Bailey's and banana), and occasional live bands draw night owls. I like it for the Wi-Fi hot spot and "show" (at 9:30, 11:30am, and 5:30pm you have the best seat in the house as the drawbridge rises to permit passage of leviathan yachts that make the fishing fleet look like toy boats in a tub). The food is incidental but good, cheap, and filling: burgers with beer-battered onion rings to baby back ribs to burritos.

Airport Rd. at drawbridge, Simpson Bay. © **599/545-3630.** www.ricsplace-sxm. com. Sandwiches, salads, and main courses $8–$12. No credit cards. Daily 8am–10pm.

2 French St. Martin

MARIGOT
VERY EXPENSIVE

Le Gaïac ✿✿ CLASSIC FRENCH Only the French would place one of the island's top restaurants in a fancy mall, albeit romantically overlooking Marigot Harbor. Handsome decor (from gilt mirrors to gleaming floors that *grand-mère* would scold you for tracking) and efficiently obsequious service (presenting dishes with a flourish on silver salvers) can be intimidating. But Chef André Morel guarantees gastronomic excess at admittedly excessive prices (though prix-fixe menus are a relative bargain). Memorable meals start with luscious *amuses bouche* like foie gras crème brûlée with mango. Indeed, foie gras lovers will not be disappointed. It's utilized creatively in both appetizers and entrees: pan-seared with gingerbread and mango bitters, paired with sea scallops and saffron on a gelatin bed, or coating beef filet with celery or black truffle ravioli. I also

---

Tips Baggin' Bargains on Baguettes & More

Put together a picnic shopping at *traiteurs* (takeout/caterers), *pâtisseries* (decadent pastry shops), and *boulangeries* (heavenly baked goods). I adore the baguettes, pastries, and cheese selection at the **U.S. Magasin du Pont** (© 590/52-87-14), a supermarket chain on the French side, especially the branch at the drawbridge in Sandy Ground, where the displays look photo-shoot ready. For all-day breakfast and lunch, try one of the many croissanteries on both sides that also serve yummy quiches, omelets, and crepes (try **Zee Best** in Simpson Bay; © 599/544-2477). Finally, the island is home to 130 nationalities, from Latino to Lebanese, Italian to Indian. Don't shy away from the glorified bodegas serving *comida criolla,* Hong Kong Chinese holes-in-the-wall, and shwarma shacks.

---

adore the seafood: lobster medallions stewed with truffles, tomatoes, *haricots verts,* and snow peas; lobster with *cèpes* in crustacean red-wine jus or vanilla-ginger sauce; and seared wild sea bass in sea urchin cream with mashed sweet potatoes. The cost and cholesterol could induce coronaries, but what a way to go!

Le West Indies Mall, second floor, Front de Mer, Marigot. © 590/51-97-66. Reservations recommended. Main courses 32€–42€ ($40–$53). AE, MC, V. Mon–Sat 6:30–10:30pm. Closed Sept 1–Oct 20.

EXPENSIVE

La Vie en Rose ✿ FRENCH   The dining room in this balconied second-floor restaurant evokes a tropical version of Paris in the 1920s, thanks to flower boxes, gold gilt mirrors, arches, ceiling fans, candlelight, and time-honored culinary showmanship to match the show-stopping harbor views. The menu is classic French, although Caribbean overtones often creep in. Lunches are relatively simple affairs, with an emphasis on fresh, meal-size salads, simple grills like beefsteak with shallot sauce, brochettes of fresh fish, and pastas. Dinners are more elaborate (attracting a dressier crowd), and might begin with a lobster salad with passion-fruit dressing. Main courses include grilled filet of red snapper simmered in champagne with pumpkin risotto; breast of duck with an orange-walnut sauce; lobster paired with boneless rabbit in honey-vanilla sauce; and an unusual version of roasted rack of lamb with mushrooms. Even if you just stop by while shopping, the near-definitive lobster bisque in puff pastry is a must.

Bd. de France at rue de la République, Marigot. ℭ **590/87-54-42.** Reservations recommended. Main courses lunch 10€–18€ ($13–$23), dinner 20€–33€ ($25–$41). AE, DISC, MC, V. Mon–Sat noon–3pm; daily 6:30–10pm.

Le Chanteclair ℱ FRENCH   This simple yet elegant eatery is positioned perfectly on the marina boardwalk. Both decor (from turquoise deck to orange and yellow napery) and owner/chef Cécile Briaud-Richard's cuisine are sun-drenched. She brilliantly fuses the warm flavors of Provence with those of the Caribbean and Asia. I can't resist the foie gras sampler: of the four variations, you might luck into sautéed foie gras with roasted mango and curried shallots or duck foie ravioli in chanterelle broth. But I won't quibble if you start with the tuna carpaccio in wasabi cream, crabmeat "egg roll" floating in coconut-citronella-infused seafood bisque, or unique tempura and tartare of lobster scented with curry in pineapple-flavored ravioli. Exceptional main courses include sautéed filet of halibut on a tart with ratatouille and Chinese seaweed and roasted lamb noisettes in basil emulsion with white beans, tomato, onions, and goat cheese crisps. Among the many delectable desserts, the Innommable (un-nameable, indescribable) stands out—pastry bursting with semi-sweet chocolate paired with vanilla ice cream in its own pastry shell swimming in vanilla sauce. The "Chef's Discovery" and "Gastronomic Lobster" menus at 50€ ($63) are comparative bargains with aperitif and four courses.

Marina Port la Royale, Marigot. ℭ **590/87-94-60.** Reservations recommended. Main courses 19€–28€ ($24–$35). MC, V. Daily 6–10:30pm.

Mario's Bistro ℱ FRENCH   The setting defines romantic, with tables staggered along a balcony overlooking Sandy Ground Bridge. The greeting from Martyne Tardif couldn't be warmer. And her husband, Mario, inspires passion with his lovely if now old-fashioned architectural, tiered presentations. His inventive cooking is spiced with Asian, Moroccan, and Southwestern accents. Asparagus chowder with crab and scallops is finished with a dollop of black pepper sour cream, the fancy and fanciful mushroom risotto with poached quail egg, portobello tempura, white truffle oil, and aged *balsamico*. I adore his fried hoisin-braised duck ravioli with Granny Smith salad, plantain-wasabi crème brûlée, and banana barbecue sauce; grilled tuna with asparagus-camembert-spinach-and-bacon quesadilla, soft cumin polenta, chimichurri, and caramelized tomato chutney; sesame-grilled foie gras napoleon with *balsamico*-Angostura bitter caramel and mango-orange marmalade kissed by cinnamon and

Sauternes; braised short ribs with creamy pumpkin risotto, orange-pistachio *gremolata* (minced parsley, lemon peel, garlic), pumpkin-nutmeg fritters, and red-wine-and-bitter-chocolate sauce. The dizzying (and often dazzling) mélange of flavors makes wine pairing difficult, but otherwise he takes the confusion out of fusion cuisine, everything in supreme balance.

Sandy Ground Bridge, Marigot. ℂ **590/87-06-36**. www.mariosbistro.com. Reservations recommended. Main courses 23€–32€ ($30–$40). DISC, MC, V. Mon–Sat 6:30–10:30pm.

MODERATE

Claude Mini-Club ⊛ CREOLE/FRENCH   For more than 3 decades, this has been a long-enduring favorite with *au courant* (in-the-know) locals and discerning visitors. The building was constructed to resemble a tree house around the trunks of old coconut palms and the Haitian decor—straw and shell handicrafts dangling from the beams and marvelous murals of local scenes (islanders liming [chilling out], Carnival, boats, and the marketplace)—captures much of the vibrancy of that troubled island. A big terrace opens onto the sea. Authentic Creole offerings include *lambi* (conch) in zesty tomato stew and *accras* (cod fritters) in shallot sauce, but you can also find entrecôte in green-peppercorn sauce, veal escalope with fresh morels, and such classic desserts as banana flambé and crème brûlée. This place is busiest on Wednesday and Saturday nights, as the restaurant stages the island's best buffets, featuring such crowd pleasers as roast suckling pig, roast beef, quail, chicken, red snapper, and Caribbean lobster, accompanied by bottomless carafes of wine.

Bd. de la Mer, Marigot. ℂ **590/87-50-69**. Reservations required for buffet. Main courses 16€–30€ ($20–$38); fixed-price menu 24€ ($30); buffet 40€ ($50). AE, MC, V. Mon–Sat 11am–3pm and 6–10pm. Closed Sept.

Le Plongeoir ⊛ FRENCH   This nautically themed diner overlooking Marigot Harbor by the Fort St. Louis trail is often overlooked, yet it's a superb choice for lunch. It appears slightly funky—royal blue with crimson awning, portholes, and fishing nets: I half expect the Marseilles merchant marine to enter at any moment. The ever-changing Asian-tinged menu highlights fresh catch. Take in the salt air and boat traffic while you enjoy such starters as camembert flambéed with calvados (wondrous texture, contrasting runny cheese with crisp crunchy slices of apple and toasted baguettes slathered with pesto). Entrees are equally simple yet beautifully prepared and presented, from a barely seared "kamikaze" tuna steak to sea scallops bathed with truffle oil to seafood swimming in coconut curry.

Front de Mer, northeast of Le West Indies Mall, Marigot. ℂ 590/87-84-71. Main courses 12€–20€ ($16–$25). MC, V. Daily 11:30am–10pm.

L'Oizeau Rare ℱ FRENCH   Creative French cuisine is served in this blue-and-ivory-colored antique house with a view of three art-fully landscaped waterfalls in the garden. The tables are dressed with snowy cloths and Limoges china. At lunch, served on the covered terrace, you can choose from a number of salads and crispy pizzas, as well as fish and meat courses (specials might include tilapia in puff pastry with tomato marmalade or sweet-and-sour duck breast with ginger-garlic/red fruit sauce). Dinner choices include fresh fish, such as snapper or salmon, and roasted rack lamb with Provençal herbs. There are numerous daily specials and prix-fixe options, they give a 1€ to $1 exchange (confirm before ordering), and the wine list features plentiful French options at moderate prices. Many guests come here at sundown to enjoy the harbor view over a kir royale and cigar from the extensive selection.

Bd. de France, Marigot. ℂ 590/87-56-38. Reservations recommended. Main courses lunch 12€–20€ ($16–$25), dinner 16€–30€ ($20–$38). AE, DISC, MC, V. Mon–Sat noon–2:30pm and 6–10pm. Closed June.

INEXPENSIVE
La Belle Epoque FRENCH   "You maybe like watching ze pretty boats in ze marina, ze pretty people on ze boats, no?" asked a waiter one time as I passed. *Mais oui,* and you won't find a better perch than this almost-clichéd blue-awning sidewalk (or rather, board-walk) cafe. After window-shopping a storm in Marigot, I often stop by for Belgian beers or a glass of proper rosé, grilled Creole specials, or hangar steak au poivre, and utterly scrumptious special minipiz-zas (I can still taste the luscious Landaise—duck breast, mushrooms, and yes, honey on the tomato-mozzarella base).

Marina Port la Royale, Marigot. ℂ 590/87-87-70. www.belle-epoque-sxm.com. Salads, sandwiches, and main courses 7.50€–19€ ($9.50–$23). MC, V. Daily 7:30am–11pm.

GRAND CASE
EXPENSIVE
Le Cottage ℱ FRENCH/CREOLE   This perennial favorite in a town loaded with worthy contenders is set in what looks like a private house on the inland side of the main road running through Grand Case. Its atmosphere is at least partly influenced by Burgundy-born

sommelier, Stephane Emorine, who shows a canny ability to recommend the perfect wine by the glass to complement the French-Caribbean cuisine. Stephane and owner Bruno Lemoine apprenticed with the great Alain Senderens at Lucas-Carton in Paris: Their attention to detail is unmatched, right down to the gray bud vases with fresh blooms. Meals begin dramatically with such dishes as a casserole of crayfish and avocados with a citrus sauce, lobster ravioli infused with ginger and basil, or sautéed foie gras coated lightly with gingerbread and served with apple-almond marmalade. Mains include both rustic *cuisine du terroir* (such as roasted rack of lamb with either rosemary or cream-based *pistou* sauce) and Creole dishes, including mahimahi filet served with a reduction of crayfish. Desserts similarly range from traditional Grand Marnier soufflé to a crystallized eggplant with anise cream and basil sorbet. The four-course lobster dinner is *magnifique.*

97 bd. de Grand Case, Grand Case. © **590/29-03-30.** Reservations recommended. Main courses 22€–49€ ($26–$59). AE, DC, MC, V. Daily 6–11pm.

Le Pressoir ☆ FRENCH   This local favorite occupies a charming, 19th-century Creole house painted yellow and blue. The interior delights the eye with blue and white napery, periwinkle shutters, mango walls hung with homey island paintings (many for sale), carved hardwood chairs, and lace doilies as lampshades. The kitchen presents an equally artful combination of old and new French cuisine, the ultra-fresh products' natural flavors enhanced by imaginative seasoning. Standout standards include crème brûlée of foie gras with smoked duck breast, filet of halibut in grapefruit sauce, rabbit breast stuffed with shrimp in horseradish sauce, tuna steak in ginger confit *nage,* and roast duck with lime-banana brown jus. The signature dish combines fresh grilled shellfish and fish in a stewpot with beurre blanc.

30 bd. de Grand Case, Grand Case. © **590/87-76-62.** Reservations recommended. Main courses 26€–35€ ($33–$44). AE, MC, V. Daily 6–10:30pm.

L'Hibiscus ☆☆ *(Finds* FRENCH/CREOLE   Ask other Grand Case restaurateurs for recommendations and they'll name this unassuming Antillean *boîte.* You know you're in the Caribbean: The tiny cottage is vividly decorated with green trellises, paintings of hibiscus blossoms, bibelots on tiny shelves everywhere, orange-yellow-and-green floral tablecloths, and earthenware pots and plants dangling from white rafters. Thierry Delaunay and Franco Burato's original "island-perfumed" cuisine is served on fancy Faïence (Thierry's

---

Finds **Ooh La La, Lolos!**

Every Caribbean island has roadside shacks (and mobile vans) serving savory local specialties. These barbecue stands are a St. Martin institution, dishing out cheap heaping helpings of scrumptious barbecued ribs, lobster, chicken or fish grilled on split metal drums, garlic shrimp, goat stew, rice and peas, blood sausage, cod fritters, and johnnycakes. There are several in Grand Case (all with sea views), including my two faves, **Talk of the Town** (✆ 590/29-63-89) and **Sky's The Limit** (✆ 690/35-67-84). In Marigot, there's Derrick Hodge's **Exclusive Bite** (no phone) by the scenic cemetery and **Enoch's** in the open-air Marigot Market (✆ 590/29-29-88). The Dutch side counters with its own versions. For lunch try **Mark's Place** (no phone) in Philipsburg's Food Center Plaza parking lot; after 6pm head for **Johnny B's Under the Tree** (no phone) on Cay Hill Road in Cole Bay.

---

hometown) plates. You're welcomed with marvelous *amuses bouche,* usually a souplike chicken-breadfruit cream. Sterling appetizers range from escargot-parsley samosas with garlic dressing to hot foie gras sprinkled with passion fruit seeds, coriander, hibiscus petals, and fried plantains. Pastas and rice are equally exquisite: prawn-zucchini risotto or vanilla-scented ground veal Marsala pappardelle. Fancy surf and turf? Opt for such creative variations as jumbo shrimp and scallops with bacon in red wine sauce. Finish with the assortment of five crèmes brûlées (rose, vanilla, banana, mint, coffee). Among several worthwhile tasting menus from 27€ to 60€ ($34–$75), my favorite is the "Lobster" (lobster soup with fennel and licorice-flavored whipped cream, crispy fried lobster meat in meat jus with sugar cane vinegar, and lobster tail in Colombo sauce). The English isn't the best here but the expressions on your face (and occasional gasp of delight) will tell the story and earn free shots of home-infused fruit rum.

15 bd. de Grand Case, Grand Case. ✆ **590/29-17-91.** www.hibiscus-restaurant. com. Main courses 22€–32€ ($28–$40). Reservations recommended. MC, V. Daily 6–11pm. Closed Sept.

Rainbow Café ✒ FRENCH I confess to a soft spot for this trim little bistro set on northeastern Grand Case's "Restaurant Row." On my first visit to St. Martin, owners Dutch-born Fleur Radd and

Buffalo, New York–born David Hendricks, took me in hand, introducing me to island society, high and low. Thankfully, the warhorse not only maintains but continually surpasses its standards, and Fleur and David remain consummate hosts. Meals are served in a striking, chicly simple dining room outfitted in shades of cobalt blue and white, accented by beach photos and opening right onto the symphonic surf. In contrast, the upstairs lounge (come here for cigars and aged rums) sports wild cherry red sponge-painted walls lined with posters for cognacs and Parisian cafes, and Asian watercolors and knickknacks in niches. Menu items evolve almost every evening—I've particularly enjoyed *crabe farci* with fresh fennel, snapper in Parmesan-onion crust with tomato vinaigrette, salmon in puff pastry with citrus-dill beurre blanc, and every dessert, including the textbook *tarte tatin*.

176 bd. de Grand Case, Grand Case. © **590/87-55-80**. www.rainbow-cafe.com. Reservations recommended. Main courses 20€–36€ ($25–$45). MC, V. Mon–Sat 6:30–10:30pm.

Sol é Luna ✿ *Finds* FRENCH   This charming, family-run Creole *caze* virtually swallowed up by luxuriant greenery crowns a hill with smashing Anse Marcel views. Set back from the road it's tricky to find, but the incomparable ambience, service, and food make "Sun and Moon" the perfect place to propose or let someone down easily. Asian influences and ingredients combine with classic French preparations to create light yet intensely flavored dishes. You might commence with their take on California rolls or a goat cheese terrine with red bell peppers, onion confit, and pesto (revealing the owners' Provençal origins, as does the short but well-priced wine list). Lamb braised for 7 hours melts off the bone and in your mouth, as do equally savory scallops and shrimp on saffron risotto or open-face sweetbread ravioli. Sumptuous scrumptious desserts are followed by a minitasting of artisan rums (plum–passion fruit, vanilla-ginger). The hideaway also offers quite handsomely appointed studios and suites from $780 a week.

Mont Vernon, Cul de Sac above Anse Marcel. © **590/29-08-56**. www.soleluna restaurant.com. Main courses 14€–28€ ($18–$35). MC, V. Daily 6–10pm. Closed mid-June to mid-July and mid-Sept to Oct.

MODERATE

Il Nettuno ✿ ITALIAN   The island's most elaborate Italian restaurant gracefully handles a cosmopolitan, international crowd. It was established by a seasoned Italian restaurateur, Raymon Losito, whose career included a 25-year stint at a French restaurant in

Washington, D.C., where he befriended the Redskins' ex-owner, the late Jack Kent Cooke. He exported his fanaticism to St Martin: One wall is devoted to the "home of a Redskins fan" (caps, pennants, "bears," reserved parking sign). It's a great watering hole, outfitted in the colors of the Italian flag, and drawing a fervent crowd of fans for U.S. football games; Raymon hosts splashy parties during the play-off season. Meals are served on a large, rambling wooden veranda that the owners bravely refurbish after hurricanes. Specialties include grilled portobello mushrooms over spinach drizzled with *balsamico*, filet of sea wolf cooked in parchment, filet of grouper encrusted with pistachios, lobster risotto, and an especially worthwhile version of sea bass baked in rock salt, prepared for a minimum of two diners. The pastas and desserts are predictably superb.

70 bd. de Grand Case, Grand Case. ✆ 590/87-77-38. www.ilnettuno.com. Reservations recommended. Main courses 20€–27€ ($28–$34). AE, DISC, MC, V. Daily noon–2:30pm and 6–10:30pm. Closed for lunch Apr–Oct; closed Aug 30–Oct 15.

La California FRENCH/ITALIAN   Everything is artful at this seaside *boîte*, from the decor to the dishes. I love the multihued gauzily flowing drapes and unframed paintings on the walls sponge-painted appetizing melon and mustard. Be sure to stop by the gallery/boutique featuring hand-tooled leather photo albums, shell artwork, and sensuous sculptures. Of course, the finest canvas is free: the ever-changing Atlantic views. The fare is simple but well-executed, adroitly incorporating tropic ingredients: shrimp and monkfish in saffron sauce with Parmesan wafers, chicken in curried coconut milk, foie gras with mango chutney. Don't miss the mussels if they're fresh (usually Thurs–Sat). Pizzas are also creative (the Trois Fromages actually features four cheeses, including chèvre and Roquefort). Already fairly reasonable prices are quoted at a 1-to-1 exchange (but double check). The owners also rent two charming beachfront one- and two-bedroom apartments for $900 to $1,100 a week in high season.

134 bd. de Grand Case, Grand Case. ✆ 590/87-55-57. www.california-restaurant. com. Main courses 16€–26€ ($16–$26 with 1-to-1 exchange). AE, MC, V. Daily 11am–10:30pm.

Spiga ✹✹✹ *Finds* ITALIAN   The ebullient, gracious husband-and-wife team of Ciro Russo (a native of Lecco, Italy) and Lara Bergamasco (second-generation St. Maarten restaurant royalty) have crafted the finest Italian restaurant on the island, if not the entire Caribbean. Simple elegance reigns, starting with the 1914 Creole home that accommodates only 10 tables (four on the patio). Many ingredients (oils, cheeses, cured meats) are flown in direct from Italy to ensure freshness and quality. Lara states they want to escape "traditional" Italian fare, yet Ciro prepares a textbook *insalata caprese* (*mozzarella di bufala*, basil, tomato) and beef carpaccio with white truffle oil. You could opt for the tuna carpaccio with scallops, mango, and pineapple or lobster ravioli with mascarpone and peas in vanilla saffron sauce—demonstrating Ciro's deft marriage of tropical ingredients and Italian techniques. Whatever your choice— red snapper with capers and asparagus, pesto-crusted rack of lamb in honey *balsamico* with arugula mashed potatoes, USDA-prime beef tenderloin in Gorgonzola sauce reclining atop velvety porcini risotto—rest assured that Lara will find an appropriate wine pairing. End your enchanted evening with passion fruit parfait with raspberry sauce or a classic tiramisu, washed down with fiery grappa or homemade *limoncello* (lemon liqueur).

4 rte. de l'Espérance, Grand Case. (C) 590/52-47-83. www.spiga-sxm.com. Reservations recommended. Main courses 19€–28€ ($19–$28 with 1-to-1 exchange). DISC, MC, V. Daily 6–10:30pm. Closed Tues May–Nov.

Sunset Café ⊘ FRENCH/INTERNATIONAL   This open-air restaurant dramatically straddles the rocky peninsula dividing Grand Case Beach from Petite Plage. Tables are strewn along a narrow terrace that affords sweeping views of the setting sun, when the water is spotlit for extra effect. A planter's punch will make the fish soup, locally smoked fish, snails with Roquefort sauce, heavenly Norman mussels in white wine–garlic broth, Chilean sea bass with Provençal sauce, or red snapper filet with vanilla sauce taste even better. Lunch items are simpler, with emphasis on sandwiches, burgers, pastas, salads—and herons dive bombing for their own meal. Servings are enormous (the waiters brag about "American-size" portions), the wine list is the most favorably priced on the island, and the restaurant often offers a 1-for-1 euro/dollar exchange. Gracious hosts Pascal and Karen Narm also own the equally fine L'Auberge Gourmande in "downtown" Grand Case and Le Montmartre at Atlantis Casino.

Grand Case Beach Club, rue de Petit-Plage, Grand Case. (C) **590/87-51-87.** Reservations recommended for weekend dinners in winter. Main courses lunch 10€–22€ ($13–$28), dinner 18€–30€ ($23–$38). AE, MC, V. Daily 7am–midnight.

BAIE NETTLE & SANDY GROUND
VERY EXPENSIVE
Le Santal ⊘ FRENCH   The approach to this dazzler, through a ramshackle, working class Marigot suburb, is forbidding, but the

glam interior glistens with mirrors, dim lighting, fresh flowers, ornately carved chairs, crystal, Villeroy & Boch china, and Christofle silver. Try to nab one of the coveted oceanfront tables, often occupied by the likes of Diana Ross to Robert de Niro, Brooke Shields to chic sheiks and minor royalty. Alas, service can sometimes be fawning (but condescending to non-celebs) and even when owner Jean Dupont appears friendly, you can't help but wonder if a piece of entrecote has stuck in your teeth (stick to English if you mangle the French pronunciation). No matter: The exquisite frozen-in-the-Eisenhower-era fare is worth it. The roasted sea scallops with gossamer prawn *mousseline* (hollandaise-whipped mousse) in tomato ginger emulsion is transcendent, as is the grilled whole red snapper flambéed in pastis with star anise beurre blanc and deboned at your table. Seafood rules the menu, though you can savor superb chateaubriand au poivre flambéed in aged Armagnac and coated with béarnaise. End your evening with classic crêpes suzette (they still consider tableside presentation the height of luxury and decadence). The restaurant offers a 1€ to $1 rate, but call ahead to verify.

40 rue Lady Fish, Sandy Ground. ℂ 590/87-53-48. www.restaurantlesantal.com. Reservations recommended. Main courses 29€–48€ ($36–$60). AE, MC, V. Daily 6–10:30pm (lunch by advance reservation for groups of 6 or more).

EXPENSIVE

La Cigale ⊛ FRENCH   *Cigale* means "cricket" in French, and discerning diners chirp at this winning combination of innovative French fare with tropical flair, beachfront setting, and the warmth and intimacy only a family-run establishment can provide. Tucked away behind the Laguna Beach hotel at the end of an alley, congenial Olivier Genet's bistro is worth a potential wrong turn or three to find. He recruited his parents from the Loire Valley to help him run the tiny operation: Mama is the hostess, papa the pastry chef (bravo to both the molten chocolate cake topped by homemade vanilla ice cream, and duo of strawberries and mango with fresh mint flambéed in Grand Marnier). The setting and ambience are casual, but Chef Stéphane Istel's subtly seasoned food is anything but. Ah, for his Guadeloupe prawns and Breton sea scallops artfully arrayed around risotto. Or the *crottin de Chavignol* (goat cheese) *en nougatine* with raspberry vinaigrette, red snapper with chorizo jam and parsley coulis, and duck breast with roasted fresh figs. My sole complaint is the comparatively high price of wines (considerably more than the same bottle at "fancier" establishments). But at least Olivier will ply you with several home-brewed rum *digestifs* and animated anecdotes of his Sancerre upbringing.

101 Laguna Beach, Baie Nettlé. ✆ **590/87-90-23**. Reservations recommended. Main courses 26€–33€ ($33–$41). MC, V. Mon–Sat 6–10:30pm.

MODERATE

Thaï Garden ✿ THAI   Given France's former colonial interests in Indochina, you'd expect scintillating Asian fare and you'd be right. The proper ambience and mood are set by raw silk cushions, red-and-black tables, lacquered bamboo, Buddhas in various incarnations, and wildly colorful Thai dragons. The kitchen utilizes fresh traditional seasonings (Thai basil, lemon grass, galangal, Kaffir lime leaves) calibrated at the right Westernized heat factor, though they make too many concessions to sensitive palates for my taste. Still, I can't fault the superlative dumplings, *tom yam koung* (shrimp lemon grass soup), snapper with red curry and coconut milk, pork *laarb* (minced pork and onion with seasonings wrapped in a lettuce leaf) salad, lacquered duck, and sugar cane–wrapped shrimp. There's also a sensational sushi bar and adaptations of such other Asian classics as Peking duck and chicken satay. The price, however, is exorbitant given the recent euro to dollar exchange rate.

Rte. des Terres Basses, Sandy Ground. ✆ **590/87-88-44**. Main courses 13€–18€ ($16–$23). MC, V. Mon–Sat 7–11pm.

5

What to See & Do in St. Maarten/St. Martin

Though St. Maarten/St. Martin is most celebrated for beaches, shops, restaurants, and nightlife, it also packs a number of man-made and natural attractions into its compact terrain. From zoos to zip lines and working farms to forts, the array of diversions here suit history buffs, eco-geeks, and active types alike—and despite the island's adult playground rep, nearly all are family-friendly.

1 Island Layout

St. Martin/St. Maarten is a rugged, hilly island; driving around you'll discover numerous lookouts with splendid panoramas of the coast and offshore islets. One main road essentially circumnavigates the island; a detour from Marigot to Cole Bay on the Dutch side hugs the eastern shore of Simpson Bay lagoon and avoids traffic around the airport and bustling Maho area during rush hours.

The island is shaped—very roughly—like a boot. The toe at the western point encompasses the French **Lowlands (Terres Basses),** a tony residential area with several stunning beaches. Following the main road east takes you through **Sandy Ground,** a strip of land crammed with tour-group-style hotels, restaurants, shops, and beach bars. It's bordered on the north by Baie Nettlé and on the south by **Simpson Bay,** the Caribbean's largest enclosed body of water. **Marigot,** the French side's capital, is just over 2km (1¼ miles) to the northeast. Ferries depart its harbor for **Anguilla.** The main route ambles north, with turnoffs west on rutted roads to fine beaches, as well as east to **Pic du Paradis** (the island's highest peak at 424m/1,400 ft.) before reaching **Grand Case,** site of the tiny inter-island L'Espérance Airport, and beloved by foodies for its superlative eateries. The highway runs east, with a fork at Mont Vernon. The north turnoff accesses **French Cul-de-Sac** (embarkation point for ferries to the offshore cays) and a side road to Anse Marcel, home of a marina and the upcoming Radisson resort. The other turnoff accesses the (in)famous nudist beach, **Orient Bay,** continuing south through the residential **Orléans** quarter, straddling the Dutch border at **Oyster Pond** and its marina.

Dawn Beach, site of increased development, is the first major strand on the Dutch side. The main highway turns slightly inland and passes the Great Salt Pond on its way to the Dutch capital, **Philipsburg,** which unfurls along **Great Bay.** The major cruise ships dock here; there are also several marinas offering boat rentals and excursions. **Pointe Blanche** forms the very flat heel. From Philipsburg, the highway parallels the south coast, rising and dipping over Cay and Cole Bay Hills. Traffic here in both directions is often dreadful, especially on weekends: the "Caribbean's longest parking lot," as locals joke. Party central begins at **Simpson Bay,** where the highway officially becomes Airport Road. Marinas, bars, restaurants, timeshare units, casinos, and strip malls line both sides, continuing almost unabated past Princess Juliana International Airport to **Maho Beach,** another nightlife nirvana. The road passes Mullet Bay and the lively **Cupecoy** area in the Dutch Lowlands before hitting the French border.

2 Recommended Tour Operators

Because most activities are geared toward the water (see "Beaches" and "Sports & Other Activities," later in this chapter, for some suggested excursions), taxi drivers (see "Getting There" in chapter 2) are your best bet on terra firma.

Paradise Tourisme, Grand Case (① **590/29-24-15;** www.paradise tourisme.com), is run by effervescent entrepreneur Frank Chance. Frank, a Grand Case native, works with several other knowledgeable local drivers, and commandeers a fleet of vans and buses. He can arrange everything from shopping to sightseeing tours.

Rendezvous Tours, Marigot (① **590/87-79-22;** www.rendezvous tour.com), caters mostly to huge cruise ship tours, but can be an excellent option for active travelers, with sightseeing via kayak, mountain bike, and your feet.

3 The Main Sights
DUTCH SIDE

Philipsburg ☞, capital of the Dutch side, is named, perhaps surprisingly, for an 18th-century Scottish governor. The town has always enjoyed an uncommonly lovely setting at the headlands of Great Bay, on a spit of land separating the Caribbean from the Great

---

> *Tips* **Mapping It**
>
> For locations of the sights listed in this chapter, please refer to the St. Maarten/St. Martin, Marigot, or Philipsburg maps on p. 50, p. 59, and p. 52, respectively.

Salt Pond. Its superb, deep natural harbor can accommodate such enormous cruise ships as the Queen Mary II. They disgorge passengers, who descend eagerly if not rapaciously on the casinos and duty-free stores lining the main drag, **Front Street** (see chapter 6). The hordes tend to obscure the many handsome colonial buildings, including the ornate white 1792 **Courthouse** (still in use) replete with cupola at Wathey Square, which roughly bisects Front Street. A series of hurricanes left Philipsburg somewhat dilapidated: one part lower-rent New Orleans, one part Reno.

Over the last several years, Philipsburg has undergone a beautification project. The face-lift added a delightful beachfront red brick boardwalk (Great Bay Beach Promenade), with newly planted royal palm trees, clock towers, and old-fashioned cast-iron street lamps and benches. The beach side of Front Street is now a delightful pedestrian-friendly place to stroll, goggle at the leviathan cruise ships and mega-yachts, hop on the sand, or enjoy the sunset over an umbrella-shaded concoction in one of the many inviting cafes.

The continuing makeover will include a revamped tourist office, marinas, and expanded ferry and cruise dock, as well as a dolphinarium (Atlantida, the developer, swears it will open by late 2007, despite protests from environmentalists and animal rights activists). Eventually, the beautification will extend to the Great Salt Pond (where locals still fish for mullet), with paving and planting all the way north to the French border.

St. Maarten Heritage Museum   Documenting island history and culture, the St. Maarten Heritage Museum starts with an impressive collection of indigenous Arawak tools, pottery shards, and *zemis* (spiritual totems) that date back over 2 millennia. The plantation and piracy era yields its own artifacts (including cargo salvaged from an 1801 wreck), period clothes (contrasted with slave beads), and weapons. The environment is represented by exhibits on typical flora, fauna, geology, and coral reefs. The final multimedia display recounts the catastrophic effects of Hurricane Luis in 1995.

7 Front St. (℮ **599/542-4917**. Admission $1, free for students and children. Weekdays 10am–4pm; Sat 10am–2pm.

Fort Amsterdam   Built in 1631 on the peninsula between Great and Little bays as the Caribbean's first Dutch bastion, Fort Amsterdam was promptly captured by the Spaniards, who made it their most important garrison outside El Morro in San Juan before abandoning it in 1648. Only one small intact storage building, a few walls, and rusted cannons remain, but it's most noteworthy for its smashing views of Philipsburg. Easiest access is via the Divi Resort on Little Bay (guards will let you pass if you tell them you're hiking to the fort).

On the peninsula between Great and Little bays. No phone.

St. Maarten Zoological Park ⚘ *Kids*   Just east of Philipsburg, this is the largest park of its kind in the Caribbean. More than 500 animals comprising 80 different species from the Caribbean basin and Amazon rainforest inhabit this safari reserve. There are no cages or bars of any kind. Rather, cannily erected, environmentally conscious "naturalistic" boundaries carefully protect both animals and visitors while duplicating typical habitats. An example is Squirrel Monkey Island: The capuchins and vervets are separated by a moat (replicating the streams that draw them in the wild) stocked with water lilies, turtles, and freshwater fish. Lovingly landscaped botanic gardens (with interpretive signs adding another edu-tainment element) alternate with various environments from a caiman marsh to a tropical forest to a boulder-strewn savannah. Walk-through aviaries hold more than 200 birds: macaws, toucans, and the Caribbean's largest display of exotic parrots. Other residents include capybaras, ocelots, peccaries, coatis, baboons, and such highly endangered species as the golden lion tamarin. Fascinating activities range from regularly scheduled zookeeper talks, feedings, and one-on-one close encounters to face-painting competitions, puppet shows, clown acts, and treasure hunts. The zoo even features the island's largest playground (slides and, of course, jungle gym). Kids of all ages will love the Night Safari, held 1 night a week (usually Sat), 7 to 9:30pm: The guided tour includes a barbecue at the Monkey Bar (a restaurant cum souvenir shop), followed by the other kind of nocturnal wildlife with Afro-Creole music and dance.

Arch Rd., Madame Estate. ✆ 599/543-2030. www.stmaartenpark.com. Admission $10, children under 12 half-price. Daily 9am–5pm (9:30am–6pm in summer).

FRENCH SIDE

Marigot, capital of the French side, is one of the Caribbean's more charming towns: gas lamps, sidewalk cafes, and traditional Creole brightly hued, gingerbread-trimmed wood houses ringing a lovely harbor, as well as a separate marina, **Port la Royale.** Aside from drinking in the marine activity (and kirs or rum punches), there are several delightful boutiques and galleries (see chapter 6) worth exploring. The waterfront **Market** is a hub nearly every day for vendors and farmers. This classic colorful Caribbean jambalaya of sights, sounds, and smells is busiest early mornings as islanders converge to buy fresh-caught fish, fruits, vegetables, and herbs.

A steep trail runs from the harbor-side Sous-Préfecture (by the splashy West Indies Mall) to **Fort Louis.** Better preserved than its Dutch side counterparts (Forts Willem and Amsterdam), the 1767 bastion was erected to repel English incursions. Its hilltop situation rewards hikers with sensational 180-degree vistas of Marigot, Simpson Bay lagoon, and most of the French coast, with Anguilla shimmering in the background.

Musée de Saint-Martin   Subtitled "In the Trail of the Arawaks," this museum details island history and culture going back 2,500 years through the colonial era. The ground floor features rotating arts and crafts exhibits. The second floor is a treasure trove of maps, prints, daguerreotypes, and newspapers spanning the 18th to early 20th centuries. Ask the clerks about guided tours of the island focusing on its cultural heritage, including visiting archaeological digs (some closed to the general public), as well as discussing natural phenomena, such as the island's volcanic origins.

Terres-Basses Rd. *©* 590/29-48-36. Admission $5. Weekdays 9am–4pm; Sat 9am–1pm.

Loterie Farm *★★* *Finds* *Kids*   Located along the turnoff to Pic du Paradis halfway between Marigot and Grand Case, this splendid sanctuary—by far the greenest spot on island—merits a stop. It was a famed sugar plantation between 1721 and 1848 (the original slave walls still hauntingly surround the property). In its modern heyday a half-century ago, the Fleming family hosted Fortune 500 elite and celebrities (Benny Goodman, Jasper Johns, Harry Belafonte). But after Hurricane Luis ravaged the property in 1995, it became derelict. Eco-centric Californian B. J. Welch purchased the land in 2003 with the goal of establishing a nature retreat, preserving the island's last remaining virgin rainforest. Literally thousands of plant species including towering mahogany, corossol (soursop), mango, papaw, and guavaberry trees (re)claim a hillside filigreed with streams and cascades, embroidered with rock formations. Iguanas,

> ### *Tips* Feeling Bush-ed
>
> Set in a *carbet* (covered wood patio) at Loterie Farm's entrance, Hidden Forest Café serves luscious lunches and dinners Tuesday through Sunday. It sports a funky-chic treehouse look, with photos of dreadlocked musicians, a blue-tile bar, oars dangling from the rafters, and hurricane lamps. There's live jazz or soca several evenings in season (perfect for an aperitif) and yoga with Dinah Saturday mornings. But this is the domain of Canadian-born, self-taught chef Julia Purkis, who says her surroundings provide inspiration (and, of course, fresh ingredients from the organic gardens and forest). Her sophisticated culinary techniques and presentation (including often-edible floral garnishes) are all the more impressive given the cramped basic kitchen and frequent power outages. You might start with cumin chicken rolls, mahimahi fingers with red pepper tartar sauce, shrimp spring roll, or brie in puff pastry with mango chutney. Standout main courses include grilled salmon with apple-ginger compote, rare duck breast with banana-mint-tamarind salsa, pan-seared sea scallops with vanilla rum sauce, and Julia's signature curried spinach-stuffed chicken.

parrots, hummingbirds, monkeys, and mongoose run wild. Well-maintained trails zig and zag from the foothills to the top of Pic Paradis, the island's highest point, where a viewing platform offers sweeping 360-degree panoramas. You can trek on your own or take one of the farm's guided tours, from a mild sunset walk and "Hidden Forest" hike (both $25) to a wild, strenuous 2½-hour "Eco-Challenge" ($45). Along the way, enthusiastic guides discourse on local history, geology, wildlife, and bush medicine (plants to "cure anyt'ing what ails ya," from impotence to impetigo). A treetop adventure park, "The Fly Zone," offers a canopy of ziplines and ropes courses suspended 11 to 23m (35–75 ft.) in the air (kids can also play Tarzan and Jane on slightly lower suspended bridges and swinging ropes).

Rte. Pic Paradis, Colombier. © 590/87-86-16. www.loteriefarm.com. Admission $5. Tues–Sun 9am–6pm.

Plantation Mont Vernon *(Kids*   Not far from Orient Beach, this restored .8-hectare (2-acre) 1786 plantation provides valuable historic perspective while maintaining the island's agricultural and craft traditions. New buildings in vernacular style cleverly blend with 18th-century structures, including an animal-powered mill and the classic stone-and-exotic-wood manor house with corrugated red tin roof. This Maison de Maître is stuffed with antique furnishings, ornaments, and objects. But the highlight is the walk-through, self-guided tour (with trilingual audio sets, bilingual interpretive signs, and several interactive elements). The botanical and herb gardens are dotted with displays on such traditional plantings as manioc, corn, tobacco, and spices that perfume the air. Along the route, several buildings act as minimuseums on different cash crops. You can visit decantation pools used to process indigo into dye. The coffee museum re-creates the gathering, drying, roasting, and grinding processes. The inevitable yet excellent rum museum not only features old equipment from sugar press to still but bottles and labels from the last 3 centuries. Free rum and coffee tastings are on tap (though neither is actually produced on-site). The site also contains a kids' playground, a pleasant restaurant (recommended for its Antillean brunch), and a fine gift shop stocking not only jams, rums, and coffee, but local crafts fashioned from mango wood, bamboo, and banana leaves.

2 Main Rd., Cul de Sac. ✆ **590/29-50-62.** www.plantationmontvernon.com. Free admission (audio wands $10). Daily 9am–5pm.

The Old House (aka Musée du Rhum)   A restored 18th-century green-and-black sugar plantation greathouse, the Old House's interior, including living room and bedroom, carefully replicates the life of a typical planter: period furniture and original family portraits and personal objects preserved for six generations. The museum's complementary second half retraces the history of rum, from the first voyages of Columbus, through the buccaneer days and the rise of the sugar plantocracy, up to the effect of Prohibition. The old posters and print ads are especially delightful, and more sober exhibits cover other French West Indies calamities, from the eruption of Martinique's Mont Pelée to the eruption of world war.

Main Rd. (across the main highway from Mont Vernon Plantation), Cul de Sac. No phone. Admission 5€ ($6.25). Daily 9am–4pm.

Butterfly Farm *(Kids*   More than 100 species of butterflies from around the world (including such rarities as the Central American postman, Malaysian malachite, and Brazilian blue morpho) flit and flutter through this miniature, very humid bamboo rainforest replica. The atmosphere is hypnotically calming, between tinkling waterfalls, ponds stocked with splashing koi, and soft classical

music. If you arrive early, you might witness butterflies emerging from their chrysalides; wear bright colors or floral scents and they might light on you. Multilingual docents conduct 25-minute hands-on tours following the typical life cycle from egg to caterpillar and on to adulthood. The shop sells butterfly earrings, wind chimes, pewter figurines, fridge magnets, and framed mounted sets.

Rte. Le Galion, Quartier d'Orléans. ℂ **590/87-31-21**. www.thebutterflyfarm.com. Admission $12, $6 children under 12. Daily 9am–4:30pm.

4 Beaches

Coves scissor the island's rugged littoral like a child's whimsical paper cutouts; with 39 beautiful beaches of varying length and hue, it's fairly easy to find a place to park your towel. All are public though access is often via a rutted dirt road and/or through a fancy resort. Beaches on the western leeward half are generally hotter and calmer; those on the eastern windward side, predictably, breezier with rougher swells (when not reef-protected). *Warning:* If it's too secluded, be careful. It's unwise to carry valuables; there have been robberies on some remote strips.

Wherever you stay, you're never far from the water. Beach samplers can sometimes use the changing facilities at bigger resorts for a small fee. Beach bars often rent chairs and umbrellas for roughly $6 and $3, respectively, but may waive the charge if you order lunch or drinks. Nudists should head for the French side of the island (where all strands are at least topless), although the Dutch side is getting more liberal.

DUTCH SIDE

Popular **Cupecoy Beach** ✿ is very close to the Dutch-French border at the island's southwest tip. It's a string of three ecru-sand beaches set against a backdrop of caves, rock formations resembling abstract sculpture, and dramatically eroded limestone cliffs that provide morning shade. Locals come around with coolers of cold beer and soda for sale, though you can also pop into two bars with absolutely stunning sunset views. My favorite is **Cliffhanger Bar** (ℂ **599/526-7837**), a wooden deck built into the bluff under the supremely ugly timeshare/condo Cupecoy Beach Club. Every Friday, Saturday, and Sunday it hosts a "Big BBQ & Beach Party" at 5pm. Come for martinis (as the sign proclaims, "You don't need alcohol to have a good time, but why risk it?") and massages, the latter courtesy of Israeli expat Varda Solomon, who uses her own blend of aromatic oils. The beach has two parking lots, one near Cupecoy and Sapphire beach clubs, the other a short distance to the west. Parking costs $2. You must descend stone-carved steps to reach the sands. Cupecoy is also the island's major gay beach. Clothing is optional toward the northwest side of the beach. The steep drop-off and high swells make the beach hazardous for younger children and weak swimmers; prevailing weather affects not only the surf but the sands' width.

The next strand down, west of the airport, palm-shaded white-sand **Mullet Bay Beach** beckons. Once it was the most crowded beach on the island, but St. Maarten's largest resort, Mullet Bay, has been shuttered (save for a timeshare section) since Hurricane Luis in 1995, so it's relatively deserted, though locals flock here on weekends. Watersports equipment can be rented at a local kiosk, while a few stands dish out local fare. Local surfers enjoy the wave action and rip currents (never swim alone here); snorkelers will find several miniature bejeweled reefs around the offshore rocks. Any beachcomber will savor the views of Saba and Statia, as well as the lovely sunsets.

Another lovely spot near the airport, **Maho Beach,** at the Sonesta Maho Beach Hotel and Casino is a classic Caribbean crescent that dances to a reggae beat, with vendors hawking colorful wares and locals inviting you to impromptu beach barbecues. This is one of the island's busiest beaches, buzzing with windsurfers—and buzzed by jumbo jets that nearly decapitate the palm trees. The blasts from 747s and 757s are so powerful they've been known to topple cars: Shield your eyes from the sand storm and hang onto your hats, towels, and partner. Food and drink can be purchased at the hotel, as well as such legendary watering holes as Sunset Beach Bar and Bamboo Bernie's (see chapter 7), where the takeoffs and landings are augmented by other entertainment.

West of Philipsburg before you reach the airport, the 2km-long (1¼-mile) white sands of crescent-shaped **Simpson Bay Beach** ring the lagoon and are set against a backdrop of brightly hued fishing boats, yachts, and town homes that resembles an Impressionist canvas. This beach is ideal for a stroll or a swim (beware the steep drop-off), with calm waters and surprisingly few crowds. Watersports equipment rentals are available, but there are no changing rooms or other facilities, and only a couple of bars. Adjacent **Kim Sha Beach** is often mistakenly considered part of Simpson Bay, though it lies outside the lagoon. It's generally livelier, with local outings, frequent promotions, sand castle competitions, watersports operators, and several eateries within walking distance.

Great Bay Beach ✦ is best if you're staying along Front Street in Philipsburg. This 2km-long (1¼-mile) beach is sandy and calm; despite bordering the busy capital, it's surprisingly clean: Think of it as St. Maarten's less trendy answer to South Beach in Miami. It's a splendid place to kick back after shopping, admiring the leviathan cruise ships from one of many strategic bars along the spanking new boardwalk. On a clear day, you'll have a view of Saba. Immediately to the west, at the foot of Fort Amsterdam, is picturesque **Little Bay Beach,** but it, too, can be overrun with tourists disgorged by the cruise ships. When you tire of the sands here, you can climb up to the site of Fort Amsterdam itself. Built in 1631, it was the first Dutch military outpost in the Caribbean. The Spanish captured it 2 years later, making it their most important bastion east of Puerto Rico. Only a few of the fort's walls remain, but the view is panoramic. Snorkeling is excellent, and several resorts offer plentiful refreshment and recreation options.

Guana Bay ✦, just north of Philipsburg up Pondfill and Guana Bay roads, is long, wide, windswept, and usually deserted (aside from a few surfer dudes and boogie boardistas hanging ten and hanging out). It's topless; the southern section is often clothing-optional. Baying guard dogs occasionally interrupt the solitude (it's a mini–celebrity enclave), the Atlantic swells can be fierce, and it lacks shade and facilities. But the rugged beauty, seclusion, and smashing St. Barts views compensate. On the east side of the island, **Dawn Beach** ✦ is noted for its underwater life, with some of the island's most beautiful reefs immediately offshore. Visitors talk ecstatically of its incredible sunrises. Dawn is suitable for swimming and offers year-round activities such as sand-castle-building contests and crab races. There's plenty of wave action for both surfers and windsurfers. Fairly undeveloped until recently, Dawn Beach has become a preferred locale for condo projects. Construction on the **Westin Resort** (slated to open by Dec 2006), in addition to expansion of **Oyster Bay Resort,** has diminished its peaceful allure. But the views of St. Barts, remarkable reef, and soft pearly sand remain unchanged. Food and drink come courtesy of **Busby's Beach Bar** (✆ 599/543-6828), reincarnated come evening as a scintillating Italian restaurant, Daniel's by the Sea; **Ms. B's** (✆ 599/557-7370), which is currently embroiled in legal action regarding licensing (ask about it and get a lesson in frustrating, yet amusing Caribbean politics); and the Oyster Bay Resort's worthy beachfront bar on the section also called **Oyster Pond Beach,** where bodysurfers take advantage of the rolling waves.

FRENCH SIDE

Baie Longue (Long Bay) ✿✿ on the west coast is one of those beaches that exudes a pull as potent as pheromones: Water of such pristine purity its colors defy gemologists' descriptions, sand the hue of antique lace, dunes as curvaceous as Goya's *Naked Maja,* limestone ironshore (a sea-weathered combination of porous limestone, coral, and fossils) resembling an abstract expressionist canvas. Chic, expensive La Samanna hotel opens onto this beachfront, but it's otherwise blissfully undeveloped and uncrowded, conducive to R&R *à deux.* Its reef-protected waters are ideal for snorkeling, but beware of the strong undertow and steep drop-off. Baie Longue is to the north of Cupecoy Bay Beach, reached via the Lowlands Road. Don't leave valuables in your car, as many break-ins have been reported along this occasionally dangerous stretch of highway.

Baie aux Prunes (Plum Bay) is a Cheshire grin of ivory sand, stretching luxuriantly like a cat around St. Martin's northwest point. This is a sublimely romantic sunset perch (bring your own champagne, as there are no facilities), which also offers some good surfing and snorkeling near the rocks. Access it via the Lowlands Road past Baie Longue.

Baie Rouge (Red Beach) ✿, is caught between two craggy headlands where flocks of gulls and terns descend like clouds upon the cliffs at dusk—hence its western end is dubbed Falaise des Oiseaux (Birds' Bluff). The other side is marked by the Trou du Diable (Devil's Hole), a collapsed cave with two natural arches where the sea churns like a washing machine. You'll find superlative snorkeling here, but beware the powerful undertow. Beachwear becomes increasingly optional as you stroll west, though the modest will find several stands hawking sarongs, shorts, and sunbonnets. Baie Rouge is a charmer, from the serene waters to the views of Anguilla to the *accueil sympa* (cordial welcome) at the two beach bars, **Gus'** (no phone) and **Chez Raymond** (✆ **690/30-70-49**). The latter cooks up blistering barbecue and delivers a knockout punch with Raymond's Special, a blend of six rums, and rocks with reggae on weekends.

Baie Nettlé (Nettle Bay) unfurls like a plush beige carpet between the Caribbean and Simpson Bay, just west of Marigot. Access is right off the main highway running through Sandy Ground. The area has become increasingly developed in the past decade, with several hotels, apartment complexes, watersports franchises (waterskiing and kiteboarding are quite popular), and tiny beach bars alternating with fancier restaurants. The view on the

Moments **Pining for Pinel**

Imagine a tropical island movie set. Breakers lap a beach dotted with *palapas* and parasols. St. Martin's curtain of jade mountains, crowned by a halo of clouds, undulates in the background. Tiny motorized fishing boats trawl vividly hued nets in the distance. Fifteen meters (50 ft.) away a mix of flirtatious locals sporting colorful knotted bandannas and rich young Parisian *flaneurs* (idlers) sip *ti' punches* chest-deep in emerald water. The sultry rhythms of zouk accompany the soft susurrus of surf, while the scents of Creole sauce and coconut oil commingle with the salt air. Welcome to Îlet Pinel, a Lilliputian landfall a few hundred meters—and worlds away—from Orient Beach.

Ferries, costing $6 per passenger, run from Cul de Sac on the northeast coast to Pinel daily on the hour from 10am to 4pm. Watch for the last return trip at 4:30pm. You can hop aboard a CNS Watersports catamaran from Orient Beach for $45 per person. The island has no residents (except wild goats) or electricity—just fine white-sand beaches, idyllic reefs with great snorkeling (especially over the hill on the even more secluded, wind-lashed northeast coast), and waters ideal for bodysurfing. You'll find two delightful beach bistros, separated by Paradise Boutique (aka Tom's Place), which sells hand-painted pareos, tie-dyed shirts, shell jewelry, and whimsical wind chimes. Right at the dock, **Yellow Beach** (© 690/33-88-33) is a series of thatched wood huts; I adore their planters punch with litchi and Creole specialties (the Salade Royale—crab, lobster, large prawns, corn, peppers, and endive—could serve a whole family). **Karibuni** (© 590/39-67-00), the country's longest running beach bar, enjoys an even more dramatic setting, its tiered decks crawling up the rocks, with a boat serving as bar. Savor fresh lobster from traps bobbing just offshore, oysters (fresh from Normandy on Wed and Sat), and house-smoked fish or eviches (the owner catches the wahoo, tuna, and mahimahi himself). At **Pinel Watersports,** a hut on the beach, you can rent pedal boats, kayaks, and snorkeling gear.

Caribbean side frames Anguilla, Marigot's harbor to the north, and the ruins of La Belle Creole along the Pointe du Bluff to the south. Among the numerous *pieds dans l'eau* (literally, feet in water) bistros,

I love Laurent Maudert's **Ma Ti Beach Bar** (✆ 590/87-01-30), where specialties include homemade duck foie gras and calamari "steak" flambéed with pastis.

Isolated **Anse des Pères (Friar's Bay Beach)** lies at the end of a winding bumpy country road that always has me begging for a chiropractor; its clearly signposted entrance intersects with the main highway between Grand Case and Marigot. Although you certainly won't be alone here, this is a less-visited beach with ample parking. Shelling, snorkeling, and sunset watching are all favored. Two beloved beach bars define shack chic and organize raucous themed bashes. At **Friar's Bay Beach Café** (no phone) you can purchase a provocative, often politically charged painting on display or order Laurent's sublime stuffed mussels. The competitor is **Kali's Beach Bar** (✆ 590/49-06-81), a thatched bamboo hut splashed in Rasta colors, where Kali himself serves some of the island's best barbecue. Ask Kali about his "full moon parties," featuring reggae bands on the beach along with a bonfire and plenty of drink. His Jazz Monday and Soca Saturday dinners are also a delight. *Tip:* Have one of the staff here point you in the direction of relatively undiscovered **Anse Heureuse (Happy Bay)** ⊕, a 10-minute walk north through underbrush over a hill from Friar's (pause to drink in the views of Anguilla). It richly deserves the name, thanks to the tranquillity, fine snorkeling, and almost clichéd blinding white sand fringed by spindly swaying palms.

White-sand **Grand Case Beach,** a long narrow ribbon right in the middle of Grand Case, is often crowded, especially on weekends. The waters are very calm, so swimming is excellent and it's a good choice for kids. A small beach, it has its own charm, with none of the carnival-like atmosphere found elsewhere. Unparalleled dining choices along the Caribbean's "Restaurant Row" run from *lolos* (essentially barbecue shacks) to gourmet bistros. For something in between, try the fun and funky **Calmos Café** (see chapter 7).

To the east of Grand Case, follow the winding road up and over Pigeon Pea Hill. The spectacular setting of **Anse Marcel** comes into view. If you'd like to anchor here, check out **Caraïbes Watersports** (✆ 590/29-57-64), offering snorkel gear, bike rentals, parasailing, or kayaks. The adjacent **Marina Port de Lonvilliers** offers several restaurants and shops, and the former le Méridien is being redeveloped as a Radisson, promising additional recreational and gustatory opportunities. The beach itself is protected, with shallow waters ideal for families. You can swim here or else take a hike for 1½ hours north over a hill and down to one of the island's most pristine beaches, **Baie de Petites Cayes.** This is also the most idyllic spot on St. Martin for a picnic. A ribbon of brilliant white sand beckons, and the waters ripple from sapphire to turquoise. Part of the fun is the hike itself, with panoramic views stretching all the way to Anguilla.

On the east coast, the only official nudist beach, **Baie Orientale (Orient Beach)** 𝕮𝕮 redefines "ocean view." Its southern end contains the naturist resort, Club Orient: Passing cruise ships actually snap the sexy Gallic 20-somethings molting thong bikinis and *grand-mères* letting it all hang out. But you needn't shed your bathing suit or inhibitions. This buoyant beach jumps with jaunty bands and bistros, vendors and *vendeuses de la plage* (swimwear models whose informal shows put the tease back in striptease), and watersports from windsurfing to waterskiing to snorkeling around the pyrotechnically colored offshore reef. Eating, drinking, and people-watching qualify as sports, and many beach bistro/bars offer not only everything from grilled crayfish Creole to Cristal, but also live music, boutiques (with fashion shows), massages, parasailing, jet ski rentals, kiteboard instruction, and more. Of those marketing themselves as "The Five Stars of Orient Bay," **Waïkiki Beach** (✆ 590/87-43-19) is a favorite of the well-heeled barefoot St. Barts set, who down beluga caviar with Belvedere shots. **Kontiki** (✆ 590/87-43-27) has two sections: the main eatery and the Tiki Hut, serving a mix of dishes from jerk chicken to paninis to quesadillas to sushi. **Bikini Beach** (✆ 590/87-43-25), which also stays open for dinner, runs from American-styled hamburgers to Spanish-influenced paella studded with lobster; its Manokini snack bar is cheaper (it stocks fine wraps). Like Kontiki, the live music and DJs (best Tues–Wed and Fri) rock. Don't miss the non-star weekend hot spot, **Boo-Boo-Jam** (✆ 590/87-03-13), with wild Caribbean music mixes, various sponsored parties, and a Sunday afternoon bash that attracts locals in droves. Remarkably for this adult sandbox, it offers a playground and kid-friendly activities. Another must is **Baywatch** (✆ 690/66-22-27), Andy and Cheryl Susko's little piece of the Jersey shore (can't beat those hot wings, meatballs, or sausage-and-pepper sandwiches). Andy's Margarita shrimp and ribs delight patrons, as do such "competitions" as Eyeball Olympics (rate passersby 1–10 on paper plates).

Baie de l'Embouchure 𝕮, embracing Le Galion and Coconut Grove, just south of Orient, is part of the St. Martin Réserve Sous-Marine Régionale, established to protect migrant waterfowl habitats

---

Fun Fact **All Cay-ed Up**

Pinel is just one of several Robinson Crusoe cays cast like dice from a gambler's hot hand off the east coast. You can haggle with fishermen at Cul de Sac, Anse Marcel, and Orient (or take an excursion, usually $55 with drinks and lunch) to go even further afield to wild, 10-sq.-km (4-sq.-mile) **Tintamarre,** patois for "noisy sea" after the nesting birds (and bleating goats). The island features pristine snow-white beaches (including the aptly named Baie Blanche), striking ocher cliffs, and wrecks such as an upright tugboat encrusted with jewel-like coral reefs. You can clamber through the scrub and woodlands, discovering the ruins of a 19th-century stone farmhouse and an airport for regional carriers abandoned half a century ago. But nothing matches slathering yourself with mineral-rich mud from the flats, adding sea water, and baking avocado-colored in the sun: nature's exfoliant.

---

and rebuild mangrove swamps. A coral reef encloses the bay: The calm shallow water (you can wade up to 100m/330ft. out) makes it ideal for kids—it's the only beach on the French side where topless sunbathing is discouraged. Yet the steady gusts also make it a wind-surfing mecca; **Tropical Wave** (see "Sports & Other Activities," below) is one of the best places to learn. Tiki carvings and blue umbrellas mark the appealing **Le Galion Restaurant** (aka Chez Pat after owner Pat Turner; ✆ **590/87-37-25**). Locals love this laid-back spot; many families make charcoal pits in the sand for impromptu barbecues.

5 Sports & Other Activities

If it's aquatic, St. Maarten/St. Martin offers it: from sailing to scuba diving, big game fishing to boogie boarding. It almost seems the island has more marinas per square mile than anywhere else on earth (one even recently changed its name to Dock Maarten, neatly combining two local economic mainstays—boating and shopping). Land-based excursions are less popular, though hiking and mountain biking can be rewarding.

ORGANIZED TOURS

Every seasoned sea salt worth his or her salt seemingly ends up on St. Maarten at some point, if only to compete in the many renowned regattas. To keep themselves two sheets (or more) to the wind, they charter their boats. Needless to say, the island offers everything from booze cruises to eco-kayaking on all manner of pleasure craft from banana boats to catamarans to dinghies.

Aquamania Adventures offers a plethora of pleasures out of Pelican Marina, Simpson Bay (© **599/544-2640;** www.stmaarten-activities.com). In addition to a parasail outfit, a PADI dive shop, ferry service to Saba and St. Barts, and a boutique abounding in beach toys and resort wear its three party-hearty boats patrol the waters several times daily. Two catamarans, *Lambada* and *Tango,* cruise to Anguilla and Prickly Pear for snorkeling and beach barbe-cues (from $75). Or simply opt for sunset sails ($25 including open bar). *Sand Dollar* clings closer to St. Martin with a 3-hour snorkel-ing excursion to Creole Rock ($35, $20 children under 12). Kids can take turns piloting the *Calypso* in Simpson's Bay's serene waters ($15), then bombard a small wreck with water balloons. Prizes and bobbing blow-up animals keep things happy. Or the family can frolic just offshore on *Playstation* ($15 for a half-day; 9:30am–4:30pm), a converted colorful "swing, slide and splash" catamaran that resembles an avant-garde art installation. The plat-form includes Tarzan swings, several slides, and plenty of room to clamber. Dinner cruises (some aboard, others stopping at restau-rants in Marigot's Marina Royale) are generally genial affairs; the return voyage toward St. Maarten's blazing neon skyline is memo-rable indeed.

Two New England expats, Donna and Susan, run **Turtle Tours** in Simpson Bay (© **599/526-4662;** www.turtletours-sxm.com); they love giving a thorough grounding (or sightsea-ing) of their adopted home. You can circumnavigate the lagoon, piloting your own unsinkable 3.3m (11-ft.) Boston Whaler Sport while admiring the homes and mega-yachts of the rich and famous. Or get cozy with a few new friends on a 4.8m (16-ft.) Boston Whaler, snorkel-ing at Creole Rock. The owners also arrange day sails (on larger craft) to Sandy Island or Tintamarre, including lunch. Prices vary because they prefer to customize excursions.

The sleek 23m (75-ft.) catamaran **Scoobidoo** (© **590/52-02-53;** www.scoobidoo.com) departs from Anse Marcel and Grand Case, sailing to Tintamarre, Anguilla, Prickly Pear, St. Barts, or some com-bination of the above. Most outings ($55–$120) include snorkeling equipment, lunch, and open bar; sunset cruises are $35. The crew spins arguably the best mix of the charter boats, from ambient to lounge to jazz to soca. You've gotta love their sense of humor (storm clouds on the horizon bring out Wagner's "Ride of the Valkyrie").

Eagle Tours at Bobby's Marina in Philipsburg (© **599/543-0068** or 599/542-3323; www.sailingsxm.com) offers lagoon sightseeing tours aboard the flatboat *Explorer,* stopping in Marigot for shopping before heading home; mimosas and rum punches flow copiously. But their pride and joy is the 23m (76-ft.), custom-designed *Golden Eagle* catamaran. Originally built for the prestigious Whitbread Around the World Race, it features a 24m-tall (80-ft.) main mast and a 7.2m (24-ft.) sail that took two men 3 weeks to paint by hand. It cruises to various deserted strands and cays for snorkeling and soaking up both tropical ambience and drinks (the pampering service includes a floating bar). The Friday jaunt ($99) sails to Tintamarre and Creole Rock, puts in at Grand Case for lunch, then stops by Baie Longue for a final cooling dip. Transportation to and from your hotel is included.

The 12m (40-ft.) catamaran *Celine* departs Skipjack's dock at Simpson Bay (© **599/545-3961;** www.sailstmaarten.com) for a mellow sunset cruise ($25; with dinner $65). But South African skipper Neil Roebert, who built *Celine* by hand, is most (in)famous for leading a Lagoon Pub Crawl around Simpson Bay, with sons Graham and Johann as occasional accomplices. Neil calls himself the "ultimate designated driver," steering guests toward four of the better local bars: Peg Leg Pub, Skipjack's, La Guinguette, and Lal's

---

Moments Come Sail Away

Ever wonder what racing a swift state-of-the-art yacht is like? The St. Maarten 12-Metre Challenge in Philipsburg at Bobby's Marina (© **599/542-0045;** www.12metrechallenge.com) gives nautical nuts a chance to crew on one of five famed America's Cup yachts specially designed for the 1987 competition off Fremantle, Australia. The marquee marques include Dennis Conner's champion *Stars & Stripes, True North,* and *Canada II.* Each boat takes nine to 18 competitors (12 and up) for a thrilling 3-hour race ($75). Previous sailing experience isn't required: The captains and mates brief their swabs-for-a-day on the basics from grinding a winch to tacking, as well as the history of the America's Cup. Or you can just drink in the experience along with rum punches, letting everyone else worry about even keels.

Indian. In addition to an open bar aboard, the first drink is free at each stop, along with a signature bite (from filet mignon cubes to mahimahi kabobs). Departures are at 7pm Wednesdays and Thursdays, with Mondays added in high season. The 3-hour bender costs a mere $65. Neil also charters *Celine* for trips to Pinel, Tintamarre, Baie Longue, Friar's Bay, and more with or without lunch; base rate is $85 per person (minimum of 10 people).

STAYING ACTIVE

BOATING   Sea dogs will happily bark (or bite) at **Lagoon Sailboat Rental** in Simpson Bay Lagoon (© 599/557-0714; www. lagoonsailboatrental.com). You can explore the lagoon and surrounding waters in state-of-the-art 6m (20-ft.) Sunfasts for $150 ($110 for a half-day). The congenial Cary and company also give a thorough 10-hour course for $200 (minimum two people, maximum three) that can be broken up however you like. The big dogs (from Beneteaus on up) are anchored at the local branch of internationally respected **The Moorings** at Captain Oliver's Marina, Oyster Pond (© 599/87-32-54; www.moorings.com).

DEEP-SEA FISHING   The island hosts several highly regarded competitions, including May's Marlin Cup and June's Billfish Tournament, that lure an impressive international roster of entrants. The waters teem with tuna, wahoo, snapper, grouper, jack, pompano, yellowtail, marlin, and other big game fish. The crew from **Lee's Roadside Grill** on Welfare Road 84, Simpson Bay (© 599/544-4233; www.leesfish.com), knows where to catch the big boys, since they supply their own wildly popular seafood haunt. Its 9.3m (31-ft.) Bertram, *Baby Blues,* is available for a minimum of four people (maximum six). Drinks are included in the half-day trip ($400) and lunch and drinks are included in the ¾- and full-day excursions ($550 and $750, respectively). And yes, they'll cook your trophy up at the restaurant.

Water Fun Tours departs from Bobby's Marina in Philipsburg or the Red Cross Building on Airport Road and Buccaneer Beach Bar in Simpson Bay (© 599/520-1581; www.watertour-stmaarten. com). Ben "Flying Dutchman" Steen's 6.9m (23-ft.) Mako features an auto-pilot chart plotter, sounder, and other top-notch equipment. Drinks flow liberally on the half- and full-day charters ($375 and $650). You can also charter the boat for $25 per person per hour, minimum of four guests. Ben also arranges snorkeling, sunset, and circumnavigation tours at competitive prices.

On the French side, **Big Sail Fish Too** at the Marigot waterfront (℃ **690/27-11-12**) will take four to eight anglers aboard a 9m (30-ft.) Blackfin. The crew is knowledgeable, the tackle high quality, and the rum punches strong. Drinks are included for half-day charters ($500); add lunch to the full-day trip ($800).

GOLF   The **Mullet Bay Resort** (℃ **599/545-3069** or 599/545-2801), on the Dutch side, has the island's only golf course. It's a battered, scrub-blanketed, slightly dusty 18-hole par-70 Joseph Lee–designed course, whose fate has hung in the balance, based on some ongoing court battles, for years. Although the resort itself is closed, the golf course is still operational. Mullet Pond and Simpson Bay Lagoon provide both beauty and hazards (holes 12 through 15 are especially tricky as they crisscross an arm of the lagoon). Greens fees are $60 for 9 holes or $88 for 18 holes, for players who opt to walk instead of ride. Renting a two-person electric cart will cost an additional $8 to $18 depending on how many holes you play. Club rentals cost $21 for 9 holes or $26 for 18 holes.

HIKING & MOUNTAIN BIKING   Despite its small size, the island offers terrain ranging from limestone plateaus to a central volcanic ridge topped by 445m (1,482-ft.) Pic du Paradis, and ecosystems from semi-desert to tropical rainforest. Birders will sight coots, black-necked stilts, and ospreys nesting amid the swamps and cliffs.

Adrenaline junkies and eco-buffs will feel at home at **TriSport** headquarters on 14B Airport Rd. in Simpson Bay (℃ **599/545-4384;** www.trisportsxm.com). When they're not running (in both senses) marathons or triathlons, the jocks and jockettes here lead hikes and mountain bike tours, all customized to participants' interests and skill/fitness levels (treks are moderate to strenuous). One popular 2½-hour nature hike around Guana Bay ($31) includes several steep pitches. But views of rock formations on the rugged east coast more than compensate, as does a dip in the natural sea pool. The guides explain the flora (including herbal folklore). Mountain bikers can rent Trek aluminum bikes ($12 half-day, $18 full day, $100 per week) or join the twice daily expeditions ($49) around Cay Bay and St. Peter's on the Dutch side, or Friar's Bay and Colombier on the French side. TriSports also ventures into the open water with snorkeling/kayaking tours around Anse Guichard's hulking Henry Moore–ish boulders and Caye Verte. The 2½-hour lagoon explorer tour ($49) includes instruction and a stop at deserted Grand Îlet, whose mangrove system houses unusual critters from sea cucumbers to upside-down jellies. You can rent kayaks for $15 per hour; a double kayak costs $19.

HORSEBACK RIDING   **Lucky Stables** in Cole Bay (© **599/ 544-5255;** www.luckystable.com) offers a romantic Moonlight Champagne ride ($65) including a marshmallow roast or a sunset jaunt (from $45). The winner is the 2-hour combo ride ($65). Guides explain local folklore, fauna, and flora along the picturesque route through the closest thing to wilderness on the Dutch side. The highlight is the descent into secluded, stony, unspoiled Cay Bay (aka Cape Bay) as Saba, Statia, St. Kitts, and Nevis drift on the horizon. Suddenly the horses wade into the warm water; your saddle feels like a flotation device as they swim with surprising grace. There's time to go shelling and snorkel in the seemingly pyrotechnic offshore reef (without your ride). Birders will also enjoy the many waterfowl sightings; it's also an excellent vantage point for whale-watching in spring. The owners also give instruction in Doma Vaquera training (Spanish dressage) and occasionally mount (pun intended) shows in traditional dress on *paso fino* horses. Lessons are $25; the little bar actually turns out terrific ribs and satays with fries for $3 to $5. Its equally worthy, eco-sensitive counterpart on the French side is **Bayside Riding Club,** rue de la Galion, Orientale (© **590/87-36-64**). Prices start at $70 for 2 hours per person (including the Champagne and Full Moon rides), $50 for 1 hour. Here too, the highlight is swimming astride your mount in the water. Children can take pony rides for $25 per half-hour.

SCUBA DIVING   Scuba diving is excellent around **St. Martin,** with reef, wreck, night, cave, and drift diving; the depth of dives is 6 to 21m (20–69 ft.). Off the northeastern coast, dive sites include Îlet Pinel and Creole Rock, for shallow diving; Green Key, a barrier reef; and Tintamarre, for sheltered coves and geologic faults. To the north, Anse Marcel and neighboring Anguilla are good choices. **St. Maarten's** crystal-clear bays and countless coves make for good scuba diving as well as snorkeling. Underwater visibility runs from 23 to 38m (75–125 ft.). The biggest attraction for divers is the 1770 British man-of-war, **HMS *Proselyte,*** which came to a watery grave on a reef 2km (1¼ miles) off Philipsburg in 1801. Other excellent sites include Tugboat Annie, Frenchman's Reef, Lucy's Barge, Pelican Rock, the double pinnacles of One Step Beyond, Moonhole (a large crater with caves and walls of sponges), and the intact fishing vessel Fu Cheng 36m (120 ft.) down.

Memorable sightings amid virtual mountain ranges of coral with crevices, ledges, and drops galore include schools of vibrantly colored fish from grunts to queen angels, sea fans beckoning like come-hither courtesans, stingrays, mantas, moray eels, barracuda, tarpon, banded coral shrimp, Caribbean spiny lobsters, endangered turtles (green, leatherback, hawksbill, loggerhead), and reef and nurse sharks. Most of the big resorts have facilities for scuba diving and can provide information about underwater tours, photography, and night diving.

Scuba Fun has offices at Marina Port Lonvilliers, Anse Marcel (© **590/87-36-13;** www.scubafun.com), and Dock Maarten Marina, Great Bay, Pointe Blanche (© **599/542-3966**). Morning and afternoon dives in deep and shallow water, wreck dives, and reef dives cost $45 per dive (certified divers only). A resort course for first-time divers with reasonable swimming skills costs $75 and includes 45 minutes of instruction in a swimming pool and a one-tank shallow dive above a coral reef. Full PADI certification costs $350, an experience that requires 5 days and includes classroom training, sessions with a scuba tank within the safety of a swimming pool, and three open-water dives. Snorkeling trips cost $30 for a half-day, plus $10 for equipment rental.

Dive Safaris in Bobby's Marina, Philipsburg (© **599/542-9001**), and Simpson Bay (© **599/545-2401;** www.divestmaarten.com) offers competitive rates and a full range of PADI certification courses, including specialty instruction in marine habitats, photography, and wreck diving. Those wanting to prove their mettle can don chain-mail-like armor (resembling fetishistic Gaultier designs) to feed the sharks at "Big Mama's Reef."

The larger-than-life owner of **Ocean Explorers** at Kim Sha Beach (© **599/544-5252;** www.stmaartendiving.com), LeRoy French, is still diving more than a half-century after he caught the bug (using some of Cousteau's first Aqua Lungs). Starry students in his 40-plus-year career have included Jackson Browne, Matthew McConaughey, and Sandra Bullock. He's been profiled by *Sports Illustrated,* and even the Cousteau team might envy his vivid videos. The personalized touch—he takes a maximum of six divers—costs a bit more ($45–$55 single dive, $100 double; $390 full certification) and means reservations are essential.

SNORKELING 🤿🤿   Calm waters ringing shallow reefs and tiny coves make the island a snorkeler's heaven. The waters off northeastern French St. Martin have been classified as a regional underwater nature reserve, **Réserve Sous-Marine Régionale,** which protects the area around Flat Island (also known as Tintamarre), Îlet Pinel, Green Key, and Petite Clef. Equipment can be rented at almost any hotel, and most beaches have watersports kiosks. The waters surrounding the entire Dutch side to a depth of 60m (200 ft.; with designated fishing, scuba, and shipping zones) are protected as the **St. Maarten Marine Park,** which also inaugurated an Artificial Reef program, utilizing special balls to imitate the appearance and function of natural coral reefs. The island's top snorkeling beaches are Mullet Bay, Cay Bay, Little Bay, Dawn Beach, Plum Bay, and Baie Rouge.

One of St. Martin's best sources for snorkeling and other beach diversions is **Carib Watersports** (© 590/87-51-87), a clothing store, art gallery, and watersports kiosk on the beachfront of the Grand Case Beach Club. Its French and U.S. staff provides information on island activities and rents kayaks and paddleboats for $20 an hour and snorkeling equipment for $10 a day. The main allure, however, are the guided snorkeling trips to St. Martin's teeming offshore reefs, including Creole Rock, an offshore clump of reef-ringed boulders rich in underwater fauna. The 2-hour trips depart daily at 10am, noon, and 2pm; cost is $30 including equipment. Reservations are recommended. **Rhino Safaris** in Simpson Bay (© 599/544-3150) allows you to pilot your own craft, a sleek Rhino Rider, on a 2½-hour guided adventure to various snorkeling spots (singles $80, tandem $49 per person).

TENNIS   You can try the courts at most of the large resorts, but you must call first for a reservation. Preference, of course, is given to hotel guests.

On the Dutch side, there are four courts at the **Maho Beach Hotel,** Maho Bay (© 599/545-2115). **Port de Plaisance,** Cole Bay (© 599/544-5222) has seven courts. **The Pelican,** Simpson Bay (© 599/54-42503) has four courts, and the **Divi Little Bay Beach Resort,** Little Bay Road (© 599/542-2333), has one court, but they are for guest play only. On the French side, **Esmeralda Resort,** Orient Bay (© 590/87-36-36) has two courts, although the new **Radisson Resort & Spa,** Anse Marcel (© 590/87-67-00), a redevelopment of the former Le Meridien, may add four courts for its anticipated opening in early 2007.

WATER-SKIING & PARASAILING   Most of French St. Martin's large beachfront hotels maintain facilities for water-skiing and parasailing, often from kiosks that operate on the beach.

An independent operator on Orient Bay, **Kontiki Watersports** (*C* **590/87-46-89;** www.sxm-game.com), rents jet skis and WaveRunners for around $45 per half-hour, $80 per hour; parasailing costs $50 for 10 minutes or $90 if two people go together. They also offer banana boats, aquajumping, and half-day guided jet ski tours with snorkeling at Tintamarre, Petite, and Grande Cayes, and/or Anse Marcel for $60. Jet-skiing and water-skiing are also especially popular in Dutch St. Maarten. The unruffled waters of Simpson Bay, the largest lagoon in the West Indies, are ideal for these sports, and outfitters have facilities right on the sands. **Club Caraïbes** at the Hôtel Mercure Simson Beach in Nettle Bay (*C* **690/33-30-01;** www.skicaraibes.net) provides wakeboard and jet ski rentals, as well as water-skiing instruction with Laurent Guy and Brigitte Lethem (the 2004 U.S. Master Champion). You can learn slalom or tricks for 30€ ($38) per set; 5-day intensive water-skiing and wakeboard courses cost 270€ to 490€ ($338–$613). Right next door (or shack) at Nettle Bay is **Sensation Jet Excursion** (*C* **590/51-15-53**), where rentals cost 40€ ($50) per half-hour. The outfit also offers tours of the lagoon (80€/$100) and island circumnavigations as well as visits to Pinel and, depending on water conditions, Tintamarre for 140€ to 150€ ($175–$188), including lunch.

WINDSURFING & KITEBOARDING   Most windsurfers gravitate to the eastern part of the island, most notably Coconut Grove/ Le Galion Beach, Orient Beach, and to a lesser extent, Dawn Beach, all in French St. Martin. The top outfitter here, **Tropical Wave,** Le Galion Beach, Baie de l'Embouchure (*C* **590/87-37-25;** www.sxm-restaurants.com/orient/chezpat), capitalizes on the near-ideal combination of wind and calm waters. Pat rents Mistrals for 20€ ($25) an hour, with instruction offered at 30€ ($38) an hour, and 45€ ($56) for a 2-hour beginner course. They also rent snorkeling gear, pedal boats, and kayaks (tours can be arranged). **Club Nathalie Simon** on Orient Beach (*C* **590/29-41-57;** www.cnsorientbay.com) is one of the Caribbean's premier kiteboarding schools. Lessons cost 40€ ($50) per hour, 55€ ($63) for 1½ hours. Kite trips for the experienced to Green Cay start at 95€ ($119). CNS also rents windsurfers and Hobie Cats from 35€ ($44) per hour, and offers both safaris and instruction (with excellent multilesson discounts). Equipment, Tatou to Tiga, is state-of-the-art.

6

Shopping on St. Maarten/St. Martin

Many visitors' favorite sport (and sightseeing activity) is window-shopping. The island teems with duty-free bargains in seemingly everything from linen to liquor, china to cameras, with prices as much as 25% to 40% lower than those in the U.S. and Canada. There's an energizing hubbub in Philipsburg every morning as cruise ship passengers scatter eagerly in search of latter-day treasure: The goods displayed in the windows along Front Street are an eye-catching, mind-boggling display of conspicuous consumption. Philipsburg's inviting French counterpart Marigot boasts smart boutiques with striped awnings and wrought-iron balconies that recall the Riviera, and galleries showcasing local artists' work: The island's charms beg for delicate watercolors. Frenetic yet stimulating, Philipsburg encourages you to "shop till you drop." Marigot murmurs seductively, "relax, the shops will still be open in an hour or two": It's the perfect place to savor the salt air, watch the ferries load for Anguilla, and enjoy a steaming cup of café au lait.

1 The Shopping Scene

Not only is Dutch St. Maarten a free port, but it has no local sales taxes. Prices are sometimes lower here than anywhere else in the Caribbean, except possibly St. Thomas. Many well-known shops from Curaçao have branches here.

Except for the boutiques at resort hotels, the main shopping area is in the center of **Philipsburg.** Most of the leading shops—Tiffany to Tommy Hilfiger—line **Voorstraat (Front Street),** which stretches for about 2km (1¼ miles). Just off Front Street, **Old Street** lives up to its name, with adorable 19th-century houses that today contain specialty stores. More shops and souvenir kiosks sit along the little lanes, known as *steegjes,* that connect Front Street with **Achterstraat (Back Street),** another shoppers' haven.

Maho Plaza (surrounding the glitzy Sonesta Maho Beach Resort) is another area for name brand offerings (and outlets), including branches of Front Street stalwarts.

In general, the prices marked on the merchandise are firm, though at some small, personally run shops, where the owner is on-site, some bargaining might be in order.

Many day-trippers head to Marigot from the Dutch side just to browse the French-inspired boutiques and shopping arcades. Since St. Martin is also a duty-free port, you'll find some superb buys here as well, even at the ultraluxe boutiques along **rue de la République, rue du Général de Gaulle,** and **rue de la Liberté** (think New York's Madison Ave. or Paris's av. Montaigne). French luxury items such as Christofle tableware, Vuitton bags, Cartier accessories, and Chanel perfume are understandably emphasized.

The waterfront **Le West Indies Mall** (© 590/51-04-19) is an overly ornate stone-wood-and-concrete architectural monstrosity with arches, skylights, curved staircases, and gazebos galore. But it does concentrate 22 big-name boutiques, from L'Occitane to Lacoste, their wares almost fetishistically lit and displayed. You'll also find branches of the famed Jacques Dessange Hair Salon and the venerable gourmet shop Hédiard (established in Paris in 1854), where you can purchase exquisite champagne, caviar, and foie gras; its aromatic tea room is a delightful stop for fresh pastries. Smaller but equally prestigious complexes include **Galerie Périgourdine** and **Plaza Caraïbes** (Cartier and Hermès outposts).

At Marigot's harbor side, there's a lively **morning market** on Wednesday and Saturday with vendors selling spices, fruit, shells, and handicrafts: an elegant bazaar.

At bustling **Marina Port la Royale,** mornings are even more active: Schooners unload produce from the neighboring islands, boats board guests for picnics on deserted beaches, and a dozen different little restaurants ready for the lunch crowd. Marina Royale is peppered with upscale boutiques and galleries selling everything from lingerie to liqueurs.

Several charming boutiques and ateliers fight for scraps of space between the bistros along the main drag of St. Martin's "second" city, Grand Case, nicknamed "Caribbean Restaurant Row." They keep unusual hours: Most are shuttered during the day, but fling their doors open come evening for pre- and post-dinner strollers.

Prices are often quoted in U.S. dollars, and salespeople frequently speak English. Credit cards and traveler's checks are generally

---

Tips   **Mapping It**

For locations of the shopping establishments listed in this chapter, please refer to the St. Maarten/St. Martin, Marigot, or Philipsburg maps on p. 50, p. 59, and p. 52, respectively.

---

accepted. When cruise ships are in port on Sundays and holidays, some of the larger shops stay open.

2 Shopping A to Z

CLOTHING 𝒢
DUTCH SIDE

Blooming Baskets by Lisa   Blooming Baskets showcases the talents of two sisters from Harrisburg, Pennsylvania. The baskets are actually straw-and-raffia handbags in various sizes adorned with silk flowers duplicating not just island blossoms but a virtual botanical garden, from irises to sunflowers. Their hand-mixed dyes, inspirations of the moment, ensure no two bags are ever quite alike. 21 Maho Marketplace, Maho Beach. ✆ 599/545-2270. www.bloomingbaskets bylisa.com.

Del Sol St-Maarten   This shop sells men's and women's sportswear. Embedded in the mostly black-and-white designs are organic crystals that react to ultraviolet light, which transforms the fabric into a rainbow of colors. Step back into the shadows, and your T-shirt will revert to its original black-and-white design. The same technology is applied to yo-yos, which shimmer psychedelically when you rock the baby or walk the dog. 23 Front St. ✆ 599/542-8784.

Rima Beach World   Rima hawks essentially any beach accessory you might need from peasant skirts to pareos, bonnets to bags, and much, much more, all bedecked in luscious tropical colors. Nisbeth (Pondfill) Rd. just north of Philipsburg. ✆ 599/542-1424.

FRENCH SIDE

Act III   Perhaps the most glamorous women's boutique in St. Martin, Act III prides itself on its evening gowns and chic cocktail dresses. If you've been invited to a reception aboard a private yacht, this is the place to find the right outfit. Designers include Alaïa, Christian Lacroix, Cavalli, Armani, Lanvin, and Gaultier. The bilingual staff is accommodating, tactful, and charming, but they know if you're truly versed in Versace or parade in Prada knockoffs. 3 rue du Général de Gaulle. ✆ **590/29-28-43.**

Desmo   This Florence-based style guru understands the wisdom of that fabulous *Steel Magnolias* line, "The only thing that separates us from the animals is our ability to accessorize." Whether it be shoes, purses, scarves, or belts, Desmo features Italian designers—Dibrera, Perla-Azzurra, Francesco Biasia—who take that quote as their mantra. 15 Marina Royale. ✆ **590/87-84-62.**

Havane Boutique   This boutique is a hyper-stylish menswear store, more couture than ready-to-wear, with mannequins draped in clothes ranging from Armani to Zegna; its adjacent sister store, **Ital-iaMania** garbs gals in Ferragamo and Dolce & Gabbana. 50 Marina Royale. ✆ **590/87-70-39.**

La Romana   This boutique specializes in elegant women's wear that's more lighthearted, even frivolous compared to the selection at Act III. Italian rather than French designers are emphasized, including lines such as Anna Club, plus La Perla swimwear, handbags, and perfumes. It's also the place for sheer ooh-la-la lingerie. A small collection of menswear, from linen to leather, is also available. 12 rue de la République. ✆ **590/87-88-16.**

L'Atelier   L'Atelier showcases such younger designers as Alexander McQueen and Narciso Rodríguez alongside legends like Paul Smith and Sonia Rykiel. 28 Marina Royale. ✆ **590/87-13-71.**

Longchamp   A branch of the famed family-run, trendsetting Parisian boutique, Longchamp specializes in exquisitely hand-crafted leather goods, as well as nylon totes in edible colors like blueberry, lime, and mango. Plaza Caraïbes, rue Général de Gaulle. ✆ **590/87-92-76.**

Luis Gomez *(finds*   Although he's only open from 3 to 5pm during the week, Luis Gomez is worth seeking out if you crave richly colored hand-stitched swimwear, sarongs, and wraps, inspired by his peripatetic wanderings through Asia. He works with several fabrics, cotton to silk, and will custom-design anything from simple to elaborate. On Orient Beach next to Baywatch bar. ✆ **599/547-2396.**

Max Mara   This, the first Caribbean franchise for the Italian Maramotti empire, carries every line from the more casual, lower-priced SportMax and Weekend to the dressy Pianoforte. Marigot, 6 rue du Président Kennedy. ✆ **590/52-99-75.**

Serge Blanco "15" Boutique   Although a relatively unknown name in North America, in France Blanco is revered as one of the most successful rugby players of all time. His menswear is sporty, fun, and elegant. Clothes include polo shirts, shorts, shoes, and truly wonderful latex jackets. Marina Royale. ℰ 590/29-65-49.

Vie Privée   Care for a python to curl around your waist? This shop offers belts in leather and various exotic skins from ostrich to crocodile with elaborate buckles designed by Philippe Jourdain that make a bold statement. Marina Royale. ℰ 590/87-80-69.

CONTEMPORARY ART ℱ

The island's charming local scenes and resplendent light have inspired such renowned artists as Romare Bearden over the years. I generally find the galleries more sophisticated on the French side; curious shoppers can also visit various ateliers.

DUTCH SIDE

Greenwich Galleries   This is the Dutch side's most urbane art gallery, with Bajan pottery in sea greens and blues, replicas of Taíno artifacts from the Dominican Republic, enameled metal cutouts that are both quirky and enigmatic, and paintings and prints from artists on both sides of the Atlantic. 35 Front St. ℰ 599/542-3842.

Planet Paradise   Also known as Island Arts of That Yoda Guy, this is the playpen of the wildly creative Nick Maley, an artist/SFX designer who was instrumental in fashioning *Star Wars*'s resident gnomic gnome and contributed to other blockbusters from *Superman* to *Highlander*. John Williams's iconic theme music wafts through the air as you examine rare Lucasfilm prints, posters signed by the director himself, and Nick's own island-themed artworks. If you're lucky, he'll be around, relating cinematic anecdotes ("I spent my first career making 53 movies, my second making piña coladas," he quips). He's slowly creating a museum in back holding his own considerable collection of film memorabilia, including casts of various stars' faces, set schematics, original drawings, and items such as a *Daily Planet* front page. There's a second location at 106 Old St. 19A Front St. ℰ 599/542-4009. www.yodaguy.com.

FRENCH SIDE

Alexandre Minguet   Yet another highly regarded French expat, Minguet's fluid canvases marry the form of Cézanne with the sensuality of Gauguin. He also exhibits other Caribbean painters of note. Rambaud Hill between Marigot and Grand Case. ℰ 590/87-76-06. www. minguet.com.

Antoine Chapon This Bordeaux-born painter's work provides a dynamic counterpoint to Eck's. Andrew Wyeth lauds Chapon's ethereal watercolors of serene marine scenes. His prints are pretty (and quite inexpensive), but the comparatively flat medium lacks the elusive, watery quality of his paintings. Terrasses de Cul de Sac. ✆ 590/87-40-87. www.chaponartgallery.com.

Atelier des Tropismes With a studio in back, Atelier des Tropismes is home to three artists. Patrick Poivre de la Fréta studied in Paris with Salvador Dalí; some works display a homoerotic undercurrent as he depicts scenes as witnessed by a sailor, but he also creates playful, witty still lifes and genre scenes in feverish Fauvist hues, and *objets* like screens. Paul Elliott Thuleau faithfully reproduces architectural facades in super-realist fashion with luminous hues. Nathalie Lépine's portraits of women, some sturdy like Léger or de Lempincka, others attenuated like Modigliani or Giacometti (with a hint of wry cartoonist Lynda Barry) are contemplative, almost hauntingly melancholy. 107 Boulevard de Grand Case. ✆ 590/29-10-60.

Digital Fusion This is the foundry of bronze sculptor Thierry Garcia (who also works in stone); his powerful figures are patterned after Arawak carvings. Bellevue outside Marigot. ✆ 590/52-36-95.

Dona Bryhiel *(finds)* Provence native Dona Bryhiel focuses on the curvaceous, even zaftig feminine form as a visual metaphor for the island and vice versa; she also produces splendid light-suffused paintings of Provence. You'll also find hand-painted T-shirts, beach towels, and textiles; stunning jewelry incorporating local materials from shells to banana wood; and the delicate enameled ceramics of fellow Provençal, Martine Azéma. 9 Residence Lou Castel, Oyster Pond. ✆ 590/87-43-93. www.donabryhiel.com.

Francis Eck An Alsatian expat inspired rather like Rothko and Gottlieb by the purity of Asian art, Francis Eck commands fabulous prices for his intense abstract genre scenes, landscapes, and seascapes. Their dramatic, almost shocking, jazzy riffs of primary color and bold brush work (combined with knife and trowel) enable him "to explore the intersection of figurative and abstract," yet reflect Nature's dichotomous simplicity and depth. The atelier is open by appointment only. 48 rue du Soleil Levant, Concordia outside Marigot. ✆ 590/87-12-32. www.francis-eck.com.

Gingerbread Gallery Gingerbread Gallery exhibits vivid powerful Haitian art, including works by such modern masters as Alphonse and Brésil. 14 Marina Royale. ✆ 590/87-73-21. www.gingerbread-gallery.com.

NOCOart NOCOart was founded in 2004 by sisters Norma and Corinne Trimborn, whose work couldn't be more different. Norma's paintings are figurative with abstract expressionist elements. Corinne's unsettling neo-surrealist melting and disfigured faces and strong, striking color fields suggest the essential duality of the female experience. 39 Falaise des Oiseaux, Terres Basses near Plum Bay. ⓒ 590/87-55-29. www.nocoart.com.

Roland Richardson Paintings and Prints Known for luminous landscapes, portraits, and still lifes, Roland Richardson's clearest influence is the 19th-century Barbizon School of Impressionists. A native of St. Martin and one of the Caribbean's premier artists, he works in numerous media: oil, watercolors, pastels, charcoal, even batik and stained glass. You can often find him working *en plein air* to capture Nature's fleeting colors and forms as rapidly as possible. His work has been exhibited in nearly 100 one-man and group shows in museums and galleries around the world. Celebrity collectors have ranged from Martha Graham to Jackie Kennedy Onassis, Harry Belafonte to Ivan Lendl, the Getty family to Queen Beatrix of the Netherlands. He and wife Laura are gracious hosts in their carefully restored landmark West Indian home with concealed courtyard garden and gallery dating back to the 1700s. 6 rue de la République. ⓒ 590/87-84-08.

HANDICRAFTS & GIFTS
DUTCH SIDE

Dutch Delft Blue Gallery The authentic source for hand-painted Delftware, visitors find the four primary types here: Delft Imari, Delft Green & Gold, traditional Delft Blue, and Delft Polychrome (including the Animal series modeled after antique Dutch tiles). 37 Front St. ⓒ 599/542-5204.

Lalique It is surprising that this store is found in Philipsburg not Marigot. The fabulous and fabulously priced art glass and stemware (as well as authentic jewelry) should tempt any collector. 13 Sint Rose Arcade, Front St. ⓒ 599/542-0763.

Linen Galore This place only looks, well, tatty: The tablecloths, napery, placemats, towels, fine lace, and runners are carefully sourced from Europe and Turkey. 97 Front St. ⓒ 599/542-2533.

Shipwreck Shop This place offers one-stop souvenir shopping, from handmade hammocks to herbs, batik sarongs to bronze geckos. Marigot's Marina Royale holds another branch (ⓒ **590/87-27-37**). 42 Front St. ⓒ **599/542-2962**.

FRENCH SIDE

Amahoro Afro-Caribbean Art & Craft Gallery This gallery showcases the island's African heritage with assorted tribal masks, wall hangings, fertility icons, and eye-catching jewelry. Le West Indies Mall, Front de Mer. ℂ 590/29-51-16.

Lagune Blue Lagune Blue sells sublime Murano glass objects, ornate Venetian masks, and an alluring array of ornaments and knickknacks in whimsical shapes. Marina Royale. No phone.

La Petite Favorite *(Finds* This is a marvelous artistic commune spearheaded by Cécile Petrelluzzi. She displays her own ceramics, which deftly balance art and function, alongside those of three other potters at Elementerre. An adjacent room showcases works by artists in various media from photographs to metal work. Other artisans' ateliers on-site include Lanmè (Tessa Urbanowicz's finely crafted jewelry) and Kaiera (Tumay Yalcin's ceramic home furnishings). There's even a fun souvenir shop (Boubou's) and a little cafe serving equally artful seafood platters and pastries. Boulevard de Grand Case. ℂ 590/87-06-55.

Les Exotiques This is the workshop and showroom of Marie Moine, a ceramicist who fires charming local scenes onto plates: Creole houses, birds flying over Monet-like ponds, tiny Antillean figures in traditional dress. 76 rue de la Flibuste, Oyster Pond. ℂ 590/29-53-76.

JEWELRY, PERFUMES & COSMETICS ℛℛ

Front Street seems like one jeweler after another (not unlike New York's West 47th St. Diamond Exchange), all selling loose stones as well as designer items. Marigot counters with its selection of luxury brands, particularly in watches. Many stores operate branches on both sides of the island. Beware of unscrupulous hucksters selling loose "gems" like emeralds and diamonds on the street.

DUTCH SIDE

Colombian Emeralds International This is yet another branch in the Caribbean-wide chain that sells unmounted emeralds from Colombia at heavily discounted prices, as well as jewelry fashioned from other precious stones. Old Street Shopping Center. ℂ 599/542-3933.

Hans Meevis Jewelry Hans Meevis is a master goldsmith, who works brilliantly in miniature. He loves using inlays such as larimar in ebony, or fashioning mosaics of tiny gems. Signature items include frolicking dolphin rings and pendants and remarkable keep-sake blued titanium disks with intricate relief of the island in bur-nished white gold—right down to salt ponds and isthmuses. But Hans also delights in customizing all manner of decorative pieces (including bric-a-brac) on-site. 65 Airport Blvd., Simpson Bay. © 599/522-4433. www.meevis.com.

Little Switzerland   This is part of a chain scattered throughout the Caribbean, whose top-of-the-line famous-name imports (watches, china, crystal, and jewelry from the likes of Tiffany) sport equally lovely price tags. 52 Front St. © 599/542-2523.

Touch of Gold   This store actually sells liquor and various luxury items as well as bejeweled baubles. Sapphires, rubies, diamonds, emeralds, tanzanite, and more are prettily mounted on platinum and gold. Brand-name watches include Daniel Mink, Skagen, and Christian Bernard; top-flight jewelry designers range from Louis Feraud to Susy Mor. 38 Front St. © 599/542-4120.

Zhaveri Jewelers   Zhaveri carries the spectrum of certified loose gems, as well as genuine cultured pearls, brand-name watches, and handsomely designed necklaces, rings, bracelets, and brooches. 53A and 103 Front St. © 599/542-5176. www.zhaveri.com.

FRENCH SIDE

Artistic Jewelers   This store carries extravagantly designed and priced jewelry and watches, ranging from frankly garish to utterly ravishing. Featured individual designers and brands include David Yurman, Mikimoto, Fabergé, Scott Kay, Van Cleef & Arpels, Piguet, and Girard-Perregaux. Visitors to the Philipsburg store, 61 Front St. (© 599/542-3456), find even more inventory. 8 rue du Général de Gaulle. © 590/52-24-80. www.artisticjewelers.com.

Carat   This is one of several upscale jewelers along this street, fea-turing a smaller but still select variety of watches from Baume & Mercier to Breitling, not to mention sparkling bracelets, chokers, and pendants. 16 rue de la République. © 590/87-73-40.

Goldfinger   Goldfinger is the island's official Rolex agent. But timepiece fanatics will find it's the ticket for designs by Tag Heur to Tissot. Other high-ticket items include designer jewelry, art glass (Kosta Boda, Orrefors, Waterford), tableware (Christofle, Daum), and porcelain (Herend, Lladró). The inventory is so vast and eclec-tic they seemingly open a new store annually: You can also stop by Rue de la République (© 590/87-55-70), Marina Royale

(℮ **590/87-59-96**), and Philipsburg at 79 Front St. (℮ **599/542-4661**). Le West Indies Mall on the waterfront. ℮ **590/87-00-11**.

Lipstick   This is another Caribbean chain noted for its top-notch selection of scents and cosmetics, from Clarins to Clinique, Chanel to Shalimar. Stylists here do makeovers, touch-ups, skin care sessions, and even facials utilizing primarily Dior products. There's a Dutch side branch at 31 Front St. (℮ **599/542-6051**). Rue de Président Kennedy. ℮ **590/87-73-24**.

LIQUORS, CANDIES & CIGARS ✻

In addition to the usual upmarket single malt and stogie culprits (remember that Cubanos are illegal in the U.S.), the island produces its own concoctions noteworthy for their attractive packaging. Though the base rums are imported from Guadeloupe, local distillers blend or infuse them creatively. Look for Rum Jumbie, whose flavored varieties include coconut, mango, vanilla, and pineapple. But its trademark is the liqueur (incorporating citrus, spices, and passion fruit), sold in a sculpted brown figurine bottle that resembles a cross between Harry Belafonte in his Calypso days and Aunt Jemima.

DUTCH SIDE

Antillean Liquors   This store has a complete assortment of liquor and liqueurs (including guavaberry), cigarettes, and cigars. Prices are generally lower than in other stores on the island, and the selection is larger. Queen Juliana Airport. ℮ **599/545-4267**.

Belgian Chocolate Shop   This place isn't entirely family-oriented, at least not around Valentine's Day when some of the velvety delectables are playfully pornographic. Otherwise, all ages will savor such specialties as Grand Marnier butter-cream truffles. It should come as no surprise that it's always bustling, especially when cruise ships are berthed at the nearby piers. 109 Old St. ℮ **599/542-8863**.

Cigar Emporium   This place claims to stock the Caribbean's largest selection of Cuban cigars under one roof, and the walk-in humidor is certainly impressive. The smoking lounge is often filled with would-be CEOs practicing one-upmanship, puffing out their chests while puffing on Partagas. The shop also carries countless cigar and pipe accessories, cutters, and cases (but sadly, no classic smoking jackets!). 66 Front St. ℮ **599/542-2787**. www.cigaremporium.biz.

Guavaberry Emporium   Guavaberry Emporium sells the rare "island folk liqueur" of St. Maarten, which for centuries was made only in private homes. Sold in square bottles, this rum-based liqueur is flavored with guavaberries, grown on the hills in the center of the island and harvested once a year near Christmas. (Don't confuse the yellow guavaberries with guavas—they're quite different.) The liqueur has a fruity, woody, smoky, bittersweet tang. I prefer it blended with coconut as a guavaberry colada or splashed in a glass of icy champagne. You can sample the line of liqueurs, including wild lime and mango, and frozen libations (free recipes available) at the counter. The charming Creole cottage also contains exotic natural perfumes and hot sauces (like habanero-lime or creole chipotle). The elegant hand-crafted specialty bottles and hand-carved wooden boxes make especially nice gifts. 8–10 Front St. 🕐 599/542-2965. www.guavaberry.com.

La Casa del Habano   This highly regarded chain, with outposts from Cancún to Kuala Lumpur, has its own walk-in humidor and a men's club–like lounge (ah, the aroma of leather, tobacco, and fresh Cuban coffee!) behind a waterfall, which I love as a respite from the shopping hordes. The selection is nearly as comprehensive, and there's a branch in Marigot, 71 Marina Port La Royale (🕐 **590/87-58-94**). 24 Front St. 🕐 **599/543-1001**.

FRENCH SIDE

Le Goût du Vin   This is the island's top source for wines (as well as brandies and rare aged rums). The inventory of 300,000 bottles showcases the best of France, but thoughtfully includes intriguing offerings from around the globe. If you're around the first Friday of the month, stop by for free tastings at 6pm. The head sommelier, Martial Jammes, offers suggestions with a soupçon of wit. Rue de l'Anguille. 🕐 **590/87-25-03**.

Ma Doudou 🦀 (Finds)   Ma Doudou occupies a tiny shack virtually obscured by overgrown foliage in the town of Cul-de-Sac. Call ahead unless you're in the neighborhood, as it keeps irregular hours. Ma Doudou means "my darling" in Creole patois. Darling certainly describes the collectible hand-painted bottles garnished with madras clippings. The products—rum-filled candies, spices, jams, and 20 flavored rums (including one starring an enormous embalmed centipede that reputedly possesses aphrodisiacal properties)—practically overflow the shelves in the cramped space. The owners often throw in a free bottle with a minimum purchase. 🕐 **590/87-30-43**.

7

St. Maarten/St. Martin After Dark

A perhaps apocryphal anecdote relates that the French/Dutch border was established by an 18th-century drinking contest. How fitting, then, that St. Maarten/St. Martin arguably contains more bars per capita than any other Caribbean island. Or maybe it just seems that way, especially given the myriad sunset booze cruises to toast the legendary elusive green flash (not a superhero but an atmospheric phenomenon caused by prismatic refraction of the sun's rays—or one margarita too many). It's more a commentary on the island's party-hearty rep than a reflection on the friendly, fun-loving locals. Bars come in all shapes and sizes, from rickety rum shops to salvaged scows to neon-streaked nightclubs. And of course, after gamboling on the beaches, you can gamble in the Dutch side's casinos. Whether you seek a (relatively) quiet sunset cocktail or after-hour boogieing to the latest urban funk, St. Maarten/St. Martin delivers.

Best of all, there's rarely a cover charge or minimum purchase, save at the occasional velvet-rope see-and-be-scene. Free entertainment abounds, aside from people-watching on the nude beaches and in the casinos. Most restaurants (notably at Simpson Bay; see chapter 4) and beach bars (especially on Orient Bay; see chapter 5) host rocking live bands at least once a week, not to mention joyous happy hours. Many hotels sponsor beachside barbecues (particularly in season) with steel bands and folkloric dancing. Outsiders are welcomed at most of these events, but call ahead to see if it's a private affair.

Then there are the regular community jump-ups. Friday nights, the Philipsburg boardwalk along Front Street percolates with activity, as does Marigot's waterfront market Wednesdays and Sundays in season. Tuesdays from January to May, the "Mardi de Grand Case" (aka Harmony Night) explodes with color and sound: brass or steel drum bands, dancers, street performers, local crafts booths, and mouth- (and eye-) watering barbecue. The late-night nexus of Maho Village is transformed weekends by scantily clad acrobats, fire-eaters, and belly dancers (earning a symphony of honks from passing Hell's Angels and wolf whistles from overgrown *South Park* brat-ernities). The Dutch side in particular resembles perpetual spring break where party animals will find plenty of zoos to their liking.

1 The Club Scene

Both sides of the island provide that endorphin rush of dancing to a great DJ's mix. A few tragically trendy spots exhibit 'tude, but fashion fascism is generally out, the better to sweat to the throbbing beat. The action usually starts at 10pm (though the beachfront discos throw afternoon theme parties).

DUTCH SIDE

Bliss ⊛   Conveniently located within walking (or staggering) distance of the Maho "strip," Bliss practically defines casual tropic chic: partly open-air, with plenty of exotic woods, miniature palms, and private cabanas swaddled in billowing eggshell curtains. The complex includes two bars (one dispensing "Blisstinis"—designer martinis flavored with espresso, watermelon, passion peach, and more), The Taste of Bliss restaurant (scrumptious fresh oysters swimming in vodka shot glasses), the requisite overcrowded laser-swept dance floor, a heated pool (with swim-up bar), and a boutique (in case you forgot your Gaultier bathing suit). Every afternoon features a different theme or promotion, usually revolving around the pool (4–6pm happy hours are ideal for sunset-watching and include half-price bottles). On Wednesdays ladies get free massages, world-renowned guest DJs spin on weekends, and Sounds of Sunday is the liquid brunch du jour. But Thursdays (two-for-one drinks all night) are really hip and happening, with Who's-the-Hugo-Boss types wearing trophy companions on their arms like Rolexes and voracious singles looking to generate heat. Caravanserai Resort, 2 Beacon Hill Rd. ⓒ 599/545-3936 or 599/554-3140. www.theblissexperience.com.

ⓘ Tips **Mapping It**

For locations of nightlife options listed in this chapter, please refer to the St. Maarten/St. Martin, Marigot, or Philipsburg maps on p. 50, p. 59, and p. 52, respectively.

Kuta Beach   The dance club sister of mega-lounge Bamboo Bernie's (see "Classic Hangouts," below), it attracts an even sexier bunch than Bliss to such popular events as "Cult Movie Classic on the Beach" (*M.A.S.H.* to *The Matrix*). Sunday's barbecue/beach competition (volleyball, *pétanque,* board games) also lures an elegantly rowdy crowd. Frequent beauty pageants and bathing suit contests add still more spice. In between, sleek writhing bodies gyrate to local, French, and Spanish DJs, or recline (with little declining) on rattan beds in the sand, lending new meaning to the term "petting zoo." Tribal Vibe Thursday and Fusion Friday are the big nights, when lasers strobe over the Balinese artifacts and flowing crimson sheets, while barely legal girls look ready to audition for the next *Girls Gone Wild* video. 2 Beacon Hill Rd., behind Caravanserai. ✆ 599/526-1331.

Mambo Dance Club   This place could generously be termed cozy. The laser-swept dance floor takes up half the space; the bar and a small seating area seem almost after-thoughts. Tuesdays (two-for-one happy hours) and Hot Fridays with DJ Silk are the big nights, when sultry *señoritas* squeeze themselves into dresses until they can barely breathe. Salsa, soul, soca, and merengue comprise the musical menu. Maho Village upstairs. ✆ 599/556-5174.

Q-Club   This is the island's loudest and dressiest (though not necessarily most fashionable) dance club—reflected by the higher cover charge. The closest thing to a big city disco, it features several bars, multilevel dance floors, wraparound catwalks, and nooks and crannies aplenty. The back-to-the-future Googie decor (think *Jetsons*)—tables lit from beneath; curved streamlined Deco touches; raised seating areas with silvery or slate blue semi-circular banquettes divided by geometric floating walls; floral, chessboard, and Miró-inspired patterns—ranks among the Caribbean's most cosmopolitan looks. The vast space pulsates not only with righteous deep house, techno, and jungle trip hop mixes (courtesy of state-of-the-art sound system and an impressive roster of local and international spin gurus), but a color wheel of fiber-optic lighting and videos. Wednesday is ladies night when the mano-a-womano action is punctuated by male strippers; otherwise go-go goddesses shimmy on seemingly every level surface. It's jammed and jamming weekends with strapping guys and strapless-dressed gals. Casino Royale, Sonesta Maho Beach Resort. ✆ 599/524-0071. www.qclubdisco.com.

FRENCH SIDE

Club One/Pulse   Formerly known as In's Club/L'Alibi, this *boîte* lies among the hotbed of cool joints peppering the marina that bop until dawn. The two main DJs, Léo and Antoine, have developed quite a following, especially for their sizzling House mixes on Friday and Saturday, classic disco on Tuesday, and Latin-themed Techno/House ("Mi Casa Es Su Casa") on Wednesday. Thursday and Friday are "Happy Bottle" nights (buy one bottle of booze, get one free). Marina Royale. ℂ 590/87-08-39.

Le Crazy   This section is the less voyeuristic part of the topless Crazy Paradise club (see "For Adults Only," later in this chapter). The get-ups are almost as wild as those at StarBar, especially during Saturday Disco Parties with DJ La Noche, when the best costume earns a bottle of champagne (though most eyes fixate on the go-go girls). Friday's Shotgun House Party is fueled by free vodka shots for every mixed drink purchase. Sunday is Ladies Night (free First Kiss and Sex on the Beach cocktails). The US$1 = 1€ exchange policy lures more Americans. It closed for renovations in April 2006 and is scheduled to reopen in late 2006. 21 rue Victor Maurasse. ℂ 690/88-96-98.

Nell's Café   Thursday through Sunday, Nell's feels like a rave as Double G pumps the volume up with the most esoteric electronica and deepest Techno/House mixes on island. Preening trust fund pretties and knowledgeable locals are packed as tightly as Gauloises in the dim, smoky room. Marina Royale. ℂ 690/54-65-46.

StarBar   This is the French side's slim-hipper-than-thou club, attracting Gallic youth (and a smattering of chic-by-reconstructed-jowl celebs) for funky House and Techno. You're really in with the sin crowd on Mondays, when reservations are actually recommended and dressing up (that means your jeans should be Ralph Lauren, minimum) de rigueur. Ladies swill Moët & Chandon free on Wednesdays, when Donna Summer rules the retro roost. "Be Free" Thursdays lure the alt lifestyle crowd: Rasta trannies dancing on tables with soccer punks. But my favorite night is Saturday, when slinky live acts such as Hanna Haïs (a bossa nova/soul genius) perform, and "Vertigo 38" with DJ Tarzan (Léo) and Nério turns the animals loose in the jungle. The tiny club is gussied up to match the showgirls *manquées* in spangled stilettos, leopard and zebra skins, plumed headdresses, feather boas, and scarlet Fu Manchu nails. No wallflowers or shrinking violets: Everyone's a star among this exhibitionist crowd begging for reality TV cameras. Nettle Bay. ℂ 590/29-65-22.

2 Classic Hangouts

DUTCH SIDE

Axum art Café ⊛ Axum was the coronation place of Christian Ethiopian kings in the 4th century A.D., and the alleged home of the Ark of the Covenant. The minimalist decor (sponge-painted apricot walls, artfully rust-colored furnishings) reinforces the vaguely revolutionist air, as nihilist neo-Goths, dashiki-ed ethnographers and disaffected European philosophy majors articulately deconstruct their contempt between puffs and riffs. With provocative art exhibits, reggae and jazz parties, poetry recitals, storytelling, open-mic nights, and more it's actually quite fun, and that *could* be the next Sartre or Miles Davis brooding one table over. It even has limited e-mail, scanning, and printing. Upstairs 7-L Front St. ℂ 599/542-0547. www.axumart.com.

Bamboo Bernie's ⊛ Next door to Sunset, Bernie's is an updated boutique-y homage to the Trader Vic's tiki bar: a United Nations garage sale riot of Buddhas, African masks, Chinese paper lanterns, totem poles, Indian tapestries, torches, painted wood barrels, wild almost racist Betty Boop–as-monkey murals, and transparent glowing tiki gods. The menu—and clientele—is almost as eclectic, from the island's best sushi (try the Tiki Roll—salmon, tuna, and yellowtail topped with salmon roe and spicy eel sauce) to house-smoked hickory barbecue. Happy hours, accompanied by flashy sunsets and Neville York and the Tropical Brothers Steel Band, offer free drinks at 5pm, rising to $1 at 6pm. The more than 30 tiki libations include the 48-ounce Flaming Bowl, 60-ounce Shark Bite, and "lethal" Dr. Voodoo, but you can order cocktails with *cojones,* from margaritas to mudslides. Wednesday night ladies drink free, while DJ Eric "The Devil" spins trance and trip hop from 10pm. Thursday stars live reggae (Barbwire) with $2 beers and a $15 beach barbecue. Add two beaches; the 9m (30-ft.) "Mushroom" climbing rock; occasional concerts by the likes of Earth, Wind & Fire and Bob Marley's Wailers; and two pools (salt- and freshwater) hosting wet parties with exotic dancers. As he-men and their mannequins emerge with that freshly ravaged look from private thatched huts and other nooks, it plays like a sequel to the old Cruise hit *Cocktail.* 2 Beacon Hill Rd. ℂ 599/545-3622. www.bamboobernies-stmaarten.com.

Buccaneer Beach Bar Head here any time of day or night for a sublimely mellow setting and kick back over pizzas or burgers and knockout rum punches (or try the BBC: Bailey's Banana Colada, with Bailey's, fresh banana, rum, and cream of coconut). The triple B is less frenzied than other sunset watching perches, though daily special $1 shooters, from Kamikazes to Green-Eyed Blondes (melon, Irish cream, and crème de banane liqueurs), and blues duo Ian & Ed ensure guests absorb alcohol and ambience in equal measure. Kim Sha Beach behind Atrium Resort. © 599/544-5876. www.buccaneerbar.com.

The Greenhouse 🍸 This breezy, plant-filled, open-air eatery with marvy marina views is a favorite among locals and island regulars who know the food is great value, especially the certified Angus steaks, poultry (luscious mango chicken), and such seafood specials as baked stuffed swordfish. They swarm the place during happy hours (4:30–7pm), downing two-for-one drinks (Margarita Mondays, Beck's Wednesdays, Samuel Adams Thursdays, Carib Fridays) and discounted appetizers from conch fritters to jalapeño poppers. Wednesday's Crab-a-ganza and Friday's Lobster Mania sate anyone's crustacean cravings. The big screen broadcasts major sporting events and pool tables and video games keep things lively. It's *the* place Tuesday: Seemingly the entire island shows up as DJs rock the house and distribute prizes to bingo champs and trivia experts. Bobby's Marina, Front St. © 599/542-2941.

Lady C **Floating Bar** Although the rickety neon-splashed craft barely seems seaworthy, *Lady C* cruises Simpson Bay lagoon Wednesday and Sunday afternoons. The deceptively decorous-sounding *Lady Carola* remains berthed otherwise, while revelers go off their moorings. Theme nights include Two for Tuesdays (from 10pm), Wacky Wednesdays with DJ Don Marco, Thirsty Thursdays ("really, really big drinks" after 10pm), and Rock the Rock Fridays and Saturdays. It's the kind of spot that posts Wall of Shame photos of inebriated customers (all in good fun) and hosts Playboy Bunny dress-up and body-painting parties. Expect lots of thong bikinis (on both sexes) and skimpy tops regardless. It should come as no surprise that nights often end up as a meat-market feeding frenzy. Airport Rd. © 599/544-4710. www.floatingbar.com.

Sunset Beach Bar 🍸 License plates, baseball caps, Christmas lights, and patrons' business cards seemingly hold this sprawling gazebo together. Just another bar, save for its utterly unique location: on the beach (delivering the name's promised pyrotechnics) . . . and 15m (50 ft.) from the main airport runway (so close that the planes' exhaust perfumes the air, while management broadcasts radio transmissions between the pilots and air traffic controllers).

Don't panic if you see the flight crews knocking them back (they're usually on layover). The human jetsam runs from waif models so thin it hurts to stringy-haired, body-pierced skater dudes. Topless gals drink free. There's no cover for this MySpace.com scene, and two-for-one Heinekens all the time take the sting out of skyrocketing prices. The ultimate all-purpose, something-for-everyone, anything-goes venue, Sunset offers decent pub grub, a huge screen for sporting events, a tiny dance floor swept by laser lights, live music daily from acoustic guitar to hardcore reggae, sunset variety shows featuring high school marching bands and the Island Heat dancers (yes, you can join them on stage), and DJs after 10pm. It's noisy, crowded, silly—but where else can you get buzzed by 757s and kamikazes? 2 Beacon Hill Rd. ✆ 599/545-3998. www.sunsetbeachbar.com.

Taloula Mango's Caribbean Café   Facing Great Bay Beach, Taloula Mango's offers magnificent views of the harbor and leviathan cruise ships. The handsome colonial room (with ceiling fans and plantation shutters) is a fine place to sample creative cocktails and Caribbean-tinged pub grub (Gouda sticks, Haitian Voodoo wings, conch and dumplings). Weekends welcome sensational jazz, blues, and funk artists such as saxophonist Sapphron Obois. Day and night, Taloula's does a brisk trade in overgrown frat boys, families, fatigued shoppers, and tired pick-up lines. St. Rose Arcade, Front St. ✆ 599/542-1645. www.taloulamangos.com.

FRENCH SIDE

Bali Bar ✸   This place puts the sin in scintillating. A bohunk bohemian crowd bellies up to Bali's bar for glorious global tapas—grilled chorizo, stuffed mussels, shrimp tempura, tuna curry samosa, fajitas, and fried calamari—costing 4€ to 6€ ($5–$8) each. Plush decor accentuates the lounge's sensuous ambience: mauve drapes, mango walls, Indian embroidered silk wall hangings, Warhol-inspired Pop Art prints, and carved teak chairs. Smoky soca and jazz chanteuses occasionally animate the proceedings, and savvy sybarites gather for Friday's Disco Party and Saturday's house call by DJ Nério. Marina Royale. ✆ 590/51-13-16.

Calmos Café ✸   This place defines beach shack chic sans attitude (a sign near the entrance warns NO SNOBS). The whole place is splashed in sunset colors, with plenty of chaises on the sand; I love the little front library, where you can borrow beach reading or snub your companion. Young slicksters (so cool they don't have to wear black) and pop culture icons like Linda Evangelista come to flirt, gossip, and drink (terrific frozen concoctions and homemade infused rums—try the banana). In winter, there's sometimes live jazz or blues from 7 to 10:30pm to accompany sublime, affordable food from "New Wave burgers" slathered with goat cheese to such tempting tapas as anchovy filets, cumin-spiced meatballs, and shrimp satay. 40 bd. de Grand Case. ✆ 590/29-01-85. www.calmoscafe.com.

Le Pub It may be on the "wrong" non-beach side of the main drag, but Le Pub is the de facto Grand Case social center: The kind of place total strangers actually smile, chat, and ask each other to dance without ulterior motives. Diversions include darts, chess, cards, and backgammon, while the adjacent Brasserie des Îles under the same management offers scrumptious pizzas (like goat cheese or smoked salmon). Locals congregate for nightly promotions and live or canned music: Monday Rock, Tuesday $2 Caribs, Wednesday Latino party, Friday '70s/'80s flashback soiree but, especially, Thursdays for two-for-one happy hour and Caribbean rhythms all night. 49 blvd. de Grand Case (not on seaside). ✆ 590/51-91-04.

3 Live Music
DUTCH SIDE
Cheri's Café ✿ American expat Cheri Batson founded this cherished institution. The rare tourist trap that even appeals to locals, this great place to meet people is outfitted in an irrepressible color scheme of scarlet, hot pink, and white (love the goofy oversize illuminated plastic pelicans!). Everybody from rock bands to movie stars, casino high rollers to beach bums makes a pit stop at this open-air pavilion. The surprisingly good, relatively cheap food (think burgers and grilled items) is a bonus, but most come for flirting and dancing to an assortment of live acts starting at 8pm nightly. Don't miss such regulars as Sweet Chocolate Band, if only to watch the guys don wigs and falsies, and Souliga Capoeira, a group of talented local kids adept at that acrobatic Brazilian martial art–cum–dance-style. 45 Cinnamon Grove Shopping Centre, Maho Village. ✆ 599/545-3361.

Citrus This upscale restaurant occupies a slinky split-level space: brick walls, arches, cool island murals and tapestries, track-lighting, and lots of red accents. The food, though creative, can be too uneven and ambitious (though the prix-fixe menu represents good value). But the lounge smokes with live music, mostly jazz, Thursday through Saturday after 10pm. Instead of lingering over coffee, head here after dinner for the espresso martini. Inn at Cupecoy, 130 Lowlands. © 599/545-4333.

Pineapple Pete 𝄢   Pete co-opts most of an alley between the lagoon and the main drag. T-shirts dangle from the rafters in the main room (with five pool tables and dart boards), where yachters, local businesspeople and timeshare owners marinate and get tight (in both slang meanings). The fairly priced fare is quite good—signature dishes include crab-stuffed shrimp, lobster thermidor, and dark rum crème brûlée. Infectious, if ear-splitting, live music keeps things rocking half the week, including Saturdays (jazz trio), Blues Inc (and reggae) Tuesdays, and Fridays starring local stalwart Ronny Santana (classic rock garnished with R&B). Airport Rd., Simpson Bay. © 599/544-6030. www.pineapplepete.com.

Red Piano Bar   This joint attracts 40-something singles looking for romance of the fleeting variety and couples looking to rekindle sparks. The grand piano is indeed quite red, and patrons are often red-faced from the killer cocktails which help lubricate the lousier acts, death-by-karaoke, or both. The performers, professional or otherwise, are variable (one recently forgot the lyrics to "Memory"), but even the worst are amusing in *American Idol* outtake fashion—and the place is comparatively refined and quiet. Pelican Resort, Billy Folly Rd. © 599/544-6008.

Sopranos   Mobbed by 30-somethings in the mood for romance, the piano bar (replete with small area for old-fashioned touch dancing) delivers a soigné ambience without thematic overkill (other than the signature Bada Bing merchandise for sale). The photos of musicians posed as Mafiosi and giant poster of James Gandolfini aka Tony Soprano glaring down at the grand piano (or maybe at the singers) are witty; the dim lighting, intimate dark wood banquettes, and red-and-black color scheme set the right tone (if only the patrons weren't so often off-key, mangling Beatles and U2 covers in a Babel of accents). But even if the musicians shoot blanks, anyone can enjoy the marvy martinis, superb cognac selection, and fine collection of Cuban cigars. Maho Village second floor. © 599/522-7088.

FRENCH SIDE
Blue Martini   Although it doesn't have beach access, this place more than compensates for it with an enchanted garden, the perfect place to savor specialty cocktails, intriguing international beers like Abbé Leffe on tap, and tasty tapas. It shakes and stirs the young clientele with live bands Tuesdays and Thursday through Saturday

at 7pm (my fave act is Mambo Loco). 63 blvd. de Grand Case. (C) 590/
29-27-93.

Gecko Café   Although nominally an Italian eatery, Gecko Café
serves tapas and emulates Japanese decorative simplicity right down
to tatami mats and low tables on the polished wood floor. It's an
ideal place to Zen and zone out, except perhaps at sunset, when an
invigorating mix of yachters and local yupsters cruise by for happy
hours and late-night live acoustic jams Thursday through Saturday.
Marina Royale. (C) 590/52-21-25.

La Chapelle   This bar is where *au courant* (savvy) locals head
when they tire of the nonstop action at the "sand" bars on Orient
Beach—but still want to drink, dine, dance, or shoot pool and the
breeze in congenial surroundings. *Chapelle* means "clique" (as well
as "chapel"), but anyone willing to let loose will click with the clientele and staff at the different themed evenings, including special
events ranging from fashion shows to CD release parties. Come for
live rock Sundays, Latin dance classes Thursdays, karaoke weekends,
and the swinging "Ibiza" party the first Wednesday of every month,
when disco and house threaten to bring the roof down. Orient Bay
Square. (C) 590/52-38-90.

4 For Adults Only

It's impossible to ignore the more titillating aspect to nightlife, especially on St. Maarten, where the international lineup of exotic
dancers entertain each evening.

DUTCH SIDE

Golden Eyes   Calling itself a topless "ultra-lounge" with "American management and European dancers," Golden Eyes gives the
Platinum Room a run for its (and your) money. In an effort to be
inclusive, it welcomes couples and women. Theme nights include
Monday amateur wet T-shirt contests and Tuesday costume nights
with DJ, lingerie, and pajama party, and two-for-one drink specials.
Specialty acts are a tad hard core. The club itself is handsomely
appointed and the balcony offers lovely marina views. 12 Airport Rd.,
Simpson Bay. (C) 599/527-1079. www.goldeneyesclub.com.

Platinum Room   The gold standard of gentlemen's clubs, this
place even offers equal-opportunity ogling (no double standard
here), with a ladies' section where buff long-haired men thrust more
pelvi than Elvis and Ricky Martin combined. It cultivates an air of

St. Maarten's Red-Lights

The Dutch are notoriously liberal and have cultivated a permissive attitude regarding prostitution on St. Maarten. This review is neither endorsement nor encouragement; it merely offers some enlightenment on a major element of St. Maarten nightlife. Brothels operate around the island and must purchase a permit and supply affidavits on their employees (mostly Dominican, Venezuelan, Colombian, Guyanese, and Jamaican immigrants who must submit to monthly medical checkups). Several brothels are situated just outside Philipsburg (if this is your thing, ask the security guards at your hotel for advice on where to go).

It all started with the aptly named **Seaman's Club** (79 Sucker Garden Rd. [you can't make this stuff up]; *C* **599/542-2978**). It was founded in the 1940s to service Japanese tuna fishermen who'd been to sea for months at a time. These single men needed a place to carouse and the government didn't want them hassling local girls, so a tradition was born.

Note: One big difference from Amsterdam's red-light district is that possession of marijuana is not tolerated here. An infraction could lead to stiff fines or even imprisonment.

---

class: neo-colonial arches and colonnades, inlaid woods, knockoffs of Michelangelo's David and Grecian urns, sequined curtains, and cheery turquoise banquettes. The gals run the gamut from gym-toned beauties to more bootylicious and dance on stage, in bamboo cages, and even in beds swaddled in diaphanous white; the Jungle Room hosts more intimate encounters. This place crowds up quickly, with everyone from suits to bikers to cyber-geeks. Maho Village. *C* **599/557-0055**.

FRENCH SIDE

Crazy Paradise Le Crazy is the only official adult entertainment venue on the French side. The "cabaret" gives way to a nightclub after 9pm (see "The Club Scene," earlier in this chapter). The place will be under renovation until late 2006, but I hope they retain the teasing decor: The stage juts out in phallic fashion, and the walls are adorned with Georgia O'Keeffe–meets–old *National Geographic* paintings of sultry beauties in silhouette. And yes, some of the ladies dress up as naughty French maids. 21 rue Victor Maurasse. *C* **690/88-96-98**.

5 Casinos

Gaming is currently only legal on the Dutch side. For all its self-pro-
motion about a Caribbean Vegas, the scene is closer to Laughlin or
Biloxi. Regardless, the 10 casinos offer wonderful free living theater,
at times of the absurd, with everyone from blue-haired fanny pack-
ers to dreadlocked Rastas robotically feeding the maw of the
machines. If you indulge, just remember there's no such thing as a
sure system (or, Lord help us, ESP)—and the odds always favor the
house, especially in games like Keno. As for any claims of "loose
slots," don't bet on it. Gambling, like life, defies prediction. Only a
very few "professionals" earn a living by making a killing. St.
Maarten's daily "grind" (low-end betting) is geared more toward
voyeurs and "virgins" (gaming-speak for first-timers) anyhow;
whale-watching is reserved for the marine mammals, not the high-
stakes types. Hours vary (only one is open 24/7), but most casinos
are generally open from 1pm to 6am.

Atlantis World Casino ⊕ This is St. Maarten's most Vegas-style
venue, if only for adopting that destination's gourmet aspirations.
The owner/developer cleverly attracted top restaurateurs by offering
competitive rents for the eight eateries. The interior is fairly posh if
you don't look too closely: mirrored ceilings, Christmas lights, faux
plants, lipstick red accents, and murals and frescoes, mostly depicting cherubs cavorting in azure skies or surreal encounters between
Renaissance figures and islanders. Atlantis features all the major
table games, as well as more than 500 slot and video poker
machines. It tends to attract a more mature, settled crowd: tonsori-
ally challenged guys chomping on cigars and tan women who look
like aging Lakers Girls, as well as junior corporate sharks in the
Texas Hold 'Em poker room, who learned the game from ESPN.
Rhine Road 106, Cupecoy. © 599/545-4601. www.atlantisworld.com.

Casino Royale ⊕ St. Maarten's largest, glitziest, and supposedly
ritziest gaming emporium, Casino Royale's splashy exterior of illuminated fountains and its huge multihued neon sign spitting lasers
almost approximates the gaudy best (and worst) of Vegas. Despite
the upscale pretensions, most people ignore the rarely enforced dress
code (no shorts or tank tops). The casino offers games from blackjack to baccarat and more than 400 slot machines. The 800-seat
Showroom Royale is the island's largest, most technologically
sophisticated theater; its glittery shows change every few months,
but generally follow the same pattern. Like a poor man's *Ed Sullivan*

Show/Star Search, the evening might include acrobatics, jugglers tossing bowling pins and bad jokes with equal aplomb, and/or magicians with the usual large-scale tricks up their sleeves (including dismemberment and disappearing tigers). Upstairs is the island's loudest dance spot, the **Q-Club** (see "The Club Scene," earlier in this chapter). Sonesta Maho Beach Resort. ℂ **599/545-2590** or 599/544-2115. www.mahobeach.com.

Coliseum Casino   Sadly, this tri-level, ancient Rome–themed establishment, doesn't approach the garish yet playfully camp excess—or style—of Caesars Palace (Nero undoubtedly would have fed the designers to the lions, though he'd appreciate the smoky ambience). Still, it supposedly offers the highest table limits, as well as free limousine pickups for high rollers, and loud entertainment. 74 Front St. ℂ **599/543-2101.**

Hollywood Casino   Although it regrettably lacks deliriously, deliciously cheesy theming, Hollywood Casino does make some half-hearted stabs: "Oscar" door handles, movie stills (*Pulp Fiction* and *Planet of the Apes*), fake stars in the ceiling, klieg lights, Rodin-like statues, and a wall devoted to Marilyn Monroe. It offers a panoramic view of the bay, roulette, blackjack, stud-poker, Let It Ride, progressive jackpot bingo, 150 slot machines, bingo, and a high-tech Sports Book with nine screens broadcasting major events via satellite, plus nightly dancing on the Pelican Reef Terrace and island shows featuring Caribbean bands. Notable offerings include an excellent fun book with $50 worth of discount coupons and free plays, as well as a tasty late-night buffet. Pelican Resort, 37 Billy Folly Rd., Simpson Bay. ℂ **599/544-2503** or 599/544-4463. www.hollywoodcasino-stmaarten.com.

Jump Up Casino   A Carnival-themed casino, it has several ornate costumes on display. Live late weekend shows showcasing the island's hottest bands (Playstation, Jump Up Stars, Xplosion, Impact) are the best reason to visit. Emmaplein 1, end of Front St. ℂ **599/ 542-0862.** www.jumpupcasino.com.

Princess Casino   ℱ   Come up aces here in terms of overall elegance, as evidenced by the dressier crowd and handsome neoclassical design (columns, arches, domes, and frescoes galore). The place has more than 650 one-armed bandits and 20 table games from craps to blackjack. Dining options include the fancy French Le Baccara, a fine buffet, a sushi bar, and a great late-night shwarma stand. The live shows are spectacularly mounted (by island standards), particularly the Brazilian ballet and Caribbean folkloric shows. Carmen Miranda had nothing on these gals for headgear, feathers, and sequins in a rainbow of colors. House lounge lizard extraordinaire, the Teddy Pendergrass/Marvin Gaye clone, Melvin Hodge, croons soulfully in between patter with the more attractive women in the audience. Port de Plaisance Resort, Cole Bay. ℭ **599/544-4311**. www.princess casinosxm.com.

Rouge et Noir *Quelle surprise!* This joint is all red and black inside, just like a roulette wheel, with a vaguely futuristic design. It offers slot machines, roulette, blackjack, bingo, and video poker. Open Monday to Saturday at 9am and Sunday at 11am, it deprives the shops at least temporarily of cruise-ship passengers and stays open until 4am. 66 Front St. ℭ **599/542-3222** or 599/542-2952. www.casino rougeetnoir.com.

8

Anguilla

Anguilla (rhymes with "vanilla") used to tout itself as the Caribbean's best-kept secret. Small, serene, and secluded, it offered old-time West Indian privacy and proximity to St. Maarten/St. Martin's gambling, shopping, and nightlife: the best of both worlds. However, the island's secret escaped in the 1990s when new superdeluxe (and superexpensive) hotels attracted a sophisticated jet set. Now one of the Caribbean's most chic destinations—its resorts and restaurants rival even those on St. Barts (a prettier island and just as luxurious)—Anguilla has nonetheless remained tranquil and unaffected. If you're looking to rest, unwind, and be pampered without pomp or snobbery, this is the place for you.

A surprising number of small, moderately priced hotels and villa complexes exist, enabling more visitors to enjoy Anguilla's posh yet relaxed vibe. Fortunately, operations tend to be intimate and informal, as the island has tried to control development and conserve natural beauty and resources. And with good reason: The coastline boasts some of the Caribbean's finest white-sand beaches—more than 30 dot the island, shaded by sea-grape trees. Still, in March 2005 the government approved plans to construct a 2,083-unit mega-mixed-use complex on the untrammeled East End. Despite the mandated gradual 10-year process, this drive to keep pace with expanding luxury developments on other islands alarms residents and regulars alike. Other planned projects are smaller scaled if resolutely upscale, but real estate developers are buying humble beach homes and building mansions in their place as if Anguilla were the Caribbean answer to the Hamptons.

The northernmost of the British Leeward Islands in the eastern Caribbean, 8km (5 miles) north of St. Maarten, Anguilla is only 26km (16 miles) long, with 91 sq. km (35 sq. miles) in land area. The island has a population of approximately 12,500 people of mostly African descent. Anguilla's scant rainfall and unproductive soil support mainly low foliage and sparse scrub vegetation. The locals work primarily in the tourist industry or fish for lobster.

Anguilla gained its independence in 1980 from an awkward federation with St. Kitts and Nevis and has since been a self-governing British possession. Many Anguillians believe that Britain has now reduced its global ambitions and wants to relinquish colonies that have become too expensive to maintain. Though islanders may fear going it alone as a nation, they know that to retain Britain's protection, they would also have to abide by the generally liberal British laws. For the most part, islanders remain arch-conservative and often homophobic—a regrettably common attitude throughout the Caribbean.

1 Essentials

VISITOR INFORMATION

The **Anguilla Tourist Board,** Coronation Avenue, The Valley, Anguilla, B.W.I. (© **264/497-2759** or 877/4-ANGUILLA; fax 264/497-2710), is open Monday to Friday from 8am to 5pm.

In the United States, contact Ms. Marie Walker, 246 Central Ave., White Plains, NY 10606 (© **914/287-2400;** fax 914/287-2404), or log onto www.anguilla-vacation.com.

In the United Kingdom, contact the **Anguilla Tourist Board,** 7A Crealock St., London SW182BS (© **208/871-0012**).

GETTING THERE

BY PLANE　More than 50 flights into Anguilla are scheduled each week, not counting various charter flights. There are no nonstop flights from mainland North America, however, so visitors usually transfer through San Juan, Puerto Rico, or nearby St. Maarten. Some visitors also come from St. Kitts, Antigua, or St. Thomas.

Anguilla's most reliable carrier, **American Eagle** (© **800/433-7300** in the U.S. and Canada; www.aa.com), the commuter partner of American Airlines, has two nonstop daily flights to Anguilla's Wallblake Airport from American's San Juan hub. In the off season flights are reduced to one daily during the week and two on weekends. Flights leave at different times based on the seasons and carry 44 to 46 passengers. Schedules are subject to change, so check with the airline or your travel agent.

From Dutch St. Maarten, **Winair** (Windward Islands Airways International; © **888/255-6889** in the U.S. and Canada; www.fly-winair.com) has eight daily flights to Anguilla.

LIAT (© **868/624-4727** in the U.S. and Canada, or 264/497-5002; www.liatairline.com) offers daily flights from Antigua. The

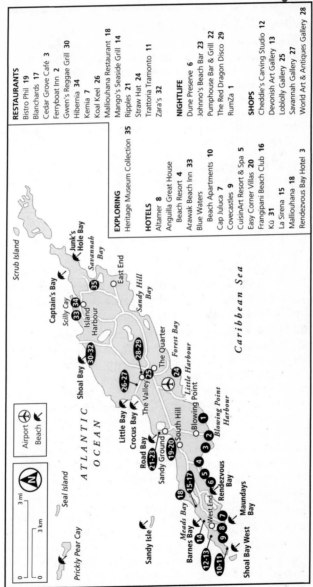

RESTAURANTS
Bistro Phil **19**
Blanchards **17**
Cedar Grove Café **3**
Ferryboat Inn **2**
Gwen's Reggae Grill **30**
Hibernia **34**
Kemia **7**
Koal Keel **26**
Malliouhana Restaurant **18**
Mango's Seaside Grill **14**
Ripples **21**
Straw Hat **24**
Trattoria Tramonto **11**
Zara's **32**

NIGHTLIFE
Dune Preserve **6**
Johnno's Beach Bar **23**
Pumphouse Bar & Grill **22**
The Red Dragon Disco **29**
RumZa **1**

SHOPS
Cheddie's Carving Studio **12**
Devonish Art Gallery **13**
Loblolly Gallery **25**
Savannah Gallery **27**
World Art & Antiques Gallery **28**

EXPLORING
Heritage Museum Collection **35**

HOTELS
Altamer **8**
Anguilla Great House
Beach Resort **4**
Arawak Beach Inn **33**
Blue Waters
Beach Apartments **10**
Cap Juluca **7**
Covecastles **9**
CuisinArt Resort & Spa **5**
Easy Corner Villas **20**
Frangipani Beach Club **16**
Kú **31**
La Sirena **15**
Malliouhana **18**
Rendezvous Bay Hotel **3**

Fun Fact **A Special Celebration**

Anguilla's most colorful annual festival is **Carnival**, held jointly under the auspices of the Ministries of Culture and Tourism. Boat races are Anguilla's national sport, and they make up much of the Carnival celebration, along with parades, concerts, and competitions from cooking to costumes. The festival begins on Thursday before the first Monday in August and lasts 10 days. Carnival harks back to Emancipation Day, or "August Monday," in 1834, when all enslaved Africans throughout the British colonies were freed. Anguilla's other prime events are the **Moonsplash Music Festival** and **Tranquility Jazz Festival,** held in late March and the second week of November, respectively.

---

airline is improving its unpunctual rep (nicknames have included "Leave Island Any Time" and "Luggage in Any Terminal").

Caribbean Star (© **866/864-6272** in the U.S. and Canada, or 264/497-8690; www.flycaribbeanstar.com) wings in daily from Antigua. Schedules are likely to change, so it's always best to call and confirm before planning any trip.

BY FERRY   Ferries run between the ports of Marigot Bay, French St. Martin, and Blowing Point, Anguilla, every 30 to 45 minutes. The trip takes 20 to 25 minutes, making day trips a snap. The first ferry leaves St. Martin at 8am and the last at 7pm; from Blowing Point, the first ferry leaves at 7:30am and the last at 6:15pm. The one-way fare is $12 to $15 plus a $3 departure tax. No reservations are necessary; schedules and fares are subject to change. Ferries vary in size, and none takes passenger vehicles. While you're waiting at Blowing Point, stop by **Big Jim's** (no phone), a rickety lean-to whose owner prepares scrumptious baby back ribs (as well as sultry island stews such as goat water and bull-foot soup).

GETTING AROUND

BY RENTAL CAR   To explore the island in any depth, it's best to rent a car, though be prepared for badly paved roads. Four-wheel-drive vehicles aren't necessary, however. Several rental agencies on the island can issue the mandatory Anguillian driver's license, which is valid for 3 months. You can also get a license at police headquarters in the island's administrative center, The Valley, and at ports of entry. You'll need to present a valid driver's license from your home country and pay a one-time fee of $20. *Remember:* Drive on the left side of the road!

Most visitors take a taxi from the airport to their hotel and arrange, at no extra charge, for a rental agency to deliver a car there the following day. All rental companies offer small discounts for rentals of 7 days or more.

A branch of **Avis** at The Quarter (✆ **800/331-1212** in the U.S. and Canada, or 264/497-2642; www.avis.com) offers regular cars and some four-wheel-drive vehicles. Local firms include **Connor's Car Rental,** c/o Maurice Connor, South Hill (✆ **264/497-6433**), **Triple K Car Rental,** Airport Road (✆ **264/497-5934**), and **Island Car Rentals,** Airport Road (✆ **264/497-2723**).

BY TAXI   Typical fixed taxi fares are $17 and $20 from the airport and ferry respectively to Cap Juluca, $7 to $12 to Rendezvous Bay Hotel, and $14 to $16 to Malliouhana. Most rides take 15 to 20 minutes. For a cab, call **Airport Taxi Stand** at ✆ **264/497-5054.** A $2 surcharge goes into effect between 6pm and 6am.

FAST FACTS: Anguilla

Banks   Banks with ATMs are open Monday to Thursday 8am to 3pm, Friday 8am to 5pm. The most reliable is **Scotiabank,** The Valley, Fairplay Commercial Complex (✆ **264/497-3333**).

Currency   The **Eastern Caribbean dollar (EC$)** is the official currency of Anguilla, although U.S. dollars are the actual "coin of the realm." The exchange rate is permanently fixed at about EC$2.70 to each $1 (EC$1 = US37¢). Rates in this chapter are quoted in U.S. dollars unless indicated otherwise.

Documents   All visitors must have an onward or return ticket. U.S., British, and Canadian citizens must have a valid passport.

Electricity   The electricity is 110-volt AC (60 cycles), so no transformers or adapters are necessary to use U.S. appliances.

Hospitals   For medical services, consult the **Princess Alexandra Hospital,** Stoney Ground (✆ **264/497-2551**), or one of several district clinics.

Language   English is spoken here.

Liquor Laws   Beer, wine, and liquor are sold 7 days a week during regular business hours. It's legal to have an open container on the beach.

Pharmacies Go to the **Health Authority** at the Princess Alexandra Hospital, Stoney Ground (© **264/497-2551**); open weekdays 8am to 5pm and Saturday 10am to noon.

Police You can reach the police at their headquarters in The Valley (© **264/497-2333**) or the substation at Sandy Ground (© **264/497-2354**). In an emergency, dial © **911**.

Post Office The main post office is on Wallblake Road, The Valley (© **264/497-5453** or 264/497-2528). Collectors consider Anguilla's stamps valuable, and the post office also operates a philatelic bureau, open Monday to Friday from 8am to 4:45pm. Airmail postcards and letters cost EC$1.50 (55¢) to the U.S., Canada, and the United Kingdom.

Safety Although crime is rare here, secure your valuables; never leave them in a parked car or unguarded on the beach. Anguilla is one of the safest destinations in the Caribbean, but you should still take standard precautions.

Taxes The government collects a 10% tax on rooms and a departure tax of $20 if you leave the island by air, $3 if you leave by boat.

Telephone Telephone, cable, and Telex services are offered by **Cable & Wireless Ltd.**, Wallblake Road, The Valley (© **264/497-3100**), open Monday to Friday 8am to 5pm. To call the United States from Anguilla, dial **1**, the area code, and the seven-digit number.

Time Anguilla is on Atlantic Standard Time year-round, which means it's usually 1 hour ahead of the U.S. East Coast—except when the U.S. is on daylight saving time, when the clocks are the same.

Weather The hottest months in Anguilla are July to October; the coolest, December to February. The mean monthly temperature is about 80°F (27°C).

2 Accommodations

VERY EXPENSIVE

Altamer ℱ Minimalist architect Myron Goldfinger designed these five-bedroom beachfront villas, similar to his controversial yet supremely comfortable Covecastles (see below) across the water. They share the same playful, carefully orchestrated geometry, all sensuous arcs, rectangles, and cylinders, including floating stairways, cantilevered walls, dramatic skylights, and floor-to-ceiling tinted sunglasslike windows: hardly the Frank Lloyd Wrong school seen elsewhere on island. Yet Altamer feels like home thanks to June Goldfinger's striking interior design, which brings the vision of peripatetic owner Rebecca Eggleton to glowing life. Every piece was carefully selected, from Murano fixtures and stemware to hand-tatted Florentine lace and linens to Turkish kilims. You'll find 18th-century Caribbean trade route maps, Constructivist paintings, wonderfully "rocuckoo" Tsarist candelabras and spittoons, embroidered slippers from an Ottoman emperor's harem. (Most are available for sale via the Altamer Collection.) Color schemes reflect the beach at dawn: silk fabrics in the cool blue-purple spectrum alternate with sunshine-y oranges and yellows. Asian wicker and bamboo contrast with specially commissioned ice-blue glass tables and shimmering seascapes. Contemporary comforts include elaborate entertainment centers (video projector to custom-made pool table), gym, kitchen, and touch-sensitive control panels. A personal butler and chef await your latest whim, completing the "if luxe could kill" mantra.

The chef of the equally striking, eponymous restaurant, Maurice Leduc began his distinguished career apprenticing at Maxim's; signature dishes include white gazpacho, gossamer goat cheese in puff pastry, coconut-and-sweet-potato-crusted snapper in orange sauce, and chocolate bread pudding with crème anglaise.

Shoal Bay West (P.O. Box 3001, The Valley), Anguilla, B.W.I. © **264/498-4000.** Fax 264/498-4010. www.altamer.com. 3 units. Winter $38,500–$44,000 per week for up to 10 guests. Continental breakfast and cocktail canapés included. **Amenities:** Restaurant; bar; pools; 2 tennis courts; kayaking; snorkeling; massage; meeting facilities. *In room:* A/C, ceiling fan, TV/DVD, fax, high-speed Internet, kitchen, hair dryer, safe, pool, Jacuzzi, gym.

Cap Juluca 🏵🏵🏵   One of the Caribbean's most boldly conceived, luxurious oases, overlooking Maundays Bay on a rolling 72-hectare (178-acre) site, Cap Juluca caters to Hollywood stars and financial barons, coddling the likes of Denzel and Donatella. Guests are welcomed with champagne, and sorbet is served on the beach. Its only peer, the classy Malliouhana (see below), has a slight edge in dining and service, but Cap Juluca fronts a longer beach, and its accommodations are even plusher.

Most of the Moorish-style accommodations have soaring domes, parapets, walled courtyards, labyrinthine staircases, and concealed swimming pools ringed with thick walls so you can take it all off. Inside, Moroccan accessories, tiles to textiles, offset elegantly comfortable wicker and Brazilian hardwood furniture. Rooms are spacious, with luxurious beds, Italian-tile floors, and louvered doors opening onto an arcaded patio with stunning sea view. If money is no object, opt for the extravagant suites with their own plunge pools. Large marble and mirrored baths are luxuriously appointed, with oversize tubs, separate shower, and bidet. The imaginative creativity extends to eco-friendly activities, from tours of the self-sufficient herb gardens (staffers will prepare healing bush teas) to unique aqua-golf driving range and putting green. The shamanic (not sham) "spa-ritual" approach integrates traditional treatments with alternative therapies, including holistic specialists utilizing storytelling, rebirthing, and channeling. And the cuisine has never been better, almost rivaling Malliouhana: witness the inventive, Asian-accented fare at the elegant **Pimms** (*©* **264/497-6666** for reservations).

Maundays Bay (P.O. Box 240), Anguilla, B.W.I. *©* **888/858-5822** in the U.S., or 264/497-6666. Fax 264/497-6617. www.capjuluca.com. 98 units. Winter/spring $780–$1,520 double, from $2,615 suite; off season $380–$730 double, from $1,240 suite. Continental breakfast included. AE, MC, V. **Amenities:** 3 restaurants; 2 bars; outdoor pool; driving range; 3 tennis courts; fitness center; spa; kayaks; sailing; snorkeling; water-skiing; windsurfing; children's programs (in summer only); rental cars; business center; room service (7:30am–9:30pm); massage; babysitting; laundry service; dry cleaning. *In room:* A/C, ceiling fan, dataport, wireless Internet, minibar, hair dryer, safe.

Covecastles *㢠㢠*   Resembling a collection of posh postmodern private homes, this is a wonderful (if shockingly expensive) small beachfront resort, with an attentive staff, that offers even more privacy than Cap Juluca, appealing to the likes of Meryl Streep and Sean Combs. Designed by award-winning architect Myron Goldfinger in 1985 and enlarged in 1998, Covecastles combines elements from North Africa, the Caribbean, and Le Corbusier's futuristic design aesthetic. The skylit duplex units include an interconnected row of town houses that accommodate two to four people, and larger, fully detached villas that house six to eight. Each building has soothing sea views, framed by the dunes and scrublands of the southwestern coast. The Point, a five-bedroom grand villa owned by Edgar Bronfman, Jr., that opens directly on the beach, ranks among the Caribbean's most fabulous accommodations.

Large bedrooms have twin or king-size beds with hand-embroidered linens and deluxe mattresses, and equally sizable, stylish bathrooms with tub/shower combinations. Living rooms have cathedral ceilings; louvered doors and enormous picture windows crafted from Brazilian walnut; terra-cotta tiles; comfortably oversize rattan and wicker furniture draped in raw silk; a fully equipped, state-of-the-art kitchen; and a hammock.

The resort's French chef, Dominique Thevenet, pampers guests (and the occasional lucky "outsider") with impeccably prepared candlelit dinners in an intimate private dining room that overlooks the beach or en suite.

Shoal Bay West (P.O. Box 248), Anguilla, B.W.I. ✆ **800/223-1108** in the U.S., or 264/497-6801. Fax 264/497-6051. www.covecastles.com. 15 units. Winter $895–$1,095 beach house, $1,395–$5,995 villa; off season $595–$695 beach house, $895–$2,895 villa. AE, MC, V. Closed mid-Aug to mid-Oct. **Amenities:** Restaurant; tennis court; aerobics; deep-sea fishing; glass-bottom boat excursions; kayaks; snorkeling; Sunfish sailboats; windsurfing; bicycles; car rental; secretarial service; room service; massage; babysitting; laundry service. *In room:* A/C, ceiling fan, TV, dataport, Wi-Fi, full kitchen, beverage maker, hair dryer, iron, safe.

CuisinArt Resort & Spa ✿

Yes, it's owned by CuisinArt, and, for all its deluxe pretensions, this beachfront resort does seem like a purée of architectural and decorative elements. Artfully aping the architecture of nearby Cap Juluca, this complex of whitewashed villas crowned by blue domes and surrounded by lush tropical foliage filigreed by "streams" seems straight out of Mykonos with stops in Sicily and Tunisia with an Art Deco garnish. It also features Anguilla's first hydroponic farm, a "kitchen stadium" offering cooking classes and demos, an herb garden, an orchid solarium, a pricey art gallery, and a spa that creatively incorporates the home-grown ingredients. Italian upholsteries, Haitian cottons, dark-wood furniture, abstract artworks in varying taste, and large tub/shower-combination bathrooms in soft-toned Italian marble characterize the enormous accommodations. The aggressively stylish, at times garish, result appeals to a cash-equals-cachet crowd.

The **Hydroponic Café**'s daily lunch features the $1-million, .6-hectare (1½-acre) hydroponic farm's fresh vegetables in salads and other light fare. The **Santorini Restaurant** is the fine-dining choice, with a French rotisserie on-site. Expect dishes infused with the flamboyant flavors of the Caribbean.

Rendezvous Bay (P.O. Box 2000), Anguilla, B.W.I. ✆ **800/943-3210** or 264/498-2000. Fax 264/498-2010. www.cuisinartresort.com. 93 units. Winter $625–$750 double, $850–$1,275 suite; off season $385–$545 double, $520–$925 suite. AE, MC, V. Closed Sept–Oct. **Amenities:** 3 restaurants; 3 bars; outdoor pool; 3 tennis courts; fitness center; spa; Jacuzzi; deep-sea fishing; kayaks; sailing; scuba diving; snorkeling; windsurfing; mountain bikes; salon; limited room service; babysitting; laundry service; dry cleaning; nonsmoking rooms; horseback riding; rooms for those w/limited mobility. *In room:* A/C, TV, dataport, Wi-Fi, minibar, hair dryer, iron, safe.

Frangipani Beach Club ⭐ Set on 1.5km (1 mile) of luscious white sand, this flamingo-pink condo complex feels like a Costa del Sol villa, with archways, stone balustrades, wrought-iron railings, and red-tile roofs. Recently renovated accommodations are light and airy, done in soft pastels with natural rattan furnishings. Upgrades range from plush down duvets to the latest in technical gadgetry. All units also have marble-and-mosaic bathrooms with tub/shower combinations, along with private terraces or balconies. The largest have full kitchens and laundry facilities, making them a fine bet for families or friends traveling together. Suites can be locked off into regular hotel rooms, but are overpriced. The restaurant's decor is more elegant and appealing than the disappointing food.

Meads Bay (P.O. Box 1655), Anguilla, B.W.I. ℂ **866/780-5165** in the U.S., or 264/497-6442. Fax 264/497-6440. www.frangipaniresort.com. 8 units. Winter $400–$500 double, from $750 suite; off season $300–$400 double, from $650 suite. Continental breakfast included. AE, MC, V. Closed Sept–Nov. **Amenities:** Restaurant; 2 bars; outdoor pool; tennis court; fishing; Hobie Cats; kayaks; snorkeling; limited room service; laundry service; dry cleaning. *In room:* TV, dataport, Wi-Fi, beverage maker, hair dryer, iron.

Malliouhana ⭐⭐⭐ *Kids* This ultrachic cliff-side retreat conjures up images of Positano in the tropics. It's even more spectacular than Cap Juluca—opulent and lavishly decorated, and situated on a rocky bluff between two alabaster beaches. Malliouhana's 10 hectares (25 acres) are lushly landscaped with terraces, banks of flowers, pools, tiled walkways, and fountains. Thick walls and shrubbery provide seclusion for a glam crowd including such regulars as Gwyneth Paltrow. Of course you'll sit chic-by-jowl with them in the resort's nonpareil restaurant (see "Dining," later in this chapter), on the beaches, or at the sumptuous spa (whose "multicultural" menu, Balinese to Hawaiian, cleverly mixes local ingredients with the latest skin care products). Fitness options range from personal training to Chi Gung (Chinese choreographed movement and breathing exercises). The pampering doesn't end there. A 224-member staff attends to 55 units; their motto is "Your wish is my command."

Lavish yet tastefully decorated public spaces and guest rooms astound with museum-quality Haitian art (one of owner Leon Roydon's passions) and objets d'art from 18th-century Indian silk tapestries to Dogon fertility sculptures. Spacious bedrooms and suites are distributed among the main buildings and outlying villas. Each room has tropical furnishings and wide private verandas; the villas can be rented as a single unit or subdivided. Three suites have private Jacuzzis, and one has a private pool. Some accommodations open onto garden views, and others front Meads Bay Beach or Turtle Cove. Many rooms have luxurious four-poster beds, plus sizable Italian marble bathrooms with tubs and shower stalls. If you're traveling with a child, this is a kid-friendly oasis, complete with a water park and faux pirate ship.

Meads Bay (P.O. Box 173, The Valley), Anguilla, B.W.I. ✆ **800/835-0796** in the U.S., or 264/497-6111. Fax 264/497-6011. www.malliouhana.com. 55 units. Winter $850–$890 double, $1,055–$3,030 suite; off season $385–$575 double, from $520–$1,945 suite. AE, MC, V. Closed Sept–Oct. **Amenities:** 2 restaurants; 2 bars; 3 outdoor pools; 4 tennis courts; gym; spa; Jacuzzi; boat trips; fishing; sailing; snorkeling; water-skiing; windsurfing; children's play area; salon; room service (7am–10:30pm); massage (spa only); babysitting; laundry service; dry cleaning; library; TV room. *In room:* A/C, ceiling fan, dataport, minibar, hair dryer, safe.

EXPENSIVE

Kú ☕ *Value* Amazingly, ultra-trendy Anguilla lacked an Ian Schrager-ish boutique hotel, so the Cap Juluca team corrected the oversight with this all-suite resort that opened in October 2005. Kú means "sacred place" in the extinct indigenous Arawak tongue, and its enviable situation fronting exquisite Shoal Bay certainly qualifies for the target clientele. The 23m-long (75-ft.) beach bar already hosts CEOs wearing model wannabes on their arms like Rolexes, bearing out the owners' goal to create an ambience "evocative of South Beach and St. Barts." Interiors adopt a fashionably minimalist look: stark (if not Starck) white furnishings and curtains set against white tile floors and pale aqua walls, enlivened by indigo, lavender, and teal pillows. Each large suite features a full kitchen, cushy duvets, and an oceanfront or oceanview terrace. The effortlessly cool result offers exceptional value on stratospherically priced Anguilla.

Shoal Bay East (P.O. Box 51, The Valley), Anguilla, B.W.I. ✆ **800/869-5827** or 264/497-2011. Fax 264/497-3355. www.ku-anguilla.com. 27 units. Winter $285–$395 double; off season $160–$200 double. Extra person $50 ($30 off season). AE, MC, V. **Amenities:** Restaurant; bar; outdoor pool; gym; spa; dive shop; snorkeling. *In room:* A/C, ceiling fan, TV/DVD, Internet access, kitchen, safe.

La Sirena ☕ Built in 1989 this Swiss-owned cliff-top resort, a 4-minute walk down to a sparkling beach, is inviting, intimate, and immaculately maintained. At least 80% of its clientele comes from Switzerland or Germany. Antiseptic accommodations, arranged in two-story bougainvillea-draped wings, feature intriguing angles, arches, and contemporary touches like halogen lamps contrasting with rattan and wicker furnishings. Some have air-conditioning; all have ceiling fans. Guests in need of a CNN fix can rent a TV with

VCR or DVD for a small surcharge. Rooms have large beds with fine linens. Bathrooms are spacious, with tub/shower combinations. Guests walk through the garden and down a sandy footpath to reach the beach where umbrellas and lounge chairs await. If possible, request rooms away from the second-floor Top of the Palms restaurant to avoid the kitchen's noise and fumes. The suites and dive packages offer exceptional value.

The **Top of the Palms** is open to cool ocean breezes and offers views over Meads Bay and the surrounding treetops. A well-trained local chef prepares specialties ranging from alpine fondues to West Indian favorites. Theme evenings featuring steel bands and folkloric troupes lure a lively crowd.

Meads Bay (P.O. Box 200), Anguilla, B.W.I. *©* **800/331-9358** in the U.S., or 264/497-6827. Fax 264/497-6829. www.sirenaresort.com. 26 units. Winter $260–$330 double, $370–$420 suite; off season $145–$190 double, $220–$250 suite. Modified American Plan (breakfast and dinner) $48 per person. AE, MC, V. **Amenities:** Restaurant; bar; 2 outdoor pools; dive center; snorkeling; windsurfing; car rental; limited room service; massage; babysitting; laundry service. *In room:* A/C (in some), ceiling fan, dataport, minibar, hair dryer, safe.

MODERATE

Anguilla Great House Beach Resort This bungalow colony's gingerbread-trimmed cottages nestle in gardens steps from the sands of Rendezvous Bay. Each bungalow contains several homey bedrooms, which can be rented in various configurations depending on your needs; virtually all boast splendid water views from their private patios. The nicest charm guests with colonial-style decor (mahogany two-poster beds and planter's chairs), coffered ceilings, and local artworks. Shower-only bathrooms are small but tidily kept. The Great House also manages **Kerwin Kottages**—four nearby self-catering one-, two-, and three-bedroom units that enjoy hotel privileges and represent superior value (starting at $197 in season).

Rendezvous Bay, Anguilla, B.W.I. *©* **264/497-6061.** Fax 264/497-6019. www.anguillagreathouse.com. 35 units. Winter $260–$290 double; off season $155–$185 double. AE, MC, V. **Amenities:** Restaurant; bar; outdoor pool; fishing; kayaks; snorkeling; Sunfish sailboats; windsurfing; limited room service; laundry service; nonsmoking rooms. *In room:* A/C, ceiling fan, TV, hair dryer, iron.

Arawak Beach Inn *⚓ (Finds* Built on the site of an ancient Arawak village only minutes from beautiful Shoal Bay Beach, this exceedingly friendly, comfortable, and inviting family-run hotel offers good value (for pricey Anguilla, anyway). Accommodations consist of studios and one-bedroom suites (some with kitchenettes) in thatch-roof, sorbet-hued, octagonal-shaped buildings; those on the upper floors open onto stunning views of Scilly Cay and Captains Ridge. Eclectic funky-chic decor runs from spartan white with dramatic splashes of color to more classic four-poster rattan beds, mahogany armoires, and teak tables. Each lodging has a smallish shower-only bathroom and private balcony or terrace. Air-conditioning, high-speed Internet access, and cable TV are available in deluxe units. The virtually private Arawak Cove's pearly sand and generally calm water sits hidden 2 minutes' walk behind the resort.

The **Arawak Café,** bedecked in bold colors, features a good Continental/Caribbean menu (look for chef Maude's creative pizzas); the bartenders are mixology magicians.

Island Harbour (P.O. Box 1403, The Valley), Anguilla, B.W.I. ✆ 877/427-2925 or 264/497-4888. Fax 264/497-4889. www.arawakbeach.com. 17 units. Winter $225–$275 double; off season $120–$185 double. Extra person $35. Children under 12 stay free in parent's room. MC, V. **Amenities:** Restaurant; beach bar; outdoor pool; canoeing; windsurfing; bike rental; car rental; limited room service; babysitting; laundry service. *In room:* Ceiling fan, TV (in some), wireless Internet (in some), fridge, hair dryer (in some), safe, no phone.

Blue Waters Beach Apartments   Fronting .8km (½ mile) of white-sand beachfront, this tranquil resort sports a vaguely modernist Moorish look. It offers well-designed and immaculately kept one- and two-bedroom apartments, cooled by ceiling fans and trade winds. Each unit offers a complete kitchen, promoting a do-it-yourself atmosphere ideal for families. Guests find ample closets, comfortable furnishings, a private balcony or terrace, and sparkling white, shower-only bathrooms.

Shoal Bay West (P.O. Box 69), Anguilla, B.W.I. ✆ 264/497-6292. Fax 264/497-6982. 11 units. Winter $303 1-bedroom apt; $429 2-bedroom apt; off season $154 1-bedroom apt; $215 2-bedroom apt. AE, MC, V. **Amenities:** Bar. *In room:* Ceiling fan, TV, kitchen, safe.

Rendezvous Bay Hotel ⟨⟩   A family-run operation in the best sense, this sprawling resort on one of the island's loveliest stretches of sand opened in 1962, jump-starting tourism on Anguilla. It will close during the next two off seasons to implement long-needed renovations and expansions, though the Gumbs family vows the upscaling mania won't diminish the down-home charm that lures the equally multigenerational loyal clientele. The cheapest rooms lack A/C and great water pressure, while the view encompasses aloes, white cedars, rusting cannons, and chicken coops, but they're still steps from the ravishing beach. Pitch-roofed villas open right onto the sand, offering large guest rooms or studios with fully-equipped kitchenettes. Golden dust ruffles, white tiles, and cobalt

bedspreads pay homage to sun, sand, and surf. As for the lack of certain creature comforts, staffers smilingly wave at the beach, observing, "That is our TV." The superlative **Cedar Grove Café** (see "Dining," below) and adjacent local art gallery reflect the younger Gumbs generation's passions, while a T-shirt sold at the hotel shop perfectly captures the mellow vibe: "Do Nothing—Then Rest."

Rendezvous Bay (P.O. Box 31, The Valley), Anguilla, B.W.I. ℂ 800/274-4893 or 264/497-6549. Fax 264/497-6026. www.rendezvousbay.com. 43 units. Winter $140–$295 double, $315–$335 studios; off season $110–$220 double, $245 studio AE, DISC, MC, V. Closed Sept to early Nov. **Amenities:** Restaurant; bar; 2 tennis courts; snorkeling; windsurfing; game room; car rental; room service. *In room:* A/C (in some), ceiling fan, dataport, kitchenette (in some), fridge, hair dryer, safe.

INEXPENSIVE

Easy Corner Villas On a bluff overlooking Road Bay, this modest villa complex is a 5-minute drive from a good beach (a car is necessary regardless). On the main road west of the airport, this property is owned by Maurice E. Connor, the same entrepreneur who rents many of the cars on the island (you can sometimes swing special deals when you book a room). His one-, two-, and three-bedroom apartments are set on landscaped grounds with beach views from their private porches. Each comes equipped with a kitchen, airy combination living/dining room, and simple but sturdy furnishings draped with attractive if blindingly bright tropical fabrics, plus small bathrooms with shower stalls. Maid service is available for an extra charge, except on Sunday.

South Hill (P.O. Box 65, The Valley), Anguilla, B.W.I. ℂ **264/497-6433.** Fax 264/497-6410. www.caribbean-inns.com. 12 units. Winter $160 1-bedroom villa, $195 2-bedroom villa, $240 3-bedroom villa; off season $125 1-bedroom villa, $155 2-bedroom villa, $195 3-bedroom villa. AE, MC, V. **Amenities:** Car rental; laundry service. *In room:* A/C, ceiling fan, TV, kitchen, beverage maker, hair dryer.

3 Dining

VERY EXPENSIVE

Malliouhana Restaurant ✷✷✷ FRENCH Malliouhana Restaurant, with the Caribbean's most ambitious French menu personally supervised by two-star Michelin chef Jo Rostang, offers fluidly choreographed service, fine food, a *Wine Spectator* Grand-Award-winning 25,000-bottle wine cellar, and a glamorous clientele. You'll dine in an open-sided pavilion on a rocky promontory over the sea. At night your candlelit table—carefully spaced to ensure no one will eavesdrop on affairs, professional to personal—will be set with French crystal, Limoges china, and Christofle silver.

The hors d'oeuvres selection is the finest on island, including delectable fresh Anguillian lobster prepared in various ways. Resort chef Alain Laurent's seasonally changing menu might offer roast breast of *poulet de Bresse* (chicken) basted with honey and cider or braised mahimahi with sweet potato purée. Dessert might be an old-fashioned slice of French-style apple tart. Its international renown is such that the resort annually holds an Epicurean Delight week in July, attracting such stellar wineries as Burgundy's Bonneau du Mar-tray and Châteauneuf-du-Pape's Château de Beaucastel, while top toques might include Hubert Keller (San Francisco and Las Vegas's Fleur de Lys), Michael Romano (New York's Union Square Café), and Paris's three-star Michelin darling, Guy Savoy.

Meads Bay. © 264/497-6111. Reservations required. Main courses $34–$48. AE, MC, V. Daily 7–11:30am, 12:30–3pm, and 7:30–10:30pm.

EXPENSIVE

Blanchards ✿✿✿ INTERNATIONAL   Bob and Melinda Blan-chard are the masterminds behind this elegantly casual, intensely fashionable restaurant on a garden-swathed pavilion beside the sea, down the beach from Malliouhana (a second outpost is scheduled to open by 2007 in the new tony Temenos Golf Clubhouse, see later in this chapter). No surprise that Blanchards has attracted a sprin-kling of celebs. But Bob and Mel are celebrities themselves: for an enduring take-home taste of the island, read their *A Trip to the Beach*, a hilarious cross between *A Year in Provence* and Herman Wouk's classic comic novel about a Caribbean hotel, *Don't Stop the Carnival*. Their latest, *Live What You Love*, is equally appetizing.

Behind tall teal shutters (which can be opened to the sea breezes), diners enjoy sophisticated food with a Caribbean flair, enhanced with spices from Spain, Asia, California, and the American South-west. Dishes change according to Chef Mel's inspiration but might include such delights as lobster-and-shrimp cakes with mixed greens and tomato-tartar sauce. The specialty (extravagant in both portions and price) is a sublime sampler: oven-crisped mahimahi with coconut, lime, and ginger, roasted Anguilla lobster with honey glaze, and jerk chicken with cinnamon-rum bananas. For a real island dessert, opt for the cracked coconut with coconut ice cream accompanied by a rum-custard sauce in a chocolate-crusted shell.

Meads Bay. © 264/497-6100. www.blanchardsrestaurant.com. Reservations required. Main courses $34–$58. AE, MC, V. Mon–Sat 6:30–10pm. Closed Aug to mid-Oct and Mon in off season.

Hibernia ⭐⭐ *Finds* FRENCH/INDOCHINESE Following Blanchards' lead closely, this is another little stunner of creativity. Chef Raoul Rodriguez and his wife, hostess Mary Pat O'Hanlon, have converted a lovely West Indian cottage into a charming restaurant with French- and Indonesian-inspired decor showcasing *objets d'art* collected from their world travels (peruse the gallery in back between courses). Chef Raoul's exquisitely prepared and presented dishes provide an equally refreshing, artful change of pace. You could feast on first courses alone: Asian mushroom soup topped with cream of cauliflower, crispy lobster medallion with pumpkin lemon grass *velouté*, foie gras duo (terrine perfumed with Gewürztraminer and mousse with Thai jasmine essence), or a selection of finely sliced, house-smoked West Indian fish with ginger horseradish. Main course dazzlers include roasted shelled lobster layered with Lao aromatic rice and papaya drizzled with lime sauce, Caribbean fish filets in a spicy Thai broth, or crayfish and scallops sautéed with shiitake mushrooms with pumpkin yam gratin infused with truffle oil. Finish with homemade ice cream and sorbets (mint to mango, green tea to tamarind) or apple ginger crumble with blackcurrant sorbet.

Island Harbour. © **264/497-4290.** www.hiberniarestaurant.com. Reservations required. Main courses $28–$41. AE, MC, V. Tues–Sat noon–2pm and 7–9pm; Sun 7–9pm. Closed Aug–Sept.

Kemia ⭐⭐ INTERNATIONAL Cap Juluca's neo-Moorish theme reaches its peak at this sultry seaside eatery. The soigné seraglio decor is all beads, sequins, tassels, billowing curtains, mosaic, and intricately inlaid woods. The "one-from-column-A" menu offers platters pitched between appetizer- and entree-size, a tapas-try weaving influences from Portofino to Peru, Cambodia to Campeche. Your culinary journey might start with Peruvian "tacu tacu" lentils with sautéed foie gras and sherry glaze or Mexican-style crayfish tail with quinoa and tequila-lime mayo, then segue to *kalbi* (Korean short ribs) with honey sesame glaze and kimchi, Moroccan lamb tagine, or *lau ca* (a smashing Cambodian seafood hot pot).

Cap Juluca, Maunday's Bay. © **264/497-6666.** Reservations required. Main courses $15–$30. AE, MC, V. Daily 7–10pm.

Koal Keel ⭐⭐ INTERNATIONAL/CARIBBEAN This romantic French/Caribbean restaurant is housed in one of the island's most historic homes, a former sugar plantation Great House from the 1790s. (Across the road you can see the oldest dwelling on the island, originally a building sheltering slaves.) Koal Keel has a type of 18th-century oven slaves built for their Dutch masters. Two French chefs (one of whom worked with the legendary Joël Robuchon in Paris), along with another chef from Punjab, turn out first-rate international dishes. Launch your meal with such delights as pan-seared foie gras with cinnamon-poached pears, going on to such mains as snapper tandoori with coconut rice or grilled chicken breast with lemon grass in orange sauce. Most dishes are reasonably priced except for the fresh lobster, which depends on the market prices of the day. Oenophiles will appreciate the sterling 15,000-bottle wine cellar and a lounge ideal for a postprandial aged rum and cigar.

The Valley. ⓒ **264/497-2930.** Reservations required. Main courses $24–$75. AE, MC, V. Mon–Sat 6:30–8:30pm.

Mango's ⓕ AMERICAN/CARIBBEAN   This pavilion a few steps from the edge of the sea, on the northwestern part of the island, fulfills anyone's fantasies of a beachfront eatery; its doors open to the breezes and its walls are brightened by local murals. Mango's serves more healthful cuisine than the island's other top restaurants. The fresh fish, meat, and produce are grilled with a minimum of added fats or calories. All the breads and desserts, including ice cream and sorbet, are made fresh daily on the premises. You might start with delectable lobster cakes and homemade tartar sauce, or creamy mango-infused conch chowder. Grilled local crayfish splashed with lime, curry, and coconut atop angel hair pasta, rum-barbecued chicken, and spicy steamed whole snapper are featured main courses, but the simple grilled fish with lemon-and-herb butter shines. Finish with intense, yet blissfully light, homemade sorbets.

Seaside Grill, Barnes Bay. ⓒ **264/497-6479.** www.mangos.ai. Reservations required for dinner. Main courses $26–$42. AE, MC, V. Wed–Mon 6:30–9pm. Closed Aug–Oct.

Straw Hat ⓕ ASIAN/CARIBBEAN   Winning rave reviews from such magazines as *Gourmet,* chef James Hassell lives up to his hype. The panoramic seaside setting and distant vistas of French St. Martin more than match the superb cuisine. A plain wooden structure, the restaurant stands on pilings overlooking a floodlit virtual aquarium of fish below. The watery motif wittily continues with vivid seascapes and tables embedded with shells or marine mosaics. Hassell's dishes, merrily marrying various culinary influences, appeal to both eye and palate. On a hot day, the mango papaya gazpacho garnished with avocado purée is refreshing, as is the cilantro-infused ceviche of local red snapper with plantain chips. Some dishes, like the jerk pork tenderloin, are traditional favorites; others are more eclectic, like the seared Anguillian red snapper with a lime, ginger, and saffron sauce or the pan-roasted duck breast with passion fruit demi-glace and garlic mashed potatoes. A cilantro, lime, and pecan pesto pasta can be served with your choice of grilled chicken, tuna, or red snapper. For dessert, order the chocolate lava cake with lavender crème Anglaise or ginger crème brûlée.

Forest Bay. ℭ 264/497-8300. www.strawhat.com. Reservations recommended. Main courses $24–$39. AE, DISC, MC, V. Mon–Sat 6:30–9:30pm. Closed Sept–Oct.

MODERATE

Bistro Phil ℛ FRENCH/ITALIAN   Perched on a cliff 15m (50 ft.) above the sea, this restaurant showcases the talents of French-born owner/chef Philippe Kim, whose culinary innovations draw a stylish crowd of diners. Many of them request a table on the terrace with its view of the sea. Kim masterfully juxtaposes flavors and textures, evident even in his scrumptious pizzas, which make splendid starters, as do the French onion soup or tuna tartare. The chef takes justifiable pride in his seafood kabob, and his tender and succulent lamb shank practically falls from the bone. For dessert, a classic chocolate mousse or crème brûlée won't disappoint.

South Hill. ℭ 264/497-6810. Reservations recommended. Main courses $22–$36. AE, DC, MC, V. Mon–Sat 6:30–9:30pm. Closed Aug–Sept.

Cedar Grove Café ℛ CARIBBEAN   More than three years after its opening, Cedar Grove remains one of the island's hottest dining tickets, thanks to the enterprising Gumbs family (the masterminds behind Koal Keel and Smokey's). In a semi-alfresco setting evocative of *Casablanca,* you can savor a series of ever-changing specialties, based on the best and freshest ingredients. Signature dishes include grilled smoked salmon tortilla with dill spread, coconut-crusted shrimp in a mango-ginger sauce, or tempura lobster with zucchini and leeks in Chardonnay beurre blanc. The wine list offers some stupendous deals.

Rendezvous Bay. ℭ 264/497-6549. Breakfast $8–$10; main courses $16–$45 at lunch or dinner. AE, MC, V. Daily 7am–9:30pm. Closed May–mid Nov.

Trattoria Tramonto ℛ *Finds* NORTHERN ITALIAN   This breeze-swept restaurant lies near the water between Blue Waters and Covecastles, but the food evokes dining on the Adriatic, thanks to chef Valter Belli, who hails from Emilia Romagna in northern Italy. The "sundowners" here are the best on island, including a peach

Bellini as good as that served at Harry's Bar in Venice. Other champagne drinks are mixed with fruits like mango, passion fruit, or guava. The chef takes special care with his appetizers, including a *zuppa di pesce* (fish soup with porcini mushrooms) and spicy hot penne with a garlic, tomato, and red-pepper sauce. All the entrees are superbly prepared, including a delectable wild striped bass with a caper-laced fresh tomato sauce or the divine house specialty, lobster-filled ravioli in a truffle-cream sauce.

Shoal Bay West. ℂ **264/497-8819.** Reservations required. Main courses lunch $8–$30, dinner $22–$36. MC, V. Tues–Sun noon–3pm and 6:30–9pm. Closed Sept–Oct.

Zara's Restaurant ☆ ITALIAN/CARIBBEAN   Shamash Brooks presides over the kitchen at this casually elegant place, a favorite among repeat visitors since its 1996 opening. The chef—known islandwide for his "Rasta pastas"—prepares everything to order, utilizing the freshest ingredients. His fish dishes, especially the crusted garlic snapper with lemon mojo sauce and roasted grouper with mango basil coulis, are delightful, but he does meat and poultry with equal élan. Try his Bahamian cracked conch, and look for various daily specials, most of them in the moderate range.

Allamanda Beach Club, Upper Shoal Bay East. ℂ **264/497-3229.** Reservations required. Main courses $16–$38. DISC, MC, V. Daily 6:30–9pm.

INEXPENSIVE

Ferryboat Inn *Value* CARIBBEAN/FRENCH   Established by the late English-born John McClean and his Anguillian wife, Marjorie, this beachfront place just a short walk from the ferry pier is one of the best deals on the island. Old-fashioned yet lovingly prepared specialties include French onion soup, black-bean soup, lobster thermidor, and scallop of veal Savoyard. Unless you order expensive shellfish, most dishes are reasonably priced.

Marjorie and son Christian also rent six spare but cozy one-bedroom apartments and a two-bedroom beach house. In winter, apartments cost $160 to $180, and the beach house is $280. Off season, an apartment is $90 to $110, and the beach house is $175.

Cul de Sac Rd., Blowing Point. ℂ **264/497-6613.** www.ferryboatinn.ai. Reservations recommended. Main courses $14–$33. AE, MC, V. Mon–Sat 11:30am–3pm; daily 7–10pm. Closed Sept. Turn right just before the Blowing Point Ferry Terminal and travel 140m (450 ft.) before making a left turn.

Ripples *Value* CARIBBEAN/INTERNATIONAL   This restaurant is earthier, rowdier and more British than most others in Sandy Ground (ground zero for island nightlife). Its jovial staff and long,

Gwen, Reggae & Barbecue

Want to spend a lazy day on Upper Shoal Bay, which arguably has the whitest sand in the Caribbean? Drop in at **Gwen's Reggae Grill** (© 264/497-2120), which has a full bar and features Gwen Webster's barbecue every day into the early evening; it's best on a Sunday when it showcases live reggae performances. Gwen's piña coladas are the best on Anguilla, as is her special slaw. Try her shrimp salad or fish sandwiches. Some easy snorkeling lies off the beach. The palm grove here is about the only naturally shady spot on island, and it comes with a fleet of hammocks.

busy bar will make you feel as though you're on the set of *Cheers,* albeit with a Cockney accent. Set in a restored clapboard house, it has a raised deck, a casual West Indian decor, and a crowd of regulars. Local fish—mahimahi, snapper, tuna, and grouper—are prepared any way you like, but the specialties are coconut shrimp, puffy brie in beer batter, and Creole-style conch. Only a few dishes are at the high end of the price scale.

Sandy Ground. © 264/497-3380. Reservations recommended. Main courses $12–$25. MC, V. Daily noon–midnight.

4 Beaches

Superb beaches put Anguilla on the tourist map. There are dozens of them, plus another handful on the outer cays. The island's interior may be barren, but there's no denying the beauty of its shores. Miles and miles of pristine, powdery-soft sands open onto crystal-clear waters. Many beaches are reached via bone-jarring dirt paths; all are open to the public, though access may be through the lobby of a deluxe hotel.

The best beaches are on the west end of the island, site of the most expensive hotels. **Rendezvous Bay** ⊛ is the island's most famous, a long curving ribbon of satiny, pale gold sand that stretches along the bay for 4km (2½ miles). With calmer, warm, shallow water, and lined by several resorts, it attracts all kinds of beachcombers, from families to romantic couples.

In the northeast, 3km (2-mile) **Shoal Bay** ⊛⊛⊛ is a Caribbean classic, with silver-white, powder-soft sands, a backdrop of coconut palms and sea-grape trees, and superb snorkeling in lavish coral gardens, home to hundreds of tiny iridescent fish This beach is often called Shoal Bay East to distinguish it from Shoal Bay West (see below). The waters are usually luminous, transparent, and brilliantly blue. At noon the sands are blindingly white, but at sunrise and sunset they turn a pink to rival any beach in Bermuda. Umbrellas, beach chairs, and other equipment are available, and you'll hear music from the terraces of the Hardbroke Cafe and Uncle Ernie's (beloved for its ribs). The Upper Shoal Bar serves first-rate tropical drinks, and souvenir shops hawk T-shirts and suntan lotion on the beach. For greater tranquillity, take the trail walk from Old Ta to little-known **Katouche Beach,** a prime site for a beach picnic under shade trees, followed by scintillating snorkeling.

Shoal Bay West has pristine white sands tinged with pink opening onto the southwest coast. Visitors find deluxe accommodations, including Covecastles, and superior snorkeling at its western tip. Adjoining it is 1.5km-long (1-mile), white-sand **Maundays Bay** ✮, site of Cap Juluca and justifiably one of the island's most popular shorelines, with good snorkeling and swimming. Though the waters are luminescent and usually calm, sometimes the wind blows enough to attract windsurfers and sailboats. On a clear day you can see St. Martin across the way.

Sandy Isle, on the northwest coast, is a tiny islet with a few palms surrounded by a coral reef, a beach bar and restaurant, and a place to rent snorkeling gear and buy underwater cameras. During the day a small ferry heads here every hour from Sandy Ground.

The northwest coast has a number of other beaches worth seeking out, notably the glittering white stretch of **Barnes Bay** beneath a bullying bluff. You can admire the offshore islands silhouetted

---

Moments **Grilled Lobster on a Remote Cay**

At Island Harbour, just wave your arms, and a boatman will pick you up and transport you across the water to **Scilly Cay,** pronounced "silly key." You wouldn't really call this place an island; it's more like a spit of sand 150m (500 ft.) off the coast of the main island's northeastern shore. At Eudoxie and Sandra Wallace's Gorgeous Scilly Cay, a glorified tiki hut, you can select a fabulous fresh spiny lobster. Grilled while you wait, the lobster (you can opt for chicken or crayfish) is marinated in a sauce of honey-laced orange juice, orange marmalade, roasted peanuts, virgin olive oil, curry, and tarragon. Lunch is daily Tuesday to Sunday from noon to 3pm.

against the horizon or join the windsurfers and snorkelers. It's usually less crowded after lunch.

Rarely crowded (save for the occasional local wedding), **Little Bay Beach** is quite dramatically set against steep cliffs. The sands are grayish, but bird-watchers, snorkelers, and scuba divers don't seem to mind.

Road Bay, also on the northwest coast, paints an idyllic old-time Caribbean scene, right down to tethered goats, spectacular sunsets and clear blue waters, often filled with yachts coming from St. Martin. A watersports center on the beach will set you up with gear. You can also watch lobstermen set out in fishing boats as brightly colored as a child's finger paints. **Johnno's** (see "Nightlife," below) is arguably the archetypal beach bar, serving fine island fare through the day and rocking at night. Indeed, many of the weathered wooden Antillean houses shaded by turpentine trees and oleander hold casual bars, making it Party Central on Friday nights.

The beaches along the northeast coast are the stuff of fantasies—especially if you've got a vehicle with four-wheel-drive. Calm and tranquil, the incredibly blue waters of **Island Harbour Beach** attract both locals and the odd visitor or two. For centuries Anguillians have set out from these shores to haul in spiny lobster. There are a few beach bars and alfresco dining rooms here, so you can make a day of it—or take a 3-minute boat ride over to **Scilly Cay.**

Savannah Bay (aka Junk's Hole) offers a long stretch of uncrowded white sand and offshore reefs full of eels, squid, and manta rays. Nat Richardson, the owner of **Palm Grove Bar & Grill** (seemingly the only building for miles), will boil or grill fresh-caught lobster, crayfish, or shrimp. *Bon Appétit* liked his johnny-cakes so much it stole and published the recipe. Hours are usually 11am to around 6:30pm daily, but vary greatly depending on Nat's mood.

Chances are you'll have **Captain's Bay** ✪ all to yourself. Near Junk's Hole, it's better for sunbathing than swimming. The undertow is dangerous, though the setting is dramatic and appealing (even to pampered guests at the super-deluxe **Exclusivity Villa,** which included Brad and Jennifer just prior to their split).

5 Sports & Other Outdoor Pursuits

CRUISES & BOATING A great way to have fun on Anguilla is to cruise to a secluded beach on an offshore cay for a picnic and some snorkeling, whether on your own or with a group. Several outfitters on the island rent vessels, including **Island Yacht Charters** (© 264/497-3744), offering an 11m (35-ft.) teak motorboat and 9m (30-ft.) Beneteau sailboat.

FISHING   Your hotel can arrange for you to cast your line with a local guide, but you should bring your own tackle. Agree on the cost before setting out, however, to avoid the "misunderstandings" that are commonly reported.

Malliouhana, Meads Bay (© 264/497-6111), has a 10m (33-ft.) fishing cruiser, *Kyra,* which holds up to eight passengers, and another 12-passenger cruiser, *Dakota.* You can charter it for fishing parties for $400 for up to 4 hours. All fishing gear and a snack basket are included. **Garfield Richardson** (© 264/497-2956) rents his sexy, supercharged Sunseeker Superhawk for $100 per hour, for four fishermen. This is one of the best deals on island for anglers.

GOLF   The 18-hole, par-72 Greg Norman–designed Temenos Golf Course, between Long and Rendezvous bays (© 264/497-7000), is slated to open November 2006 on a 111-hectare (274-acre) site that by 2008 will develop into a luxury spa and residential complex (the first three villas are utterly splendid and stratospherically priced). Four holes will play to and from the ocean. Check with your hotel desk or the tourist office for the latest details on this development.

SCUBA DIVING & SNORKELING   Most of the coastline is fringed by coral reefs, and the crystalline waters are rich in marine life, with sunken coral gardens, brilliantly colored fish, caves, miniwalls, greenback turtles, and stingrays. Conditions for scuba diving and snorkeling are ideal. In addition, the government of Anguilla has artificially enlarged the existing reef system, a first for the Caribbean. Battered and outmoded ships, deliberately sunk in carefully designated places, act as nurseries for fish and lobster populations and provide new dive sites. At **Stoney Bay Marine Park** off the northeast coast, you can explore the ruins of a Spanish galleon that sank in the 1772. Offshore cays **(Prickly Pear, Sandy Island)** offer pristine conditions.

Anguillian Divers, Meads Bay (© 264/497-4750; www. anguilliandivers.com), is a one-stop dive shop that answers most diving needs. PADI instructors are on hand, with a two-tank dive costing $70, plus another $10 for equipment. Another good choice is **Shoal Bay Scuba & Water Sports** (© 264/497-4101; www.shoalbayscuba.ai), with a custom-built, state-of-the-art boat. A two-tank dive costs $80, plus $10 for equipment. They also provide windsurfer rentals and lessons. Both offer packages of three to five dives at deep discounts.

Several places rent snorkeling gear on the island's most popular beaches, if your hotel doesn't provide it. The snorkeling's great at Shoal Bay, Maundays Bay, Barnes Bay, Little Bay, and Road Bay.

TENNIS Most of the resorts have their own tennis courts (see "Accommodations," earlier in this chapter). **Malliouhana,** Meads Bay (© 264/497-6111), has a pro shop and four championship Laykold tennis courts. All courts are lit for night games. The Anguilla Tennis Academy (www.tennis.ai) is developing a major 672-sq.-m (7,235-sq.-ft.) complex in Blowing Point with pro shop, locker rooms, gym, and six lit courts modeled after the U.S. Open facility in Flushing Meadows, New York. Anticipated opening is December 2006.

6 Exploring Anguilla

The best way to get an overview of the island is on a **taxi tour.** In about 2 hours, a local driver (all of them are guides) will show you everything for about $40. The driver will also arrange to let you off at your favorite beach after a look around, and then pick you up and return you to your hotel or the airport. Call **Airport Taxi Stand** at © 264/497-5054 or **Blowing Point Ferry Taxi Stand** at © 264/497-6089. If you want more organized sightseeing, call **Bennie's Tours** at Blowing Point (© 264/497-2788). This is the island's most reliable tour operator.

For that rare rainy day, there is the **Heritage Museum Collection,** East End at Pond Ground (© 264/497-4092), open Monday to Saturday 9am to 5pm, charging $5 admission. Artifacts on display range from the golden age of the Arawak Indians to the British "invasion" of the island in 1969, as well as fascinating photographs such as those documenting a visit from Queen Elizabeth II in 1964.

Former chief minister Sir Emile Gumbs, an Anguilla National Trust volunteer, runs $10 eco-tours (© 264/497-2711) spiked with wonderful, often wry historical and political anecdotes every Tuesday morning at 10am. Tours explore the Sandy Ground area, with stops at the recently restored 1900 "Manse," Old Salt Factory, and pink-tinged Caul Pond ("salting" was once Anguilla's economic mainstay) to view migratory fowl from pintails to peregrines.

7 Shopping

For serious shopping, take the ferry (see earlier in this chapter) and visit the big stores in Marigot on French St. Martin. Some bigger stores have little branches on Anguilla, but better merchandise and selection are just a ferry ride away.

On Anguilla itself, the most fun shopping is at **World Art & Antiques Gallery,** Old Factory Plaza, The Valley (© 264/497-5950), where Nik and Christie Douglas have assembled a fascinating array of collectibles from around the world. Treasures include Chinese bronzes and jades, exotic jewelry, tribal and pre-Columbian sculptures and masks, and antiques and paintings.

Anguilla does have a thriving local arts and crafts scene. The best of these are on display at the **Savannah Gallery,** Coronation Street, Lower Valley (© 264/497-2263; www.savannahgallery.com), on the road to Crocus Bay, and the **Devonish Art Gallery,** West End Road (© 264/497-2949). Courtney Devonish is a well-known potter and sculptor. You can also view original paintings by local artists at **Loblolly Gallery,** in Rose Cottage, Crocus Hill Road (© 264/497-6006; www.loblollygallery.com). **Cheddie's Carving Studio,** West End Road, The Cove (© 264/497-2949; www.cheddie online.com), is the domain of self-taught Cheddie Richardson, who sculpts intricate, whimsical figures (and majestic furnishings) from driftwood, stone, and coral.

8 Anguilla After Dark

Nightlife on Anguilla centers mainly on the various hotels, especially in winter, when they host barbecues, West Indian parties, and singers and other musicians. The hotels hire calypso combo groups and other bands, both local and imported.

Open-air **Johnno's Beach Stop,** Road Bay, Sandy Ground (© 264/497-2728), is a favorite of Hollywood types when they visit Anguilla. The club offers Beck's beer on the beach, barbecued spareribs, grilled chicken, and fresh fish for lunch and dinner. Live entertainment takes place Wednesday and Friday from 8pm to 1am. A weekly Sunday barbecue begins at noon, with live light jazz music starting mid-afternoon in winter. Try the Johnno Special (similar to a piña colada, but made with rum and guavaberries).

Pumphouse Bar & Grill, Sandy Ground (© 264/497-5154), is the perennial hot spot, boasting 30 different rums and a disco occupying a funky space with an uneven concrete slab floor that served as the original salt works, then as a repair station for heavy trucks. Standard but satisfying menu items include platters of fish or chicken, steaks, and a Caesar salad with slices of jerk chicken. Go any time from 6pm to 2am, except Sunday, when it's closed. Reggae lovers should show up on Wednesday and Saturday nights; Thursday nights are often devoted to merengue.

There are some other little nighttime joints on Anguilla that seem to keep irritatingly irregular hours. Most are active only on the weekend, including the riotously hued, old boat-and-driftwood shack, **Dune Preserve** at Rendezvous Bay (© 264/497-2660; www. dunepreserve.com), where the best-known singer on island, "Bankie" Banx, performs for such fans as Jay-Z, Kevin Bacon, Beyoncé, and Uma Thurman. You might also check out another weekend hot spot, **The Red Dragon Disco,** The Valley (© 264/497-2687), where dancers gyrate to the latest recorded music.

RumZa, Lockrum Bay (© 264/498-6RUM), was created when Jason and Robin Howe were married on the island. Wanting "to stay forever," they founded this hot spot offering live acts as well as the best DJs on island. In addition to dancing the night away, you can enjoy full dinners, from two versions of Anguillian lobster to coconut curry breast of chicken or guava-glazed loin of pork.

9

St. Barthélemy

St. Barts: Two words practically synonymous with glitz, glamour, and glorious beaches. This is Cannes in the Caribbean, as eternally chic as a Chanel cocktail dress and every bit as pricey. St. Barts has its historic sites and ambitious aquatic activities, but visitors go for pampering without pomp, inimitable French fare and flair, sandy strands like powdered ivory, and sybaritic sanctuary. Yet despite its chichi reputation, casual dress—jeans, sarongs, sometimes little else—prevails, though the well-heeled do prefer Manolo sandals.

New friends call it "St. Barts," while old-time visitors prefer "St. Barths," short for St. Barthélemy (San Bar-te-le-*mee*), named by its discoverer Columbus in 1493. With its arid climate and poor rocky soil ill-suited to sugar production, St. Barts never developed a slave-based agro-economy. Most longtime residents are descendants of Breton and Norman fisherfolk, intermingled with Swedes (whose colonial influence lingers in place names) as evidenced by their fair skin, blond hair, and blue eyes. The year-round population of about 6,500 occupies some 21 sq. km (8¼ sq. miles), 24km (15 miles) southeast of St. Martin and 225km (140 miles) north of Guadeloupe.

Despite an influx of young French arrivals, the old ways endure. Many locals still speak 18th-century Norman, Breton, or Poitevin dialect. In little **Corossol,** you might glimpse wizened *grand-mères* wearing the traditional starched white bonnets known as *quichenottes* (a corruption of "kiss-me-not"), which discouraged the close attentions of English or Swedish men on the island. The bonneted women can also be spotted at local celebrations, particularly on August 25, **St. Louis's Day.** Many of these women are camera-shy, but they offer their homemade baskets and hats for sale to visitors.

For a long time, the island was a paradise for a few millionaires, such as David Rockefeller, who had a hideaway on the northwest shore, and Edmond de Rothschild, whose compound graces the "other end" of the island. Development was inevitable, but perhaps conscious that *le jetset* is slowly decamping for other hot spots, the island diligently maintains its quaintness and quiet exclusivity. Cruise ships are discouraged and there are no high-rise sterile all-inclusives. Indeed, new hotels are restricted to 12 rooms maximum (the largest by far offers only 69). Nevertheless, the A-List, from real to reel royalty who need only be identified by first name (Brad, Beyoncé, Tom, Harrison), still makes a beeline to its golden coves—or the leviathan yachts bobbing just offshore. In February, the island guest list reads like a roster from *Lifestyles of the Rich and Famous,* seeking refuge from personal trainers and stalking paparazzi (the latter often unsuccessfully).

1 Essentials

VISITOR INFORMATION

For information before you go, contact the **French Government Tourist Office** (② 202/659-7779; www.franceguide.com). There are offices at 444 Madison Ave., New York, NY 10022 (② 212/745-0960); 9454 Wilshire Blvd., Suite 715, Beverly Hills, CA 90212 (② 310/271-6665); and 205 N. Michigan Ave., Suite 3770, Chicago, IL 60601 (② 312/327-0290).

On the island, go to the **Office du Tourisme** adjacent to La Capitanerie (the Port Authority Headquarters) on the pier, quai du Général-de-Gaulle (② 590/27-87-27; www.st-barths.com).

ISLAND LAYOUT & NEIGHBORHOODS

Enchanting **Gustavia,** the island's capital and only seaport, is named for a Swedish king. This seemingly dollhouse-scale port tiptoes around a splendid harbor where Lilliputian fishing boats bob alongside leviathan yachts. Its narrow streets—lined with 18th-century Swedish or French stone buildings housing gourmet eateries, galleries, chic boutiques, and an excellent **Municipal Museum**—are easily explored on foot. Traveling northwest from Gustavia, you reach the typical villages of **Corossol** and **Colombier,** where women weave lantana straw handicrafts from hats to handbags in cotton-candy-colored *cazes* (traditional wooden houses) garlanded with flowerpots and fishing nets.

Right by the airport, **St-Jean** is the closest thing to a resort town: a tropic St-Tropez, brimming with smart boutiques, beachfront bistros, and bronzed bodies. A few minutes' drive east is serene **Lorient,** site of the first French settlement with a popular locals' beach; beautifully adorned graveyards; 19th-century Catholic church, convent, and bell tower; and reconstructed 17th-century Norman manor. Further east, **Grand Cul-de-Sac** (Point Milou) is the island's

St. Barthélemy

ATLANTIC OCEAN

Pointe Milou

Colombier Beach
Petite Anse
Flamands Beach **2-3**
Colombier **1**
Corossol
Public Beach
Anse des Cayes
Baie de St-Jean
Airport **4-6**
L'Orient
L'Orient **14**
L'Orient **16** **15**
Marigot Beach
Hôtel Guanahani **17**
Grand Cul-de-Sac Beach
18-21
40-45
46
30 **7**
10
St-Jean Beach
11-13
Vitet **22**
23
Toiny
Ferry to St. Martin
33-39
27-28
31-32
29
Gustavia
8-9
Shell Beach
Lurin
Mt. Lurin
24
25 Grand Fond
26

Airport ⊕
Beach ⌐
Mountain ▲
Ferry Route - - -

Gouverneur Beach
Grande Saline Beach

Caribbean Sea

0   1 mi
0   1 km
N

HOTELS
Baie des Anges **2**
Carl Gustaf **29**
Eden Rock **10**
Hostellerie des Trois Forces **22**
Hôtel Christopher **16**
Hôtel Guanahani and Spa **17**
Hôtel St. Barth Isle de France **3**
La Normandie **11**
Le P'tit Morne **1**
Le Sereno **18**
Le Toiny **23**
Le Village St-Jean **9**
Les Mouettes **14**
Les Ondines **21**
Manoir de Marie **12**
Salines Garden Cottages **26**
Tropical Hôtel **8**

RESTAURANTS
Au Port **31**
Bartoloméo **17**
Club Lafayette **19**
Eddy's **38**
The Hideaway **5**
L'Esprit de Saline **25**
La Mandala **30**
La Route des Boucaniers **33**
Le Gaïac **23**

Le Rivage **20**
Le Sapotillier **32**
Le Ti St. Barth **15**
Le Tamarin **24**
Maya's **46**
Wall House **28**

NIGHTLIFE
Bar de l'Oubli **40**
Bar'Tô **17**
Bête à Z'ailes **41**
Le Select **42**
Nikki Beach **7**
Taïno Lounge **16**
Yacht Club **27**

SHOPS
Diamond Genesis **35**
Gold Fingers **44**
L'Atelier de Fabienne Miot **43**
La Ligne St. Barth **13**
Laurent Eiffel **37**
Le Comptoir du Cigare **34**
Les Artisans **36**
Made in St-Barth **6**
St. Barts Style **39**
Stéphane et Bernard **45**
Sud Sud **4**

second major resort center, its wide swath of sand surveyed by top-notch eateries.

GETTING THERE

BY PLANE   Before you book your own airfare, read the section on "Packages for the Independent Traveler" in chapter 2—it can save you a bundle!

The makeshift landing strip on St. Barts has been the butt of many jokes. It's petite and accommodates only STOL (short takeoff and landing) aircraft no bigger than 19-seaters. And even on these small planes, landing on St. Barts has often been compared (and not favorably) to touching down on an aircraft carrier. The pilot must divebomb between two mountains (one with a giant white Swedish cross), then pull up abruptly: no extra charge for the thrill ride. No landings or departures are permitted after dark.

There are no nonstop flights from North America. From the United States, the principal gateways are St. Maarten, St. Thomas, and Guadeloupe. At any of these islands, you can connect to St. Barts via interisland carriers.

From St. Maarten, your best bet is **Windward Islands Airways International** (known by everybody as **Winair;** ℂ **866/466-0410** in the U.S. and Canada, or 590/27-61-01; www.fly-winair.com), which usually offers 10 to 20 daily flights to St. Barts. One-way passage excluding taxes and surcharges costs around 64€ ($80); flight duration is a mere 10 minutes. **St. Barth Commuter** (ℂ **590/27-54-54;** www.stbarthcommuter.com) flies several times daily from L'Espérance Airport in Grand Case, St. Martin, and once daily from St. Maarten's Princess Juliana Airport; fares from 40€ ($50).

Air Caraïbes (ℂ **877/772-1005** in the U.S. and Canada, or 590/82-47-00 and 590/27-71-90; www.aircaraibes.com) flights depart four or five times a day from Pointe-à-Pitre's Pôle Caraïbes Aéroport in Guadeloupe. One-way passage to St. Barts starts at 130€ ($164); trip time is 45 minutes.

BY BOAT   The *Voyager* vessels (ℂ **590/87-10-68;** www.voyager-st-barths.com), which operate from a base in Gustavia harbor, make frequent (usually daily, sometimes twice a day) runs between St. Barts and either side of St. Maarten/St. Martin. The schedule varies according to the season, but the *Voyager II* (a catamaran with room for 150 passengers) usually departs Marigot Harbor for St. Barts every morning at 9am, arriving in Gustavia at 10:30am, and at 6:15pm, arriving at 7:45pm. *Voyager I,* a single-hulled sailboat with room for 120 passengers, travels from Oyster Pond to Gustavia

> ## ⟨Tips⟩ Airline Advice
>
> Always reconfirm your return flight from St. Barts with your interisland airline. If you don't, your reservation will be canceled. *Note:* On rare occasions, a flight will be rescheduled if the booking doesn't meet its fuel quota. Also, don't check your luggage all the way through to St. Barts, or you may not see it for a few days. Instead, check your bags to your gateway connecting destination (usually St. Maarten), then take your luggage to your interisland carrier and recheck it to St. Barts. Just in case pack a change of clothes, any required medicine, and a bathing suit in your carry-on.

Wednesday and Sunday at 9am and 6:15pm, arriving 45 minutes later in Gustavia. Both vessels charge 52€ ($65) round-trip on the same day or 65€ ($81) round-trip on different days, with a one-way passage going for 37€ ($46). Fares for children under 12 are reduced in half. Advance reservations are a good idea. The technologically advanced, speedier, more luxurious, and stable catamaran **Rapid Explorer** (✆ **590/27-60-33;** www.st-barths.com/rapid-explorer) offers three daily 40-minute crossings (7, 9am, and 5pm) between St. Maarten's Chesterfield Marina in Pointe Blanche (there's an additional 12:45pm departure on Mon and Fri, and no 7am departure on Sun). The round-trip fare is 89€ ($112), children under 12 half-price, with a 60€ ($75) one-way tariff; reservations are essential.

GETTING AROUND

BY TAXI   Taxis meet all flights and are not very expensive, mostly because destinations aren't far from one another. Dial ✆ **590/27-75-81** or 590/27-66-31 for taxi service. A typical rate, from the airport to Cul-de-Sac, is 20€ ($25). Fares between 8pm and 6am, and on Sundays and holidays are 50% higher. Taxi service must be arranged between midnight and 6am—call ahead. There are taxi stands at the St-Jean airport and in Gustavia.

The government imposes official fares on **tours by taxi.** Many travelers simply approach a likely looking taxi driver and ask him to show them around. The official rates for one to three passengers are 40€ ($50) for 45 minutes, 44€ ($55) for 60 minutes, and 60€ ($75) for 90 minutes. For four or more passengers, add 8€ ($10) to each of the above-mentioned prices.

BY RENTAL CAR Nowhere will you see so many open-sided Mitsubishi Mini-Mokes, Mercedes-Benz Smart Cars, and Suzuki Samurais (the last usually included in packages, though it lacks A/C and power steering) as on St. Barts. You'll enjoy driving one, too, as long as you're handy with a stick shift and don't care about your coiffure.

Budget (© **800/472-3325** in the U.S., or 590/29-62-40; www. budget.com) offers the least stringent terms for its midwinter rentals, and some of the most favorable rates. It rents various 4WD Suzukis and automatic Daihatsus for 60€ ($75) a day or 376€ ($470) a week, with unlimited mileage. A collision-damage waiver (CDW; in French, *une assurance tous-risques*), absolving renters of all but 307€ ($384) of responsibility in the event of an accident, costs 14€ ($18) a day. For the lowest rate, you should reserve at least 3 business days before your arrival.

Hertz (© **800/654-3131** in the U.S. and Canada; www.hertz. com) operates on St. Barts through a local dealership, **Henry's Car Rental,** with branches at the airport and in St-Jean (© **590/27-71-14**). It offers open-sided Suzuki Samurais for 65€ ($81) a day, and more substantial Suzuki Sidekicks for 70€ to 90€ ($88–$113) per day. The CDW is about 12€ ($15) per day (with a 576€/$720 deductible).

At **Avis** (© **800/331-1212** in the U.S. and Canada, or 590/27-71-43; www.avis.com or www.avis-stbarth.com), you'll need a reservation a full month in advance during high season. In the winter, cars range from 68€ to 98€ ($87–$126) a day. In the off season, rentals are 44€ to 90€ ($56–$116) a day. The CDW costs 11€ to 14€ ($14–$18) extra per day (with a $625–$1,250 deductible).

Tips Staying *Au Courant*

The English-language *Saint-Barth Weekly* is an excellent (re)source for events and local gossip; you can also download the latest edition in a PDF file from the tourist office website. The bilingual *Ti Gourmet Saint-Barth* is a free, invaluable, pocket-size guidebook providing contact information, mini-reviews, and general prices of restaurants; pick one up almost anywhere. The Web-only *Insider's Guide to St. Barths* (www.sbhonline.com) offers the unvarnished dirt on arts, dining, shopping, and nightlife listings, as well as constructive readers' forums and trip reports.

Driving is on the right and maximum speed is 50kmph (31 mph). Never drive with less than half a tank of gas on St. Barts. There are only two gas stations on the island: one near the airport (closed on Sun and otherwise open only 7:30am–noon and 2–7pm—with an all-night automatic pump that usually accepts MasterCard and Visa), the other in Lorient (closed on Sun, occasionally Thurs and Sat afternoon, otherwise open 7:30am–noon and 2–5pm). All valid foreign driver's licenses are honored. *Warning:* Honk your horn furiously while going around the island's blind corners to avoid having your fenders sideswiped. The corkscrewing roller coaster roads could make a Grand Prix racer blanch: Always inspect brakes and gears before accepting a vehicle.

BY MOTORBIKE & SCOOTER   **Denis Dufau** operates two affiliates (© **590/27-70-59** and 590/27-54-83). A helmet is provided, and renters must either leave an imprint of a valid credit card or pay a 400€ ($512) deposit. Rental fees vary from 24€ to 35€ ($31–$45) per day, depending on the size of the bike. For all but the smallest models, presentation of a valid driver's license is required and you must be 21 or older.

FAST FACTS: St. Barthélemy

Banks The two main banks, which both have **ATMs,** are in Gustavia. The **Banque Française Commerciale,** rue du Général-de-Gaulle (© **590/27-62-62**), is open Monday to Friday from 7:45am to 12:30pm and 1:35 to 4pm. The **Banque Nationale de Paris,** rue du Bord-de-Mer (© **590/27-63-70**), is open Monday to Friday 8am to noon and 2 to 3:30pm, and closes at noon on Wednesday.

Currency As of press time 1€ equaled US$1.25. Before you leave home, check the current exchange rate on the Web at **www.xe.com.**

Documents U.S. and Canadian citizens need a passport to enter St. Barts. If you're flying in, you'll need to present your return or ongoing ticket. Citizens of the European Union need only an official photo ID, but passports are always recommended.

Electricity The electricity is 220-volt AC (50 cycles); U.S.-made appliances will require adapter plugs and transformers.

Emergencies Dial ② **17** for **police** or **medical** emergencies, ② **18** for **fire** emergencies.

Hospital St. Barts is not the greatest place to find yourself in a medical emergency. Except for vacationing doctors escaping their own practices in other parts of the world, it has only seven resident doctors and about a dozen on-call specialists. The island's only hospital, with the only emergency facilities, is the **Hôpital de Bruyn,** rue Jean-Bart (② **590/27-60-35**), about .4km (¼ mile) north of Gustavia. Serious medical cases are often flown to St. Maarten, Martinique, Miami, or wherever the person or his/her family specifies.

Language The official language is French, but English is widely spoken.

Pharmacies The **Pharmacie de Saint-Barth** is on quai de la République, Gustavia (② **590/27-61-82**). Its only competitor is the **Pharmacie de l'Aéroport,** adjacent to the airport (② **590/27-66-61**). Both are open Monday through Saturday from 8am to 7:30pm; on Sunday, one or the other remains open for at least part of the day.

Safety Although crime is rare, it's wise to protect your valuables. Don't leave them unguarded on the beach or in parked cars, even if locked in the trunk.

Taxes You're assessed a $5 departure tax if you're heading for another French island. Otherwise, you'll pay $10. Taxes are included in your airline ticket.

Telephone St. Barts is linked to the Guadeloupe telephone system. To call St. Barts from the United States, dial **011** (the international access code), then **590** (the country code for Guadeloupe), then **590** again, and finally the six-digit local number. To make a call to anywhere in St. Barts from within St. Barts, dial only the six-digit local number, and ignore the prefix 590. To reach an AT&T operator from anywhere on the island, dial ② **0800-99-00-11.** To reach **MCI,** dial ② **0800-99-00-19,** and to reach **Sprint,** dial ② **0800-99-00-87.**

Time When standard time is in effect in the United States and Canada, St. Barts is 1 hour ahead of the U.S. East Coast and 4 hours behind Greenwich Mean Time. When daylight saving time is in effect in the United States, clocks in New York and St. Barts show the same time—5 hours behind Greenwich Mean Time.

Tipping Hotels usually add a service charge of 10% to 15%; always ask if this is included in the price you're quoted. Restaurants typically add a service charge, too. Taxi drivers expect a tip of 10% of the fare.

Water The water on St. Barts is generally safe to drink.

Weather The climate of St. Barts is ideal: dry with an average temperature of 72°F to 86°F (22°C–30°C).

2 Accommodations

Excluding the priciest hotels, most places here are homey, comfortable, and casual. In March, it's often difficult to find lodgings unless you've made reservations far in advance. Small surprise that accommodations in high season often exceed the cost of minor plastic surgery, nearly doubling during Christmas week; a service charge of 10% to 15% is usually added to your bill. Several properties close between August and October; off-season rates plummet and often include a rental car for stays of a week or more. It should be noted that one of my favorites, the colonial-style hillside **François Plantation** (© 800/207-8071), is under new ownership which planned on changes; it may be worth checking out.

St. Barts has a sizable number of villas and apartments for rent by the week or month. Most are dotted around the island's hills—very few are on the beach. Instead of an oceanfront bedroom, you get a panoramic view. Because beach-hopping is de rigueur, regardless of where you bunk, many regulars prefer the villa experience. One of the best agencies to contact for villa or condo rentals is **St. Barth Properties,** 693 E. Central St., Suite 201, Franklin, MA 02038 (© 800/421-3396 or 508/528-7727 in the U.S. and Canada; www.stbarth.com). Peg Walsh, a longtime St. Barts aficionado, and her capable son, Tom Smyth, will make arrangements for car rentals and air travel to St. Barts, then upon your arrival book babysitters, chefs, personal trainers, and restaurant reservations. Rentals can range from a one-room "studio" villa away from the beach for $980 per week off season, up to $40,000 per week for an antiques-filled mini-palace at Christmas. Most rentals average between $2,500 and $4,000 a week between mid-December and mid-April, with discounts of 30% to 50% the rest of the year. Amenities vary according to villa, from built-in gyms to wine cellars to pools. Ms. Walsh can also arrange accommodations in all categories of St. Barts's hotels. Another excellent option with similar rates and services is **Wimco** (P.O. Box 1481, Newport, RI 02840; ℭ **800/449-1553** or 401/847-6290; www.wimco.com), whose on-island partner, **Sibarth** (ℭ **590/27-62-38;** www.sibarth.com), was founded 30 years ago by Brook and Roger Lacour. Rates and services are similar; Mrs. Lacour represents nearly 250 villas in every conceivable style (hilltop Spanish hacienda, postmodern beachfront stunner, or cozy *caze*) and size, from one to seven bedrooms.

VERY EXPENSIVE

Carl Gustaf ⟨⟨ Gustavia's most glamorous hotel oversees the town's harbor from a steep hillside. Each state-of-the-art unit is in one of a dozen pink or green, red-roofed villas. Access to each building is via a central staircase, which tests the stamina of even the most active guests. The wood-frame units are angled for maximum views of the boats bobbing far below in the bay and panoramic sunsets, best enjoyed from the plunge pool on the private patio bisecting each suite. Bedrooms aren't as large as might be expected at such prices, but they are exceedingly well furnished, especially suites nos. 30 through 33. Guests walk across Italian marble floors under a pitched ceiling to reach their luxurious bed fitted with elegant fabrics. Bathrooms are also well equipped with mosaic-clad showers (no tubs) and makeup mirrors. Beaches are within a 10-minute walk.

Chef Emmanuel Motte has revitalized the classic French kitchen (the dining room was beautifully refurbished last year), and the "Goose," as it's nicknamed, remains *the place* for sunset libations.

Rue des Normands, 97099 Gustavia, St. Barthélemy, F.W.I. ℭ **800/322-2223** in the U.S., or 590/29-79-00. Fax 590/27-82-37. www.hotelcarlgustaf.com. 14 units. Winter 1,000€–1,050€ ($1,250–$1,310) 1-bedroom suite, 1,545€ ($1,925) 2-bedroom suite; off season from 550€–600€ ($685–$750) 1-bedroom suite, from 790€ ($990) 2-bedroom suite. Rates include continental breakfast and airport transfers. AE, MC, V. **Amenities:** Restaurant; piano bar; outdoor pool; health club; sauna; deep-sea fishing; sailing; scuba diving; water-skiing; windsurfing; room service; massage; laundry service; dry cleaning; nonsmoking rooms; helicopter rides. *In room:* A/C, TV/DVD, fax, dataport, kitchenette, minibar, fridge, hair dryer, iron, safe.

Eden Rock ⟨⟨⟨ Greta Garbo checked out long ago, but this legendary hotel still occupies the most spectacular site on St. Barts, a quartzite promontory cleaving St-Jean Bay into two perfect white-sand crescents. When the island's former mayor, Remy de Haenen, bought the land years ago from an old woman, she ridiculed him for paying too much. Today, the story is part of island lore.

In 1995, the new British and Zimbabwean owners David and Jane Spencer Matthews embarked on a continuing reinvention that transformed Eden Rock into one of the Caribbean's most glamorous addresses, where even celebrities people-watch. A $25-million renovation/expansion, completed in December 2005, absorbed the adjacent Filao Beach property without sacrificing intimacy or style. Individually decorated accommodations either climb the rock or are perched steps from the water on either side. The original "Rock" rooms enchant with antiques, family heirlooms, silver fixtures, steamer trunks, four-poster beds, and watercolors of local scenes by Jane (an accomplished artist who added a marvelous gallery to the premises) and her children. Larger suites might chicly and cheekily contrast lemon chairs with lavender throw pillows, or mauve walls with mahogany armoire and marble accents. Most bathrooms are compact with shower-only. The new units include eight suites with decks opening onto the beach as well as five one- to three-bedroom beach houses with outdoor Jacuzzis and plunge pools (two have full swimming pools). The 450-sq.-m (1,500-sq.-ft.) Howard Hughes Loft Suite, atop the Main House on "the rock," features hardwood floors, three verandas offering 360-degree panoramas, and two bathrooms uniquely clad in welded copper being oxidized a luminous green by salt air.

The casual beachfront Sand Bar is a must lunch for the in-crowd. An equally incomparable dinner (and people-watching) is served at the swanky On-The-Rocks Restaurant.

Baie de St-Jean, 97133 St. Barthélemy, F.W.I. ✆ **877/563-7105** in the U.S., or 590/29-79-999. Fax 590/27-88-37. www.edenrockhotel.com. 33 units. Winter 650€–950€ ($815–$1,180) double, 1,225€–2,975€ ($1,530–$3,725) suite; off season 475€–550€ ($595–$690) double, 760€–2,015€ ($950–$2,520) suite. Extra person 105€ ($131). Rates include buffet breakfast, airport transfers, taxes, and service charges. AE, MC, V. **Amenities:** 2 restaurants; bar; snorkeling; windsurfing; room service; babysitting; laundry service; dry cleaning. *In room:* A/C, TV, dataport, minibar, hair dryer, safe.

Hôtel Christopher 🏨🏨 Set on a dramatic promontory above the ocean, this full-service hotel offers views of St. Martin and nearby islets. Its four low-rise, slate-roofed, white-sided buildings nestle amid gardens, forming a semicircle above the rocky coastline. As guests must drive about 10 minutes to reach the nearest beach, Lorient, most activities revolve around the 405-sq.-m (4,359-sq.-ft.) infinity swimming pool, the island's largest. Roomy lodgings are furnished in comely neo-colonial style and have ceiling fans and a balcony or terrace with teak lounges affording smashing water views. Oceanfront rooms have separate tub/shower combinations, while garden rooms contain semi-alfresco showers only.

Le Mango, a poolside daytime restaurant, specializes in light fare; the more formal French/Creole Le Taïno ranks among the island's top kitchens and its lounge has become an evening hot spot.

9 Pointe Milou (B.P. 571), 97133 St. Barthélemy, F.W.I. © 800/221-4542 in the U.S., or 590/27-63-63. Fax 590/27-92-92. www.st-barths.com/christopher-hotel. 42 units. Winter 421€–527€ ($526–$660) double, from 884€ ($1,125) suite; off season 275€–380€ ($344–$475) double, from 612€ ($765) suite. Rates include American breakfast, airport transfers, taxes, and service charge. 1 child under 12 can stay free in parent's room. AE, MC, V. Closed Sept–Oct 25. **Amenities:** 2 restaurants; bar; outdoor pool; gym; scuba; snorkeling; car rental; room service (noon–9:30pm); massage; babysitting; laundry service; dry cleaning; nonsmoking rooms; rooms for those w/limited mobility. *In room:* A/C, ceiling fan, TV/VCR, dataport, Wi-Fi, minibar, beverage maker, hair dryer, safe.

Hôtel Guanahani and Spa 🏨🏨 *(Kids*   Better equipped than its nearest rivals, Hôtel Manapany Cottages and Le Sereno (see below), St. Barts's largest and commercial hotel enjoys a spectacular situation on its own peninsula bracketed by two scenic beaches. In 2005 the resort underwent major restoration, blossoming with a trendy lime-plum-and-turquoise theme that mirrors the surrounding gardens where butterflies and hummingbirds flit and flutter. An openair oceanview Clarins spa facility was integrated discreetly into the bungalow village, with *hammam* (Turkish bath), lily pond, Indonesian-style daybed, and swimming pool. The pitched-roof Lilliputian cottages, trimmed in gingerbread details and painted in bold tropical colors, climb the promontory, guaranteeing broad sweeping sea views. Guanahani is not for those who have mobility problems or just don't relish huffing up and down steep slopes. There's a huge variation in price, view, size, and decor, though all units have a private patio, the latest gadgetry from DVD to LCD plasma TVs, and a brightly tiled, shower-only bathroom. Glossy interiors might contrast fabrics or walls in cocktail colors, grass mats and clusters, vivid Pop and primitive artworks, and retro Philippe Hurel to Regencystyle exotic hardwood furnishings.

Though intimately scaled, Guanahani presents an amazing array of activities. The two restaurants, airy alfresco Indigo and the formal Bartoloméo (see "Dining," later in this chapter), offer creative fusion cuisine. Staffers are remarkably cordial and beyond competent; little luxuries include chilled Hermès towels in the airport shuttle.

Grand Cul-de-Sac, 97133 St. Barthélemy, F.W.I. © 800/223-6800 in the U.S., or 590/27-66-60. Fax 590/27-70-70. www.leguanahani.com. 69 units. Winter 566€–906€ ($708–$1,133) double, from 1,025€ ($1,282) suite; off season 340€–665€ ($425–$831) double, from 685€ ($840) suite. Extra person 100€ ($125). Rates include American breakfast and round-trip airport transfers. AE, MC, V. **Amenities:**

2 restaurants; 3 bars; 2 outdoor pools; 2 tennis courts; fitness center; spa; Jacuzzi; boat rental; catamaran; fishing; sailing; scuba; windsurfing; children's programs (ages 2–6); car rental; salon; room service; massage; babysitting; laundry service; dry cleaning; horseback riding. *In room:* A/C, ceiling fan, TV, dataport, minibar, hair dryer, safe.

Hôtel St. Barth Isle de France ☪☪☪ Effortless elegance distinguishes this small, family-run hotel opening right onto glorious Flamands beach. The architecture blends the richly saturated colors of Corsica with Caribbean and colonial New England influences. Guest rooms are unusually spacious for St. Barts. Each top-notch unit contains a private patio or terrace overlooking the pool, beach, or lavishly landscaped grounds. Individual decor marries antique mahogany and rattan furniture, contemporary *bergères* (wing chairs), local straw work, Limoges porcelain, dainty French fabrics, 19th-century engravings collected from neighboring islands, and the odd dramatic flourish (cherry red lampshade or magenta throw pillow). Beds are luxurious, fitted with fine linen. Commodious marble-clad bathrooms are well-equipped with dual basins, large tubs (some with whirlpool jets), and showers.

The exquisite garden spa and quintessential beachfront *boîte,* La Case de l'Isle (sophisticated island-tinged French fare and impromptu weekly fashion shows that draw the likes of Elle MacPherson), complete the sybaritic experience.

97098 Baie des Flamands, St. Barthélemy, F.W.I. ✆ **800/810-4691** in the U.S., or 590/27-61-81. Fax 590/27-86-83. www.isle-de-france.com. 33 units. Winter 680€–1,035€ ($850–$1,295) double, from 1,250€ ($1,513) suite; off season 495€–750€ ($599–$938) double, from 995€ ($1,249) suite. Rates include continental breakfast. AE, MC, V. Closed Sept 1–Oct 15. **Amenities:** Restaurant; bar; 2 outdoor pools; tennis court; exercise room; spa; car rental; room service; babysitting; laundry service. *In room:* A/C, TV, minibar, fridge, beverage maker, hair dryer, safe.

Le Sereno Lighting designer Arnold Chan (Miami's Delano, L.A.'s Mondrian) and French decorator Christian Liaigre (New York's Mercer) collaborated on the sleek, minimalist, "ethno-Zen" design aesthetic of this latest entrant in the super-deluxe category, which debuted in December 2005. Standard rooms are cramped (in great part due to trendily oversize beds) but include private mini-gardens; larger units offer private access to the resort's 180m (600-ft.) beachfront. Scandinavian and Asian influences predominate: white-on-white color scheme with wood accents, the severe geometry (elevated black granite square wash basins, triangular chrome lamps) softened by billowing white gauzy curtains and plush armchairs. Add custom-made D. Porthault linens, Ex-Voto Paris toiletries, personal iPods and docking stations, plasma-screen TV/DVDs, in-room Wi-Fi access, individual parking spaces, not to mention beach beds and designer martini bar, and *voilà:* instant boutique hotel buzz. A much-ballyhooed spa should debut by late 2006, ratcheting up the already stratospheric chic factor.

Grand Cul-de-Sac (B.P. 19), 97133 St. Barthélemy, F.W.I. ✆ 590/52-83-00. Fax 590/27-75-47. www.lesereno.com. 37 units. Winter 600€ ($750) double, 1,100€– 1,400€ ($1,375–$1,750) suite; off season 450€ ($563) double, 750€–1,100€ ($938—$1,375) suite. Rates include breakfast and airport transfers. AE, MC, V. Closed Sept—Oct. **Amenities:** Restaurant; bar; outdoor pool; room service; massage; laundry service; dry cleaning. *In room:* A/C, ceiling fan, TV/DVD, dataport, minibar, hair dryer, safe.

Les Ondines ✿ *(Finds)* This postmodern suite-hotel, cleverly sequestered by a private garden lagoon opening onto Grand Cul-de-Sac beach, is named for a mythical sea nymph. The one- and two-bedroom suites, most with glorious ocean views, range from 60 to 139 sq. m (643–1,500 sq. ft.)—enormous by St. Barts standards. The decor stylishly fuses classic and contemporary elements. Beamed vaulted ceilings and natural wicker or teak furnishings (including four-poster beds) contrast with trompe l'oeil jungle artworks, ethereal paintings depicting the eponymous sea creatures, and brilliantly hued fabrics. All feature such necessities as high-speed Internet access and fax (two-bedroom units have washer/dryer and dishwasher). Creative touches extend to modish kitchens (carved handles of leaping fish, cool ladle-shaped black or baby blue counters) and track-lit bathrooms (stunning bas relief moldings and mosaics).

Grand Cul-de-Sac, 97133 St. Barthélemy, F.W.I. ✆ 590/27-69-64. Fax 590/52-24-41. les.ondines@wanadoo.fr. 6 units. Winter 350€–690€ ($438–$863) double; off season from 215€ ($269) double. Winter rates include continental breakfast, airport transfers, tax, and service charge. AE, MC, V. Closed Sept–Oct. **Amenities:** Outdoor pool; kayaks; 20% discount on activities at the nearby watersports center; room service. *In room:* A/C, ceiling fan, TV/DVD, kitchen, hair dryer, safe.

Le Toiny ✿✿✿ One of the Caribbean's most glamorous and chillingly expensive resorts, this Relais & Châteaux enclave contains only 15 suites, scattered among a half-dozen pastel-hued buildings clinging to a gently sloping hillside overlooking the wild windswept east coast. The nearest swimming beach, Grande Saline, is a 5-minute drive but such guests as Steve Martin and Halle Berry happily unwind and wallow by each suite's private pool. Abundant flowering shrubs protect privacy-seekers from prying eyes, though Brad Pitt was supposedly so relaxed that he dropped inhibitions and more for the paparazzi. Each sumptuous suite features chinoiserie, plush Italian fabrics, and mahogany armoires and four-poster beds swaddled in Frette linens, down pillows, and mosquito netting. Floors and coffered ceilings utilize tropical woods from teak to gaïac (a rare species that grows on-site), while giant bathrooms impress with impeccable hand-painted moldings, walk-in closet, and separate outdoor garden shower. Service ranges from merely attentive to downright intuitive, thoughtful extras from snorkeling gear to jet lag lotions. The outstanding restaurant, **Le Gaïac,** is reviewed in "Dining," below.

Anse de Toiny, 97133 St. Barthélemy, F.W.I. ℂ **800/278-6469** in the U.S., or 590/ 27-88-88. Fax 590/27-89-30. www.hotelletoiny.com. 15 units. Winter 1,550€ ($2,000) 1-bedroom suite for 2, 2,600€ ($3,250) 3-bedroom suite for up to 6; off season 775€ ($975) 1-bedroom suite for 2, 1,450€ ($1,810) 3-bedroom suite for up to 6. Rates include continental breakfast and airport transfers. AE, DC, MC, V. Closed Sept 1–Oct 25. **Amenities:** Restaurant; bar; outdoor pool; bike rental; car rental; 24-hr. room service; massage; babysitting; laundry service; dry cleaning; rooms for those w/limited mobility. *In room:* A/C, TV/DVD, fax, dataport, kitchenette, minibar, beverage maker, hair dryer, iron, safe, stair-stepper and stationary bike available upon request.

EXPENSIVE

Baie des Anges 🦀   Opening right onto the white sands of Flamands beach, this retreat has a laid-back, carefree atmosphere, as opposed to the island's many snootier, pricier options. Surrounded by gardens, the two-story property is relatively simple, yet brims with warmth and charm courtesy of truly angelic owner, Annie Turbé-Ange. Rooms open onto the sea or the courtyard with its pool, where guests gather when the Atlantic waves get too rough for swimming. Each airy, spacious unit has a balcony with kitchenette and chaise longues. Fresh decor emphasizes iridescent Caribbean blues and greens, accented by white tile floors, beamed ceilings, and quaint local crafts. Even non-guests should try the inn's sophisticated La Langouste, especially for lunch. Annie will seize your choice of crustacean barehanded from the island's largest lobster tank, then cook it perfectly with three luscious dipping sauces (start with the warm goat-cheese salad or intensely flavored fish soup).

Baie des Anges, Flamands, 97133 St. Barthélemy, FWI. ℂ **590/27-63-61.** Fax 590/ 27-83-44. www.hotelbaiedesanges.fr. 10 units. Winter 210€–350€ ($265–$435) double, 24€ ($30) additional person; off season 120€–230€ ($150–$285) double, 32€ ($40) additional person. MC, V. **Amenities:** Restaurant; bar; outdoor pool; limited room service; babysitting; laundry service. *In room:* A/C, ceiling fan, TV, dataport, kitchenette (in some), hair dryer, safe.

MODERATE

Hostellerie des Trois Forces ⭐ *(Finds)*   Breton astrologer Hubert Delamotte (a Gemini) and wife Ginette created this hilltop sanctuary dedicated to enriching the flow between life's primary three forces: mind, body, and spirit. Yet it's too special to be labeled just another New Age retreat; patrons of all persuasions—seers to CEOs, Meryl Streep to Ram Dass—seek refuge and refreshment here. Even the site was divined by the ancient eco-art of geomancy: organizing environments to optimize harmony between user and space. The inn occupies panoramic grounds in Vitet about a 10-minute drive from Cul-de-Sac and Lorient beaches. The gingerbread bungalows are staggered to maximize privacy and sweeping ocean vistas. Each is named for a sign of the zodiac and decorated with the appropriate color scheme: theatrical scarlet for Leo (natural performers), meditative navy for Pisces, womblike pink for nurturing Cancer. Astrology even influenced Hubert's handmade beds (Libras, the Zodiac's romantics, wallow in a stately four-poster with lacy linen and gauzy mosquito netting). Holistic services include massage therapy, yoga, past-life regression therapy, osteopathy, and psychic readings. Hubert believes, "The stomach is a spiritual gate," and his on-site restaurant's superlative French fare earned him membership in France's prestigious gastronomic order Confrérie de la Marmite d'Or. The excellent, affordable wine list will delight any oenophile.

Morne Viet, 97133 St. Barthélemy, F.W.I. ⓒ **590/27-61-25.** Fax 590/27-81-38. www.3forces.net. 7 cottages. Winter 202€ ($250) double, 40€ ($50) additional person; off season 118€ ($148) double. AE, MC, V. **Amenities:** Restaurant; outdoor pool; laundry service. *In room:* A/C, kitchenette (in 2 units), fridge, safe.

Le P'tit Morne ⭐ *(Value)*   This is hardly the most luxurious lodging on an island legendary for its glamorous five-star hotels. But its relatively low rates, remote but remarkably pretty hillside setting 10 minutes' drive from Petite Anse and Flamands beaches, and the warm welcome extended by island-born owners, M. and Mme. Felix and their daughter Marie-Joëlle, make it a worthy vacation site. Colonial-influenced buildings hold commodious units with completely unpretentious furniture, comfortable king-size beds, aging but functional kitchens, and compact shower-only bathrooms. Each has a terrace or balcony units designed to catch the trade winds while offering breathtaking views of the crashing surf and tiny offshore cays. The best and newest room, "New Moon," offers tasteful hardwood furnishings, dramatic red-and-black color scheme, a panoramic sun deck cleverly carved from the cliff, a private pergola, and its own outdoor dining room.

Colombier (B.P. 14), 97095 St. Barthélemy, F.W.I. ☎ **590/52-95-50.** Fax 590/27-84-63. www.timorne.com. 15 units. Winter 163€–230€ ($204–$288) double; off season 75€–150€ ($94–$188) double. AE, MC, V. Closed Sept. **Amenities:** Outdoor pool; limited room service; babysitting. *In room:* A/C, TV, kitchen, fridge, beverage maker, iron.

Les Mouettes *(Value* While these well-kept if basic bungalows are nothing special, their price and admirable beachfront situation rank them among the island's better bargains. Families particularly appreciate the convenience: Each unit features an additional twin bed or pullout sofa, and outdoor patio with kitchenette and grill, which you can stock at the minimart and sublime *boulangerie* (bakery) revered for its almond croissants and éclairs across the street. The location, sandwiched between sand and a major intersection, is also its biggest drawback; weekend noise and traffic snarls are common but only the cheapest bungalow, no. 7, abuts the street itself (and lacks full ocean view). The mostly duplex bungalows sport red corrugated iron roofs, white gingerbread trim, and bright aqua railings; interiors are similarly simple yet appealing with handsome armoires, handcrafted straw lamps, and shell-patterned fabrics. The cordial, English-speaking owners (the Gréaux family) genuinely enjoy sharing advice and anecdotes with guests.

Lorient, 97133 St. Barthélemy, F.W.I. ☎ **590/27-77-91.** Fax 590/27-68-19. www.st-barths.com/hotel-les-mouettes. 7 units. Winter 135€–190€ ($169–$238) double; off season from 80€ ($100) double. No credit cards. *In room:* A/C, ceiling fan, kitchen.

Le Village St-Jean *(R* This family-owned cottage colony hideaway, a 5-minute hike uphill from St-Jean Beach, typifies what the French call a *hôtel bourgeois,* offering charm, warmth, comfort, and value. Stone-and-redwood buildings cling precariously to the hill, holding five basic rooms (with fridge only) and 20 cottages with well-equipped kitchens, tiled shower-only bathrooms, sun decks or gardens, tiered living rooms, and balconies with retractable awnings and hammocks strategically placed to enjoy the breeze and spectacular ocean views. Each is attractively appointed with polished hardwood furnishings, abstract or primitive artworks, fresh flowers daily, and striped or solid fabrics in bold colors. The complex has a popular Italian restaurant, **La Terrazza,** with a sprawling terrace on a platform above the sloping terrain.

Baie de Saint-Jean (B.P. 623), 97133 St. Barthélemy, F.W.I. ☎ **590/27-61-39.** Fax 590/27-77-96. www.villagestjeanhotel.com. 25 units. Winter 190€ ($238) double, 230€–420€ ($288–$525) 1-bedroom cottage, 570€ ($713) 2-bedroom cottage; off season 110€ ($138) double, 145€–280€ ($182–$350) 1-bedroom cottage,

330€ ($413) 2-bedroom cottage. Extra person 40€–70€ ($50–$88). Hotel rooms include continental breakfast. AE, MC, V. **Amenities:** Restaurant; bar; Internet cafe; outdoor pool; Jacuzzi; car rental; limited room service; babysitting; laundry service; dry cleaning. *In room:* A/C, ceiling fan, kitchen, fridge, hair dryer.

Manoir de Marie ✹ *(Finds)*   The centerpiece and *pièce de résistance* of this unusual retreat is a 1610 Norman manor disassembled and rebuilt two minutes' walk from Plage de Lorient in the 1970s. Shortly thereafter, eight half-timbered bungalows in ersatz Norman style were erected in the enchanted garden, each facing a reflecting pool accented with water lilies, a natural stone waterfall, a fountain, and Rodin-inspired statuary. Guests won't have a lot to do with the main house, other than to check in and chitchat from time to time with the on-site managers. But beachcombers will enjoy prized privacy, seclusion, and cost-efficiency, thanks to kitchens within six units. Antillean rustic accommodations complement the beamed ceilings and stone floors, with brown, white, and pink color schemes, embroidered white-linen hassocks, and brass or four-poster beds draped in tulle. Each bathroom has either a small, tub/shower combination or a separate alfresco shower. Although there is no restaurant, guests can enjoy custom-catered picnics (yes, even lobster and champagne) on the pool's palm-shaded wooden deck.

Route de Saline, Lorient, 97133 St. Barthélemy, F.W.I. ℂ **590/27-79-27.** Fax 590/27-65-75. www.lemanoirstbarth.com. 8 units. Winter 130€–300€ ($163–$375) double; off season 90€–210€ ($113–$263) double. AE, MC, V. **Amenities:** Bar; outdoor pool; babysitting; laundry service; dry cleaning. *In room:* A/C, ceiling fan, TV, kitchen (in most), minibar, beverage maker (in most), hair dryer, no phone.

Salines Garden Cottages ✹ *(Finds)*   These stylish gingerbread *cazes* (traditional Creole houses), three with kitchenette, nestle amid flowering trees and bushes just steps from one of the island's loveliest beaches. Each has a private tiled terrace shaded by bougainvillea. Interiors enchant with brilliant batik fabrics, baby blue basins, island crafts in various media, and four-poster or cast-iron beds. Asian and African antiques, collected by the peripatetic owners, enliven public spaces and grounds. Romantics and independent types can cherish utter seclusion while finding sustenance at two fine restaurants within walking distance.

Anse de Saline, 97133 St. Barthélemy, F.W.I. ℂ **590-51-04-44.** Fax 590/27-64-65. www.salinesgarden.com. 5 units. Winter 140€–190€ ($175–$263) double; off-season 70€–100€ ($88–$125) double; 25€ ($31) additional person. Continental breakfast, airport transfers, taxes, and service charges included. AE, MC, V. **Amenities:** Outdoor pool; babysitting; laundry service. *In room:* A/C, ceiling fan, kitchen (in some), hair dryer, safe.

Tropical Hôtel *(Value)*   The facade of this small, unpretentious hotel looks like a picture-postcard Caribbean colonial inn. Originally built in 1981 and restored in 1997, it's perched on a hillside about 40m (130 ft.) above St-Jean Beach. Each immaculate room contains a shower-only bathroom, a king-size bed with good mattress and lace coverlet, tile floors, beamed ceiling, charming straw or brick accents, and a fridge. Nine units have sea views and balconies; no. 11's patio opens onto a garden so lush it resembles a miniature jungle.

The hotel has an antiques-filled hospitality center where guests read, listen to music, or order drinks and snacks at a paneled bar. The pool is small, but watersports are available on the beach.

St-Jean (B.P. 147), 97133 St. Barthélemy, F.W.I. ℂ **800/223-9815** in the U.S., or 590/27-64-87. Fax 590/27-81-74. www.tropical-hotel.com. 21 units. Winter 200€– 230€ ($250–$288) double; off season 95€–145€ ($119–$184) double. Rates include continental breakfast. AE, MC, V. Closed June to mid-July. **Amenities:** Outdoor pool; car rental; babysitting; laundry service. *In room:* A/C, TV, ceiling fan, dataport, fridge, hair dryer.

INEXPENSIVE

La Normandie   This modest, unassuming, family-owned hotel (what the French term an *auberge antillaise*—Antillean inn) offers no facilities other than its clean, though somewhat dreary, accommodations. But what do you expect for this kind of money on St. Barts? Set near the intersection of two major roads, about 200m (660 ft.) from Lorient Beach, it offers motel-inspired bedrooms brightened slightly by pink or powder blue walls and local crafts. The more expensive, larger units lie adjacent to the tiny pool and contain TVs. Less expensive, smaller rooms open to the highway. The shower-only bathrooms are too cramped, but well kept.

97133 Lorient, St. Barthélemy, F.W.I. ℂ **590/27-61-66.** Fax 590/27-98-83. 8 units. Winter 58€–69€ ($73–$86) double; off season 54€–58€ ($67–$73) double. MC, V. **Amenities:** Outdoor pool. *In room:* A/C, TV (in some), dataport, fridge, beverage maker.

3 Dining

Fueled by young French chefs on the fast-track to Michelin favor, the St. Barts dining experience is exquisitely epicurean yet exasperatingly expensive. It remains one of the few destinations where hotel dining rooms almost invariably excel. But more casual beachfront, hilltop, and harbor-side *boîtes* abound. Many specialize in Creole fare that detonates the palate. Prized tables are often booked along with hotel reservations in high season (unless you tip your concierge quite well). You might sneak in at lunch or the bar (tapas and sushi are growing trends), both generally cheaper options. Many eateries also offer a less expensive *plat du jour* or *table d'hôte* prix-fixe menu.

IN GUSTAVIA

Au Port FRENCH Unpretentious ambience, straightforward brasserie fare, generous portions, and an utter lack of snobbery have made this restaurant an enduring island favorite. Set one floor above street level, in the center of town, it features neo-colonial decor with sailboat models and antique accessories. Appetizers feature such treats as creamy, vanilla-infused Caribbean pumpkin soup and a homemade duck foie gras. Fine fresh seafood specialties include sautéed scallops in a lime sauce and shrimp dumplings with Caribbean vegetables. Meat and poultry are also treated with tender loving care, especially the breast of honey-roasted duck and the typical island dish—goat stew with bananas au gratin.

Rue Sadi-Carnot. ✆ **590/27-62-36.** Reservations recommended, especially for veranda tables. Main courses 16€–32€ ($19–$38); fixed-price menu 33€ ($40). AE, MC, V. Mon–Sat 6:30–10pm. Closed June 15–July 31.

Eddy's *(Value* CREOLE Charismatic Eddy Stackelborough has long satisfied in-the-know locals and regulars with simple but honest island fare (scrumptious green papaya salad, barbecued ribs, chicken in coconut sauce, passion fruit mousse). The setting resembles a Caribbean translation of *The Secret Garden* with a virtual jungle punctuated by ethno-tropic trappings (masks, boldly hued art naïf, vetyver grass mats, and woven ceiling). It's a miracle how Eddy keeps prices affordable by most standards (perhaps the roving location keeps rents down).

Rue du Général du Gaulle, Gustavia. ✆ **590/27-54-17.** Main courses 15€–22€ ($19–$27). No credit cards. Daily noon–10:30pm.

La Mandala *★★* *(Finds* THAI/EUROPEAN The location alone—a house on Gustavia's steepest street with a dining deck overlooking a swimming pool—guarantees memorable cocktails and tapas as the setting sun fireballs across the harbor. But owner/chefs Kiki and Boubou (Christophe Barjettas and Olivier Megnin) animate every facet with their fun, funky sensibility from whimsical decor (Buddhas, hand-shaped ashtrays, enormous earthenware frogs) to creative globetrotting cuisine (snapper tempura with kimchee, mahimahi with mango salad and coriander sauce, or duck glazed with soy sauce and caramel). Kiki's exemplary French culinary training shines through in such decadent desserts as the warm chocolate tart.

Rue de la Sous Prefecture. ℂ **590/27-96-96.** Reservations recommended. Main courses 22€–32€ ($28–$40). AE, MC, V. Daily 7–11pm; sushi and cocktails 5–7pm.

La Route des Boucaniers *Finds* CREOLE

Having written a five-volume primer, owner/chef Francis Delage is considered the definitive authority on Creole cuisine. The decor evokes a rum shack—there's even a boat wreck—but this belies his sophisticated fare, which has lured the likes of Cameron Diaz and Steven Seagal. The chef's pride and joy is a large bowl of fresh fish, shellfish, and octopus huddled together in a silken red-bean purée. Other surprises await, especially the avocado salad given zest by chewy flakes of dried cod swimming in fiery *sauce chien* (spicy pepper-based sauce). Generous use of *beurre rouge* (lobster butter) and heavily-spiced *lardons* (strips of salt pork) enhance the menu's rich flavors and textures. Not what your doctor ordered, but irresistible.

Rue de Bord de Mer, Gustavia. ℂ **590/27-73-00.** Reservations required in winter. Main courses 18€–36€ ($22–$43). AE, MC, V. Daily 10am–10pm.

Le Sapotillier FRENCH/SEAFOOD

Dashing Austrian-born Adam Rajner presides over one of the most elegant evenings on St. Barts. Dine outside on the candlelit patio under a magnificent sapodilla tree or inside the clapboard-covered Antillean bungalow where brick and stone walls hung with vivid art naïf and hand-painted chairs contrast with splendid china and linens. Rajner's presentation and preparation are equally bold and artful. He dazzles with simple yet textbook frogs' legs meunière or duck confit, as well as more innovative juxtapositions: witness snail lasagna with spinach and walnuts in Roquefort zabaglione, or sautéed foie gras with caramelized pineapples and a dusting of Szechuan pepper. Two classic French specialties utilize chicken and pigeon flown in fresh from Bresse, a city revered throughout Europe for its poultry. The chicken is served *en cocotte* (in a stew) and the pigeon with snow peas and spaetzle (tiny egg noodles). Ask Adam to suggest the perfect pairing from his comprehensive if pricey wine list, then let the flavors, ambience, and service transport you.

Rue Sadi-Carnot. ℂ **590/27-60-28.** Reservations required. Main courses 28€–36€ ($35–$45). MC, V. Nov–Apr daily 6:30–10:30pm. Closed May–Oct.

Wall House FRENCH/SEAFOOD

Charming owners Franck Mathevet and Denis Chevallier perfected the recipe for success: dazzling harbor views, warm service, lively ambience, and bistro fare with flair at fair prices. Franck specializes in rotisserie items—witness spit-roasted five-spice honey-pineapple duck. He

---

Finds **Picnic Fare on St. Barts**

St. Barts is so expensive that many visitors buy at least one meal (perhaps a "gourmet lunch to go" package) from an epicurean takeout deli aka *traiteur*. The most centrally located, **La Rôtisserie,** rue du Roi Oscar II (℃ 590/27-63-13), is proud of its endorsement by Fauchon, the world-famous food store in Paris. On display are bottles of wine, crocks of mustard, pâté, herbs, caviar, chocolate, and exotic oils and vinegars, as well as takeout *plats du jour* from pâtés to *pissaladière* (onion tart) usually sold by the gram, costing around 8€ to 18€ ($10–$22) for a portion suitable for one. The place is open Monday through Saturday from 7am to 7pm, Sunday from 7am to noon; go early for the freshest items. American Express, MasterCard, and Visa are accepted. There are two other worthy *traiteurs* in St-Jean. **Maya's To Go** (℃ 590/29-83-70) is operated by the famed eponymous island restaurateurs (see below). Its windswept patio (with Wi-Fi access) is a great place to watch the planes and enjoy such takeout specialties as delectable salads (tabouleh, lentil), quiches, lasagna, lobster, and rack of lamb. American-born I. B. Charneau named **Kiki é Mo** (℃ 590/27-90-65) after her sons Keefer and Marlon. It channels the Italian *salumerias* of her Short Hills, New Jersey, childhood with predictably delish pizzas, pastas, and panini—and the best espresso on island.

---

also juggles ingredients and influences like a culinary prestidigitator: signature dishes include monkfish with black pepper sauce and merlot-poached pears, mahimahi in lime-ginger mayonnaise, sautéed foie gras on gingerbread with rhubarb compote, and poached egg-and-lobster brioche. The prix-fixe lunch and five-course dinner are remarkable values. The cozy salon-wine bar, which hosts rotating art exhibits, is a marvelous spot to sip an aperitif or after-dinner cordial.

La Pointe. ℃ 590/27-71-83. www.wall-house-stbarth.com. Reservations recommended. Main courses 14€–29€ ($18–$36). AE, MC, V. Lunch Mon–Sat noon–2pm; dinner daily 7–9:30pm. Closed Sept–Oct.

IN THE GRANDE SALINE BEACH AREA

L'Esprit Salines ℛ ASIAN/CREOLE   Three Maya's alumni—Christophe Cretin, Guillaume Hennequin and chef Jean-Charles (J. C.) Guy—collaborated on this supremely sensual beachside bistro. The open-air, pastel-painted cottage nestles between a virtual jungle garden and a gunmetal bluff. Crashing waves, slinky Europop, and a model (in both senses) waitstaff enhance the seductive ambience. The daily-changing menu takes the confusion out of fusion cuisine: you might begin with Moroccan pumpkin soup, segue into Thai seared scallops with passion fruit sauce or grilled free-range chicken with rosemary, *balsamico*, and St. Barts honey, then finish with sublime *gâteau aux deux chocolats Valrhona*. Beware the luscious but lethal lemon grass rum that caps dinner.

Plage de Saline. 𝄐 **590/52-46-10.** Reservations recommended. Main courses 23€–35€ ($27–$42). AE, MC, V. Open Wed–Mon noon—10pm. Closed Sept–Oct.

Le Tamarin 𝄐 FRENCH/CREOLE   This offbeat bistro sits isolated amid rocky hills and forests on the road to Plage de Saline, in a thatched gingerbread cottage with teak-and-bamboo interior. Lunch is the more animated meal, with most customers dining in T-shirts and bathing suits. If you have to wait, savor an aperitif in one of the hammocks stretched under a tamarind tree. The menu focuses on light, summery fare that complements the streaming, steamy sun. Examples include gazpacho, carpaccio of fresh salmon and tuna, chilled spiny lobster with curried mayonnaise, and chicken roasted with soy sauce, lemon, and ginger. Service can be erratic (as is the schedule—call ahead), but if you're in a rush, you shouldn't be here. It's the perfect place for a lazy afternoon on the beach.

Plage de Saline. 𝄐 **590/27-72-12.** Reservations required for dinner. Main courses 24€–36€ ($30–$45). AE, MC, V. Nov 16–Apr 30 daily noon–5pm; Tues–Sun 7–9pm. Closed May 1–Nov 15.

IN THE GRAND CUL-DE-SAC BEACH AREA

Bartoloméo 𝄐 FRENCH/MEDITERRANEAN   Although this deluxe dining choice is located at one of the island's most exclusive hotels, Bartoloméo manages to be unthreatening, informally sophisticated, and gracefully upscale. Incomparable pianist Charles Darden sets the soigné tone while diners choose from a frequently changing menu. The chefs inventively counterpoint ingredients: Standouts include Chilean sea bass with ratatouille, sautéed cod with goat cheese and black truffles, or saddle of lamb with black peppercorns and oranges. No wonder it serves as main venue for the Guanahani's annual month-long Gourmet Festival that precedes high season, with such guest chefs as Burgundy's triple-Michelin-starred Marc Meneau and top Napa toque Cindy Pawlcyn (from Mustards, Cindy's Backstreet Kitchen).

In the Hôtel Guanahani, Grand Cul-de-Sac. ✆ **590/52-90-14.** Reservations recommended, especially for nonguests. Main courses 35€–55€ ($44–$69). AE, DC, MC, V. Daily 7:30–10pm. Closed Sept.

Club Lafayette FRENCH/INTERNATIONAL This is no fast-food beach joint. Lunching in the sun here, at a cove on the eastern end of the island, is like taking a meal at your own private beach club—and a very expensive one at that. The congenial owner/chefs, Toulouse-born Nadine and Georges Labau justly if cheekily claim "the elite meet to eat" here. Fortunately their tongue-in-chic attitude informs everything from the hot pink pavilion itself to impromptu fashion shows highlighting the latest finds from the on-site boutique. Needless to say, the generally competent food is outrageously overpriced, but you're paying for the view (of beach and celebrity alike). You might begin with a warm foie gras with apples. Next, try the veal with morel sauce; Chinese mahimahi in ginger, soy, and sesame oil; or the island's best and costliest meal-size lobster salad. Desserts include everything from a rich chocolate *marquise* to *croustillant au chocolat* (phyllo dough filled with chocolate). Grand Cul-de-Sac. ✆ **590/27-62-51.** Reservations required. Main courses 20€–70€ ($25–$88). AE, MC, V. Daily noon–5pm. Closed May–Oct.

Le Rivage ✿ FRENCH/CARIBBEAN This restaurant offers the kind of offhanded charm and oversize Gallic egos that you'd expect in a chic but somewhat disorganized beach resort in the south of France. Set on a covered veranda built on piers above the lagoon, about half the tables are open to views of the stars. During the day, no one objects to bathing suits at the table; at night, fashionably casual is the preferred dress. Sterling signature items include beef carpaccio; tempting "supersalads," the most popular of which combines shrimp with smoked salmon and melted goat cheese; any grilled catch of the day; a seafood platter of raw shellfish (scallops, clams, and crayfish), artfully arranged on a bed of seaweed; a full complement of such Creole specialties as *boudin noir* (blood sausage) and *accras de morue* (beignets of codfish). Finish with the textbook *tarte tatin*.

St. Barth Beach Hotel, Grand Cul-de-Sac. ✆ **590/27-82-42.** Reservations recommended in winter. Main courses 16€–25€ ($20–$31). AE, DISC, MC, V. Daily noon–10pm.

IN THE PUBLIC BEACH AREA
Maya's ✿ CREOLE/THAI/FRENCH After several seasons, this beachfront *boîte* just northwest of Gustavia remains the island's premier stargazing (in both senses) spot, thanks to its artful simplicity

and preferential treatment for regulars. The much-rebuilt Antillean house with almost no architectural charm attracts crowds of luminaries from the worlds of media, fashion, and entertainment. It's the kind of *pieds dans l'eau* (feet in the water), picnic table–on-the-beach place you might find on Martinique, where its French Creole chef, Maya Beuzelin-Gurley, grew up. Maya stresses "clean, simple" food with few adornments other than island herbs and lime juice. You might follow tomato, arugula, and endive salad, with grilled fish in sauce *chien* (hot) or "sailor's chicken" marinated in fresh chives, lime juice, and hot peppers. Almost no cream is used in any dish, further endearing the place to its slim-hipper-than-thou clientele. Views face west and south, ensuring glorious sunset watching.

Public Beach. ✆ **590/27-75-73**. Reservations required in winter. Main courses 30€–36€ ($36–$43). AE, MC, V. Mon–Sat 7–10pm. Closed Sept–Oct.

AT POINTE MILOU

Le Ti St. Barth FRENCH/CARIBBEAN   You'll either love or hate this hilltop aerie, depending on how you fit into an environment that manages to be frenetic, stylishly permissive, and Franco-chauvinistic all at the same time. Thierry de Badereau and partner Carole Gruson have crafted a winkingly naughty place where the food is almost incidental to the hip, hopping, happening scene. Very pretty, provocatively garbed diners gyrate atop tables theatrically swathed in Indian silk to blaring Euro-pop and soca. Anything from high tides to full moons provides an excuse to celebrate with pagan abandon; theme parties are legendary (Thursday's "Sexy Fashion Show" features lingerie that would make Frederick's of Hollywood blush). Wildly uneven dishes range from the affordable and practical (locally smoked fish, barbecued ribs, wahoo in Creole sauce, grilled filet of duck with cranberry sauce) to the exorbitant (local lobster garnished with truffles). Afterward, dance off such suggestively named desserts as "Daddy's Balls" (passion fruit sorbet) and "Nymph's Thighs" (lemon cake with vanilla custard).

Pointe Milou. ✆ **590/27-97-71**. Reservations recommended. Main courses 27€–64€ ($32–$77). AE, MC, V. Daily 7pm to around midnight or later, depending on business.

IN THE ST-JEAN BEACH AREA

The Hideaway ☆ *Value* INTERNATIONAL   How can you not love a place that advertises "corked wine, warm beer, lousy food, view of the car park" with a staff "hand-picked from the sleaziest dives, mental institutions, and top-security prisons?" Savvy locals and celebrity regulars (Cameron Diaz, Paul Simon) know that the sound system, food, and prices rock at this beloved, boisterous haunt nicknamed Chez Andy after droll Brit owner Andrew Hall. Worthy specialties include Gorgonzola salad with walnuts and bacon, snapper with coriander and lime, and thin-crust pizzas (try the four-cheese or tuna) from the wood-burning oven. Andy will finish your evening (and you) off with a bottomless carafe of free vanilla or orange rum.

Vaval Center, St-Jean. ✆ **590/27-63-62**. Reservations recommended. Main courses 16€–24€ ($20–$30). AE, MC, V. Tues–Sun noon–2pm and 7–10:30pm.

IN THE TOINY COAST AREA

Le Gaïac 𝕽𝕽 FRENCH   This swooningly romantic restaurant is for folks who want to dine among the rich and jaded at Le Toiny—St. Barts's most expensive hotel—but aren't willing to mortgage their futures for a room. Guests dine in an open-air pavilion adjacent to the resort's infinity pool, with a view that sweeps out over the wide blue sea. Lunchtime menu items—perhaps ravioli with red pepper and goat cheese—are simple yet exquisitely prepared, and the sumptuous all-you-can-eat Sunday champagne brunch is a must for island movers-and-shakers. At dinner, Alan Landry's piano stylings complement the beautifully orchestrated tastes and textures. Top examples include rack and saddle of lamb perfumed with rosemary, thyme, and laurel served with eggplant marmalade; wood pigeon baked in a clay shell; roast duck in orange-cardamom sauce; and shrimp and truffle risotto with garlic cream. The first-rate cuisine, setting, and service make for a memorable meal.

In Hôtel Le Toiny, Anse de Toiny. ✆ **590/27-88-88**. Reservations recommended in winter. Main courses lunch 20€–29€ ($25–$37), dinner 30€–40€ ($38–$50). AE, DC, MC, V. Mon–Sat noon–2:30pm and 7–9:30pm; Sun 11am–2:30pm. Closed Sept 1–Oct 23.

4 Beaches

St. Barts has nearly 20 white-sand beaches. Few are crowded, even in winter; all are public and free. Topless sunbathing is common (nudity is officially permitted on two). The best known is **St-Jean Beach** 𝕽𝕽, which is actually two beaches divided by the Eden Rock promontory. It offers watersports, restaurants, and a few hotels, as well as some shady areas: There's fine snorkeling west of the rock. Lovely, comparatively uncrowded **Flamands Beach** 𝕽𝕽, to the west, is a wide, long beach with a few small hotels and some areas shaded by lantana palms. In winter, the surf here can be rough, though rarely hazardous.

Lorient Beach, on the north shore, is quiet and calm, with shady areas. An offshore reef tames breakers save on the wilder western end, where French surfer dudes hang out and hang ten.

For a beach with hotels, restaurants, and watersports, **Grand Cul-de-Sac Beach** ☞, on the northeast shore, fits the bill. It's narrow, breezy (the preferred site for windsurfing), and protected by a reef.

North of Gustavia, the rather unromantic-sounding **Public Beach** is a combination of sand and pebbles more popular with boaters than swimmers—it's the location of the St. Barts Sailing School. There is no more beautiful place on the island, however, to watch the boats at sunset, perhaps over the imaginative Asian/Creole/Latin tapas—cod carpaccio to coconut ceviche—at trendy **Do Brazil** (a favored lunch spot as well), run by Kiki and Boubou of La Mandala (see "Dining," earlier in this chapter). Located near a small fishing village, **Corossol Beach** offers a typical glimpse of French life, St. Barts style. This is a calm, protected beach, with a charming little **seashell museum.**

South of Gustavia, **Shell Beach** or **Grand Galet** is awash with seashells. Rocky outcroppings protect this beach from strong waves. It's also the scene of many a weekend party.

Gouverneur Beach ☞☞, on the southern coast, can be reached by driving south from Gustavia to Lurin. Turn at the Santa Fe restaurant (stop for drinks on the way back to savor sensational sunset views) and head down a narrow road. The uncrowded strand is gorgeous (as are the mostly nude beachcombers), ringed by steep cliffs overlooking St. Kitts, Saba, and Statia (St. Eustacius), but there's no shade. You'll find excellent snorkeling off the point. **Grande Saline Beach** ☞☞, to the east of Gouverneur Beach, is reached by driving up the road from the commercial center in St-Jean; a short walk past disused salt ponds over the sand dunes and you're here. Lack of shade doesn't deter the buff sunbathers in the buff (the late JFK, Jr., was famously photographed here), or the many families who find the shallow ocean bottom ideal for swimming.

Colombier Beach ☞ is difficult to get to but well worth the effort. It can only be reached by boat or by taking a rugged goat path from Petite Anse past Flamands Beach, a 30-minute walk. The lookouts here are breathtaking; several adjacent coves are usually patrolled only by peacocks and mules. Shade, seclusion, and snorkeling are found here, and you can pack a lunch and spend the day. Locals call it Rockefeller's Beach because for many years David Rockefeller owned the surrounding property (Harrison Ford allegedly bought his blue pyramidical house).

5 Sports & Other Outdoor Pursuits

FISHING   Anglers are fond of the waters around St. Barts. From March to July, they catch mahimahi; in September, wahoo. Atlantic bonito, barracuda, and marlin also turn up frequently. **Marine Service,** quai du Yacht-Club, Gustavia (℃ **590/27-70-34;** www. st-barths.com/marine.service), rents a 9m (30-ft.) Phoenix specifically outfitted for big-game fishing. A full day for four costs 1,300€ ($1,625), which includes a captain and first mate. The outfitter also offers shore fishing on a 7.6m (25-ft.) day cruiser, which tends to remain close to the island's shoreline, searching for tuna, barracuda, and other fish. A full-day excursion, with fishing for up to four, costs 457€ ($561).

SCUBA DIVING   **Marine Service,** quai du Yacht-Club, in Gustavia (℃ **590/27-70-34;** www.st-barths.com/marine.service), is the island's most complete watersports facility. It operates from a one-story building at the edge of a marina on the opposite, quieter side of Gustavia's harbor. Catering to both beginners and advanced divers, the outfit is familiar with at least 20 unusual sites scattered throughout the protected offshore Réserve Marine de St-Barth. The most interesting include Pain de Sucre off Gustavia harbor and the remote **Grouper,** west of St. Barts, close to the uninhabited cay known as Île Forchue. The only relatively safe wreck dive, the rusting hulk of *Kayali,* a trawler that sank in deep waters in 1994 is recommended only for experienced divers. A resort course, including two open-water dives, costs 70€ ($93), as does a "scuba review," for rusty certified divers, while a one-tank dive for certified divers begins at 55€ ($69). Multidive packages are available. An equally reliable Gustavia outfit for both diving and snorkeling is **Plongée Caraïbes,** Quai de la République next to the post office (℃ **590/27-55-94;** www.plongee-caraibes.com); rates are competitive.

SNORKELING   Hundreds of shallow areas right off beaches such as Anse des Cayes teem with colorful aquatic life. **Marine Service** (see above) runs daily snorkeling expeditions. An 8-hour excursion (9am–5pm), including a full French-style picnic, open bar, all equipment, and exploration of two separate snorkeling sites, costs 105€ ($131). They can also rent snorkeling gear and suggest top locations.

WINDSURFING   Windsurfing is one of the most popular sports here. Try **Wind Wave Power,** Grand Cul-de-Sac (℃ **590/27-82-57),** open daily from 9:30am to 5pm. Windsurfing costs 25€ ($31) per hour, and professional instructors are on hand. Reservations are recommended, especially in high season.

6 Shopping

Duty-free St. Barts offers liquor and French perfumes at some of the lowest prices in the Caribbean—often cheaper than in France itself. You'll find good buys, albeit a limited selection, in haute couture, crystal, porcelain, watches, and other luxuries. Gustavia's Quai de la République (nicknamed "rue du Couturier") matches Paris's rue du Faubourg St. Honoré or avenue Montaigne for designer boutiques, including Bulgari, Cartier, Dior, and Hermès. If you're in the market for **island crafts,** look for intricately woven straw goods (baskets, bags, bonnets) and striking art naïf including quaint models of Creole *cazes* and fishing boats.

Diamond Genesis   This well-respected jeweler maintains an inventory of designs strongly influenced by European tastes. Although the prices can go as high as 10,000€ ($12,500), an appealing and more affordable 18-karat-gold depiction of St. Barts sells for around 200€ ($250). You can also peruse the selection of watches by Jaeger Lecoultre, available only through this store, as well as Breitling, Chanel, and Tag Heuer. 12 rue du Général-de-Gaulle/Les Suites du Roi Oscar II. (C) **590/27-66-94.**

Gold Fingers ⌖   This is the largest purveyor of luxury goods on St. Barts. The entire second floor is devoted to perfumes and crystal, the street level to jewelry and watches. Prices are usually 15% to 20% less than equivalent retail goods sold stateside. Ask about sales when you visit. Rue de la France. (C) **590/27-64-66.**

La Ligne St. Barth ⌖   This store features Hervé Brin's scents and skin care products extracted from Caribbean flora according to generations-old recipes. Exquisitely packaged offerings include papaya peeling cream, melon tonic lotion, pineapple masks; vetyver grass shower gel, algae shampoo, various eaux de toilette, soaps, sponges, scented candles, and lovely boxes fashioned of papier-mâché or banana leaf. Route de Saline, Lorient. (C) **590/27-82-63.** www.lignestbarth.com.

L'Atelier de Fabienne Miot   This shop features Fabienne's stunning creations, such as black pearls or turquoise set in jagged gold nuggets, as well as jewelry by such noted designers as Kabana and Bellon. Rue de la République, Gustavia. (C) **590/27-63-31.**

Laurent Eiffel   Found here is clever *"comme-il-faux"* fashion—everything at this upscale boutique is either "inspired by" or crafted "in imitation of" designer models that cost 10 times as much. Look for belts, shoes, and bags—knockout knockoffs of Versace, Prada, Hermès, Gucci, and Chanel. Rue du Général-de-Gaulle. ✆ 590/27-54-02.

Le Comptoir du Cigare This place caters to the December-to-April crowd of villa and yacht owners. It's sheathed in exotic hardwood, and enhanced with a glass-sided, walk-in humidor storing thousands of cigars from Cuba and the Dominican Republic. Smoke the Cubans on the island—it's illegal to bring them back to the United States. There's also a worthy collection of silver ornaments, lighters, pens suitable for adorning the desk of a CEO, artisan-quality Panama hats from Ecuador, and remarkable cigar boxes and humidors. 6 rue du Général-de-Gaulle. ✆ 590/27-50-62.

Les Artisans This top gallery specializes in fanciful crafts. They can also arrange visits to ateliers of leading local artists in various media (names to watch include Robert Danet, Jackson Questel, and Hannah Moser). Rue du Roi Oscar II. ✆ 590/27-50-40.

Made in St-Barth This is the best place for handicrafts. The women of Corossol sell their intricate straw work, including those ever fashionable wide-brim beach hats. Other crafts include local paintings, pottery (gorgeous glazed tiles), infused rums, essential oils, and decorative ornaments. Villa Créole, St-Jean. ✆ 590/27-56-57.

St. Barts Style This store offers racks of beachwear and shoes by such makers as Banana Moon and Claire Mercier in citrus colors like lemon, lime, grapefruit, and orange, chic accessories like toe rings, and psychedelic-looking T-shirts from about a dozen different manufacturers. Rue Lafayette, near rue du Port. ✆ 590/27-76-17.

Stéphane et Bernard This is the playground of Stéphane Lanson and Bernard Blancaneau, who often best the prices and inventory of individual couturier boutiques thanks to their flawless fashion sense and high-powered connections. Expect the latest handpicked Gaultier, Kenzo, Leger, Mugler, and Rykiel creations. Rue de la République, Gustavia. ✆ 590/27-65-69.

SUD, SUD This store carries stylish women's-only clothing, both day and evening wear, for the high-fashion model or heiress trying to look like one. Galerie du Commerce (adjacent to the airport), St-Jean. ✆ 590/27-98-75.

7 St. Barts After Dark

Most visitors consider a sunset aperitif followed by a French Creole dinner under the stars enough of a nocturnal adventure. Beyond that, the lounge and live music scenes have exploded, enlivening the once quiet evenings.

In Gustavia, the most popular gathering place is **Le Select** ⋒, rue de la France (ⓒ **590/27-86-87**), a 50-year-old institution named after its more famous granddaddy in the Montparnasse section of Paris. It's utterly simple: vaguely nautical decor inside the glorified shanty, though most patrons congregate at tables in the open-air garden (called "Cheeseburgers in Paradise" in homage to honorary St. Barthian Jimmy Buffett), where a game of dominoes might be under way as you walk in. You never know who might show up here—perhaps Mick Jagger. The place is open Monday to Thursday 10am to 10pm, and Friday to Saturday 10am to 11pm. There's live entertainment weekly, but the schedule is erratic; expect anyone, including Mr. Parrothead himself. Locals adore this classic dive where many a rumor is started on its speedy path around the island.

Bar de l'Oubli, 5 rue de la République (ⓒ **590/27-70-06**), occupies Gustavia's most prominent corner, at the intersection that most locals simply term "Centre-Ville." The setting is hip, the color scheme marine blue and white, and the background music might be the Rolling Stones. It's open daily from 7am (when breakfast— yummy runny *croque monsieurs*—is served to oh-so-Gallic patrons puffing Gauloises while recovering from various stages of their hangovers) to midnight or later, depending on business.

Nikki Beach ⋒, Baie de St-Jean (ⓒ **590/27-64-64;** www.nikki beach.com), may well be the notoriously exclusive chain's most decadent outpost. The anything-goes ambience (think runway show–meets–frat party) starts with staffers arguably even more gorgeous than the celeb crowd. They float around in white tees and diaphanous pants sans underwear by day (changing to less potentially revealing black at night since they often end up in the water). Don't miss them modeling the Nikki Beach clothing line on Sundays to the DJ's pulsating mix or Wednesday's Caribbean barbecue night. Expect the Hilton girls, Sean Combs, Ivanka Trump, and Mariah Carey competing over who can buy the most champagne to shower fellow guests and recruiting other glam folk to table dance.

Ex-Swedish model Alex Dumas defected from Nikki Beach to supervise proceedings at the Guanahani's sizzling new **Bar'Tô,** Grand Cul-de-Sac (ⓒ **590/27-66-60**), a virtual U.N. of sights, sounds, and tastes (the latter courtesy of supper menus and desserts from Bartoloméo next door). **Taïno Lounge** in the Christopher, Pointe Milou (ⓒ **590/27-63-63**), headlines chanteuse Nilce and pianist

Philippe Nardone. Oh, how the sultry Brazilian Nilce smokily wraps her throat around classics from Aznavour to Astrud Gilberto.

Bête à Z'ailes *✹* (aka BAZ) on the harbor in Gustavia (© **590/ 92-74-09**) has become the live music club du jour (or should that be, *de la nuit?*). Owner Jean Marc LeFrance books an eclectic international roster of up-and-coming acts, accompanied by excellent sushi and creative cocktails. Le Ti St. Barth's Carole Gruson transformed the **Yacht Club,** 6 Rue Jeanne d'Arc (© **590/27-86-39**), into the dawn patrol's favored disco haunt, with bottle service only, breathtaking harbor views through billowing white drapes, and competitive dressing. Celebrities, regulars, the filthy rich, and gawking tourists shimmy cheek-by-reconstructed-jowl to the righteous spinning of DJs Franky and Chaya.

Index

See also Accommodations and Restaurant indexes, below.

FROMMER'S® COMPLETE TRAVEL GUIDES

FROMMER'S® DAY BY DAY GUIDES

PAULINE FROMMER'S GUIDES! SEE MORE. SPEND LESS.

FROMMER'S® PORTABLE GUIDES

FROMMER'S® CRUISE GUIDES

Alaska Cruises & Ports of Call
Cruises & Ports of Call
European Cruises & Ports of Call

FROMMER'S® NATIONAL PARK GUIDES

Algonquin Provincial Park
Banff & Jasper
Grand Canyon
National Parks of the American West
Rocky Mountain
Yellowstone & Grand Teton
Yosemite and Sequoia & Kings Canyon
Zion & Bryce Canyon

FROMMER'S® MEMORABLE WALKS

London
New York
Paris
Rome
San Francisco

FROMMER'S® WITH KIDS GUIDES

Chicago
Hawaii
Las Vegas
London
National Parks
New York City
San Francisco
Toronto
Walt Disney World® & Orlando
Washington, D.C.

SUZY GERSHMAN'S BORN TO SHOP GUIDES

France
Hong Kong, Shanghai & Beijing
Italy
London
New York
Paris
San Francisco

FROMMER'S® IRREVERENT GUIDES

Amsterdam
Boston
Chicago
Las Vegas
London
Los Angeles
Manhattan
Paris
Rome
San Francisco
Walt Disney World®
Washington, D.C.

FROMMER'S® BEST-LOVED DRIVING TOURS

Austria
Britain
California
France
Germany
Ireland
Italy
New England
Northern Italy
Scotland
Spain
Tuscany & Umbria

THE UNOFFICIAL GUIDES®

Adventure Travel in Alaska
Beyond Disney
California with Kids
Central Italy
Chicago
Cruises
Disneyland®
England
Florida
Florida with Kids
Hawaii
Ireland
Las Vegas
London
Maui
Mexico's Best Beach Resorts
Mini Mickey
New Orleans
New York City
Paris
San Francisco
South Florida including Miami & the Keys
Walt Disney World®
Walt Disney World® for Grown-ups
Walt Disney World® with Kids
Washington, D.C.

SPECIAL-INTEREST TITLES

Athens Past & Present
Best Places to Raise Your Family
Cities Ranked & Rated
500 Places to Take Your Kids Before They Grow Up
Frommer's Best Day Trips from London
Frommer's Best RV & Tent Campgrounds in the U.S.A.
Frommer's Exploring America by RV
Frommer's NYC Free & Dirt Cheap
Frommer's Road Atlas Europe
Frommer's Road Atlas Ireland
Great Escapes From NYC Without Wheels
Retirement Places Rated

FROMMER'S® PHRASEFINDER DICTIONARY GUIDES

French
Italian
Spanish